The book of Odin's runes
For questioning
Doing magic
and gaining self-knowledge

Odin's runes are like a magic rod
For the soul to tune in on the path to God

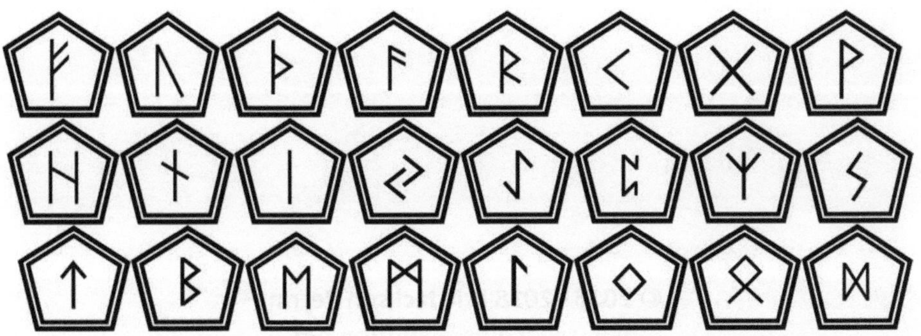

Erik Jackson Perrin

1

Books by the same author

The New I Ching - Kindle Amazon and Bod

The Birth Diamond – Sacred numerology – Kindle Amazon and Bod

Practical Mayan astrology – Kindle Amazon

To come when I translate them from French to English:

Eternal Tarot - Essence
Eternal tarot - Practicing and mastering
The path to your deep inner truth
9 astrology books

© 2016 –2018 Eric Jackson Perrin
www.coaching-evolution.net

**Published by Eric Jackson Perrin
69300 Caluire et Cuire – France**

Printed in Germany by BoD – Books en Demand

ISBN: 979-10-94871-508

Legal deposit: July 2016 – Dec 2018

Summary

Introduction

Hi and welcome! For a long time, I was called Erik Jackson. My name then became Eric Jackson Perrin as I took my French father's name. A branch of my ancestors came from northern England, from Germany, from Norway and from Sweden. Some of them lived using runes both before and after the arrival of Christian missionaries. Since the day runes arrived in my life, I have always felt a deep and close connection with Odin whom I feel is well alive somewhere in the invisible realms. Though this connection I wrote this book. This book of runes, as they originally existed and were used, was written to share this legacy with you and to pay tribute to my ancestors and to the gods. Hope you enjoy!

What are German runes? Original and genuine German runes are a set of 24 symbols that follow a specific order, which begins with a rune called Fehu, meaning the creation of wealth and which ends with the rune called Daeg, which means the returning of daylight. These 24 symbols make up an information system. They bring about energy, information and meaning. Runes were originally created to describe reality and to help men and wemen to adapt to both the visible material world and the invisible worlds. Runes are also letters that can be used to communicate, to write and to send messages amongst men themselves but also between men and gods or angels, between men and their ancestors or between men and their various inner components amongst which is the spiritual body or self. They are thus an alphabet, called the Futhark because the first six letters of that alphabet are the letters f, u, th, a, r and k. Runes are also magical symbols that can help create events so as to fulfill needs in the physical world. Finally, runes are also a tool that can be used for divination, i.e. as a communication tool between consciousness and the subconscious, to seek answers and to clarify the meaning of past, present and future events so that one can adapt.

Where do they come from? They were created in an area which now corresponds to Germany, Holland and Denmark. When were they invented, by whom and to do what? We don't know precisely. However, the roman politician and historian Tacitus describes, in a book about German people that he wrote in the year 98 AD, a divination ritual where small circular pieces of wood, carved with signs, are thrown on a white cloth and interpreted or else chosen out of a bag and put on a table. One can very easily suppose that the symbols carved on the pieces of wood were runes. Runes were more than likely created between year zero and year 98 AD, which is 2000 years ago, by members of what were then called German tribes and to be more precise by men and wemen that today we call shamans or healers or therapists. Historians suspect that they were created by members of 3 tribes called of Batavians (now called Dutch), Chats and Ubiens. These men and wemen had the ability to reach higher states of consciousness and to experience amongst other things what is called "out of body" experiences or "astral travel".

They were able to meet, to find help and to share information amongst themselves not only in the physical world but also in the astral world. Runes were created to acknowledge, to represent with symbols and to honor the gods, the forces of nature and the various life forms that thrive in this world.

They were created so that men could communicate with the gods, interpret messages received from them and synchronize their lives with the gods wills. They were created so that men and wemen could use symbols to do magic, that is to create events with the power of faith. What events are we talking about? Well, people at that time were concerned about the same things as they are now like for example having enough to eat, being healthy, being able to have children, being safe, living a meaningful life and accomplishing one's destiny. The local healer or shaman helped people achieve all this as best he or she could.

Lastly, they were created to serve as a communication system used for writing or to be more precise for sending messages. Only noblemen and wemen, shamans, certain soldiers and craftsmen had the right and the ability to carve runes. Runes were used from the time of Jesus-Christ till today all over Europe, from Russia to Island, by the people living there, like for example the Goths, the Anglo-Saxons, the Vikings, the Scandinavians and the Germans. They are now used all over the world by the descendants of these people.

What does the word rune mean? It can have two meanings. First, it means a secret concerning something magical, a mystery of life, a secret code and so a magical symbol. It also means whispering specific secret information in someone's ear so that only that person hears what has been whispered and so to communicate something secret or a secret message.

How is the runic information system organized? Runes are organized into 3 groups, into 3 families of 8 runes called « Aetts ». Each Aett is named after the first rune of its group. The first Aett is called Freyr's Aett, the second Hagl's Aett and the third Tiw's Aett. Men and wemen that use runes also have the habit of classifying runes according to the nature of the rune's vibration and the magical effects created by a rune. There are thus for example love runes, joy runes, victory runes, luck runes, health runes but also deceiving runes and conflict runes.

What's in this book? You will first learn about the people who created the runes and how the use of runes evolved from when they were created to nowadays. You will then get to know the 24 runes, learn how to interpret them, learn how to make your own set of runes and how to use them as magical symbols. You will finally, with the runic birth diamond, discover who you are and the paths of your destiny.

Hope this book changes your life.
Sincerely. Erik Jackson PERRIN. June 2016.

Chapter 1: The origin of runes

Who were the people living in Germany?

Runes were created by German people, who were people that settled in Europe, coming from present day Russia, about 200 BC. They gradually replaced the Celts that were there. They lived together forming clans or tribes that gave themselves names. Some of them were always on the move because that was their way of life while others settled down in villages. Their houses were made with earth, wood and thatch roofs. Germans were very active people. They were clever, brave, practical and very good craftsmen. They were also very efficient warriors. They had a keen sense of trade and business. Human dignity, healthy human relationships and happiness of wemen were of great importance to them. Wemen were highly respected and what they felt and said was taken into account. They also highly valued freedom and acting the right way according to the idea of destiny they had. They had a tendency to ignore any rule or law that brought about unfair limitations yet they could be very disciplined, totally dedicated and fierce when fighting or when facing adversity. Knowledge was passed on orally, though experience and decisions were taken by all during meetings called "Thing", as it is still done in Switzerland nowadays.

If we consider the historical context, at the time, between year 1 AD and year 80 AD, Europeans are in the Iron Age since about 700 ou 800 years and the Roman Empire is strongly expanding since about 100 years. Romans have just taken over Gaul (today's France) a few decades back. From the North Sea to the Black Sea, a frontier was created by them using wooden barriers. Many roman camps were built in strategic areas. Romans and Germans had permanent, complex and intensive relationships. Some Germans worked as soldiers in the roman armies. Many Germans made trade with Romans. Many also fought the Romans. Men and goods went to and fro between German lands and the Roman Empire. The cult of Mithra and Roman gods were worshiped south of the border and the new Christian religion was making its way in some people's hearts.

German people had their own way of seeing life and the world. They had their own culture and their own gods.

There are very few written documents about encounters between Romans and German.

One man however, called Tacitus, who was a politician and a historian, was very interested about German people. He wrote about them and even if he mingled facts and his personal vision of things, what he wrote helps us know more about German people.

Map of Europe in Year 1 AD

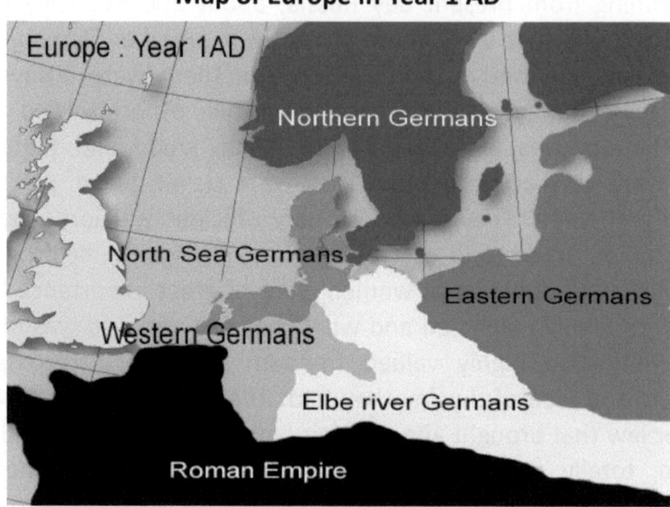

Alphabets existing at the time of Jesus-Christ:

The first symbols: Very few people stare at the sky nowadays because in most cities, there is too many things to do but also too much light and too much pollution so that one just cannot see the stars.

Before however, men and wemen spent hours and nights just watching the sky. They naturally grouped certain stars together with their imagination and gave them names.

Geometrical graphics based on the stars were thus created by people living in present day Germany and Scandinavia more than 12 000 ago. These figures, called « Hallristningar » in Scandinavia, were used during rituals to do magic. They were carved on stones or wooden objects during the Bronze Age (3000 BC to 800 BC) and during the Iron Age (800 BC to year 1 AD) when Runes were created. They are a part of human history and inspired the creation of Runes.

Source : http://racines.traditions.free.fr

The birth of writing:

In our current era, writing was invented in Mesopotamia (current day Iraq) and in Egypt about 3500 BC. Archeology reveals that a writing system called "Linear A" was used in Greece and in the Greek islands between 2500 BC and 1400 BC. An alphabet called the "Cypro-Minoan syllabary" was then used in Greece, Cyprus and Crete between 1600 BC and 1450 BC. It was followed by an alphabet called the" Linear B" between 1450 BC and 1200 BC. These alphabets latter gave rise to the Phoenician alphabet and inspired the creation of the Runic alphabet.

Here is a tablet engraved with Linear A alphabet.

Archeological museum of Crete: Tablet engraved with Linear A characters
(The last 3 carvings at the bottom are very similar to runes 11, 6 and 10)

Cypro-Minoan writing - Cyprus Museum - Source Wikipédia
(Some carvings are very similar to runes 2, 11, 16 and 23)

Somewhere between 1400 BC and 1200 BC the Phoenician alphabet was created in present day Lebanon. This alphabet inspired the creation of the Aramean, Sabean, Modern Greek, Etrusquan and Latin alphabets. Around 1275 BC groups of people, called "People from the sea", coming from present day Denmark, Holland and Germany, invaded Mediterranean lands. They were finally defeated and expelled by the Egyptian army. They surely saw the existing writing systems were they went! Below are compared various Mediterranean and Alpine alphabets with the runic alphabet that was inspired by them. The runic writing system was obviously created before year 95 AD, when Tacitus talks about it, probably between year 1 AD and year 80 AD and possibly much earlier.

Forbidden archeology: There exists a secret branch of archeology called Forbidden Archeology because it totally shatters all beliefs concerning human history on this planet. It states that civilizations with technology existed long before ours, one millions of years ago and another thousands of years ago. Forbidden archeology states that humanity faced a man-made natural disaster and a nuclear war that almost wiped everyone out and that Humanity started again from scratch, back to prehistory!

Runic character A called Ass ᚨ means a god and runic character T ↑ means a star person or a star on earth or a person connected to his inner star, to his spiritual body. Combining these 2 letters gives the word AT meaning the gods or beings that come from the stars. Their land or the place where they lived on Earth, mentioned by the Greek Plato who heard about it, was called AT-Land or Atlantis. According to Forbidden Archeology, runes come from Atlantis, from the land of gods and they are a self-knowledge writing system which allows one to recover one's eternity and to reach the heavens.

In 1984, near the town of Noleby in Sweden, a stone engraved with runes about 500 AD was found. It said "I engrave these runes that come from the gods or from the stars". Other stones found elsewhere say the same thing. So, the origin of runes could well be much more mysterious that it seems!!!

Comparing Phoenician, Etrusquan and Runic alphabets

Phoenician Alphabet 1400 BC to 500 BC				**Etrusquan Alphabet** 700 BC-100 AD		**Runic Futhark alphabet** 1 AD to 1600 AD			
Letter	**Name**	**Meaning**	**Sound**	**Letter**	**Sound**	**Letter**	**Old Norse/ Old English**	**Meaning**	**Sound**
1 𐤀	Aleph	ox	ʻ	**A**	a	ᚠ	Fe/Foeh	Creating wealth	f
2 𐤁	Beth	house	b	**B**	b	ᚢ	Ur/Ur	cow/rain	u/ou
3 𐤂	Gimel	camel	g	<	c	ᚦ	Thurs/ Thorn	Giant/ Efficient person/ thorn	th
4 𐤃	Daleth	door	d	**D**	d	ᚨ	Az/Oz	Divine power	a
5 𐤄	Hé	Door wing	h	𐌄	e	ᚱ	Reidh/ Radh	ride wagon	r
6 𐤅	Waw	hook	w	𐌅	v	<ᚴ	Kan/Ken	torch, boil	k
7 𐤆	Zayin	weapon	z	I	z	ᚷ	Gift/ Gyfu	gift, strength by unity	g/ hr

#	Name	Meaning	Sound		Sound		Rune name	Meaning	Sound
8	Heth	wall	h		h		Vend/ Wynn	Pleasure, joy, harmony	v/ w
9	Thet	wheel	t		o		Hagall/ Haegl	hail, ice egg	h
10	Yodh	hand	y		i		Naudhr/ Nyd	needs, necessity	n
11	Kaf	palm	k		k		Eis/Is	ice, strength of being	I
12	Lameth	stick	l		l		Ar/yar	year, good harvest	y/j
13	Mem	water	m		m		Ihwr/ eow	Yew tree safety	Ay
14	Nun	snake	n		n		Peordh/p erth	Luck tool	p
15	Samek	fish	s		o		Ihwar/ Eolh	Bow, Defensive fighting, , deer	z
16	ayin	eye	'		p		Sol/Sigil	Sun spark	s
17	Pe	mouth	p		S		Teiws/ Tiw	God's light/sky god	t
18	Sade	papyrus	s		q		Bjork/ Beorc	Birch tree Purification	b
19	Qop	monkey	q		r		Ior/eh	horse, man-god unity	e
20	Res	head	r		s		Madhr/ Man	Father of all men	m
21	Sin	sun	s		t		Laukr/ Lagu	water, ocean, onion, leek	l
22	Taw	mark	t		U		Ing/Ing	freedom god Ing	ng
23					X		Odhal/Ethel	Land of origin/ ancestors	o
24	Shadowed areas show similarities between Etruscan alphabet and runes				phi		Dagr/ Daegh	daylight/ awakening	d
25					xi				
26					f				

Runes and the stars:

Many seekers underlined similarities between runes as graphical forms and certain graphics that one could draw by visually joining various stars together. There is no proof that runes were inspired by looking at the stars but there is no proof that this is not so. Germans travelled a lot on both land and water. Looking at the stars and using sky marks to find one's way during night time is something men have done for a very long time. The people of Egypt who built the pyramids displayed them on the ground so as to reproduce graphically the Orion constellation. From a graphical or artistic point of view, one naturally tends to connect stars together and when one does so, runes and letters do appear, as show further down. Every civilization on earth did map stars each in its own way. Chinese, Arabs and latter the Greeks made different geometrical figures with the same stars. If you seek you will find connections between stars and runes.

What you will find will depend on the time of the year, on your way of connecting the different stars, on your vision of things and on your imagination. Below are a few examples that show similarities between what certain runes symbolize and corresponding constellations. Research on this topic remains open.

Similarities between the 24 runes and northern hemisphere constellations: Zodiac signs are in capital letters.

Rune 1 – Fehu: ᚠ The big dipper standing and ARIES

Rune 2 – Ur: ᚢ TAURUS constellation

Rune 3 – Thorn: ᚦ SCORPIO and VIRGO Constellations

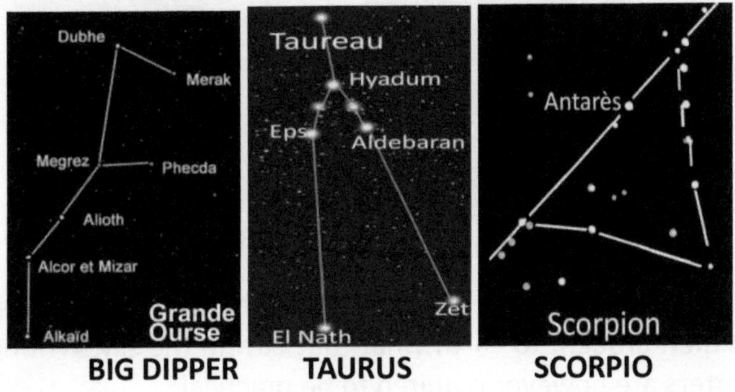

BIG DIPPER   **TAURUS**   **SCORPIO**

Rune 4 – Ass: ᚠ Andromeda cloud

Rune 5 – Raidh: ᚱ Cepheus or Pegasus.

Rune 6 – Ken: ᚲ or ᚴ VEGA-DENEB-ALTAIR. ARIES or sextant constellation

Rune 7 – Gyfu: ᚷ Cygnus constellation also called the Northern Cross

Rune 8 – Wynn: ᚹ Little dipper, LIBRA and SCORPIO

Rune 9 – Hagl: ᚺ Dolphin constellation

Rune 10 – Nyd: ᚾ CAPRICORN or Cygnus constellation

Rune 11 – Eis: ᛁ Aries or AQUARIUS

Rune 12 - Yer: ᛂ Constellation of CANCER

Rune 13 – Eih: ᛇ CAPRICORN

Rune 14 – Peordh: ᛈ Constellation of AQUARIUS

Rune 15 – Eohl: ᛉ Constellation of SCORPIO.

Rune 16 – Sigl: ᛋ Constellation of AQUARIUS

Rune 17 – Tiw: ᛏ Aquila constellation

Rune 18 – Berkano: ᛒ Cassiopeia

Rune 19 – Eh: ᛖ Constellations of GEMINI and SAGITTARIUS

Rune 20 – Mann: ᛗ Constellation of GEMINI

Rune 21 – Lagu: ᛚ PISCES

Rune 22 – Ing: ᛜ Constellation of Lyra and LIBRA

Rune 23 – Othala: ᛟ Constellation of Orion.

Rune 24 – Daeg: ᛞ Constellation of GEMINI

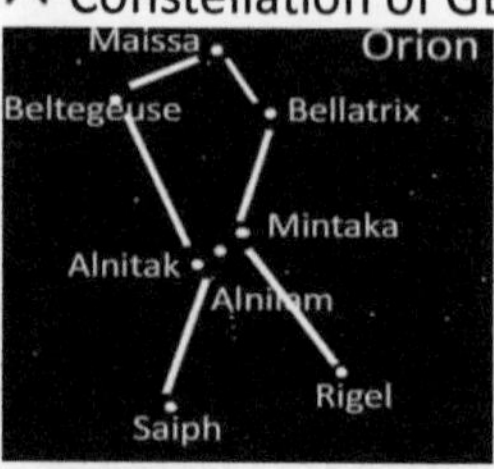

ORION (Rune 23)

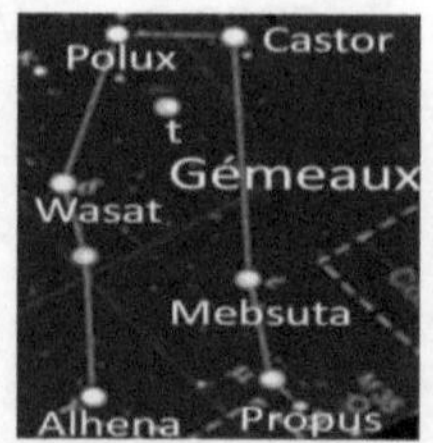

GEMINI (Rune 24)

Observing stars more than likely inspired the various existing writing systems as men brought to earth what they saw in the sky. Writing and the shape of letters are however required to be practical.

Forms and graphics thus depend very much on the tools used to draw them as well as on what type of material they are drawn on, which can be and has been stone, bone, shells, wood and latter paper.

Runic alphabets and where information about them was found:

Latin alphabet gradually replaced runes in Anglo-Saxon lands but both alphabets existed for a long time, till today, as the elite used them. We don't precisely know who created the runic alphabet though historians suppose that members of a tribe called the "Batavi" did as they were well acquainted with roman and Etruscan culture because they were hired as soldiers and were part of special roman troops called the « Cohortes Germanorum ». Legend says Odin created the runes.

Information sources enabling us to gain knowledge about the existence, the meaning and how runes were used are scarce and not very clear. There is a time span of 800 to 1200 years between the time when runes were created and the first texts that can help us understand them! In Sweden, a project called Rundata listed, classified and named, with letters and numbers, all found sources of information concerning runes. Knowledge concerning runes was originally shared orally only. There was no need to write things down.

Apart from very specific cases, the idea was to use runes without leaving any visible traces. It was considered important to give back to nature what nature gave to Men and not to leave anything behind. Things then changed and men started engraving runes on stones and on objects to do magic or to pass on messages.

First time-space: The old Futhark. From 1 AD to about 600 AD

The first runic alphabet was created following numerous war raids and intensive trade between Germans and the people living in the Roman Empire. It was used in present day Germany and in the south of Scandinavia. We then enter a time that History calls "the great migrations". Groups of fierce people coming from present day Russia, China and Mongolia invaded Europe from the east, looting and killing wherever they went. German tribes thus immigrated westwards to present day France, Spain and England, in great numbers, during a time span of 200 years, between years 400 AD and 600 AD

Source 1: Legacy of Roman historian and politician Tacitus (58 AD to 120 AD). He wrote a book about German people and life called « De Origine et Situ Germanorum » around year 98 AD. His book mixes history, roman morale and personal political opinions. Despite the fact that he makes confusion between Celts and Germans, Tacitus's book brings in much information about the German people he encountered. It also gives a precise description on how divination was carried out. Here is the famous section from chapter 10 that describes how divination was carried out. It also shows how important horses were for German noblemen. Horses were considered to be an expression of divine light.

"There is no place were divination is of greater importance. Their way of consulting the gods is very simple: they find or cut a branch from a fruit tree, cut it in small pieces, engrave special signs on each piece and then throw them up in the air so that they land on a white piece of cloth.

The local priest if stately affairs are at stake or the head of the family for personal affairs calls upon the gods and looking up at the sky, he picks and raises three pieces one by one to the sky and interprets them according to the sign on each slice of wood. If the answer is no, then one no longer asks questions concerning that specific issue. If action is required, then signs are seeked for to confirm the given answer: as these people also know how to read the flight and the songs of birds.

They have a peculiar practice which is to ask horses for omens and signs. The state feeds special white horses in fields or forests. These horses are never used for any other work. Horses are coupled to a sacred chariot and the king, with the priest or the city mayor, observed the horse's whinnies and the sound of their nostrils. Such omens from horses are considered to be the most important of all omens not only for the people but also for the priests who believe that horses are the confidants of the gods while they themselves are mere servants or ministers".

Source 2: Weapons and household objects: Example: The Vimose comb which is in the Copenhagen national museum. This object was created around year 150-180 AD. Archeologists say it is the oldest known object with runes engraved on it. We however don't know when the runes were engraved on it. The inscription is said to be either a first name or a word showing belongingness to a specific clan. Harya or Harja.

The oldest runic inscriptions (years 200 to 500 AD) were found on bones, spear heads, sword scabbards, ax handles or on helmets.

Source 3: The Kylver tombstone discovered in 1903: The grave is said to be from year 400 AD. It is labeled as object G88. It is the oldest object with a complete Futhark alphabet engraved on it. The two small bars belonging to the first are barely visible. The order of the last two runes is reversed while runes A, S and B are rotated at an angle of 180°.

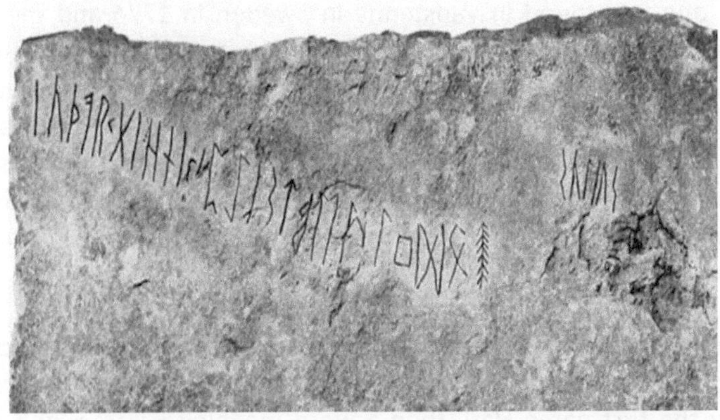

The habit of engraving runes on stones and on gravestones began around year 400 AD and took place until the middle ages. Over 50 known tombstones with runes engraved on them are dated from the era of the great migrations (400 to 700 AD) and over 3000 tombstones with runes engraved on them exist throughout Europe. The website below show a great number of rune engraved tombstones.

http://www.arild-hauge.com/sweden.htm

Source 4: Bracteates (talismans): Example 1: Vadstenna Bracteates which are kept in the Stockholm history museum

The first one was found in Vadstenna in Sweden in 1774 and the second nearby in Motala more recently. It bears the inscription "luvatuva" ou "luwa tuwa" and the three Aetts or rune families which are futharkgv, hnijeprs and then tbemlod. Linguists suppose that « luwa tuwa » is a magical phrase. Odin is represented at the center with two animals. These talismans enabled the elite to be recognized as such. They were also used as offerings or gifts in relationships between people or in relationships with the gods.

Example 2: Zealand bracteate found in Denmark: The following words are engraved on this jewel: farauisa: gibu auja: ttt ». This is interpreted as meaning: the first name Hari, then a word meaning « i am » or « me », a word meaning « wise danger », a word meaning gift and a word meaning "luck" and then 3 t letters that call upon the sky god Tiw.

One could translate that as follows: I, Hari as I am called, am wise when facing danger and I receive luck, God, God, God". So this is obviously a talisman to attract luck. More than 300 similar bracteates or pieces of jewelry from that period of time have been discovered.

Zealand bracteate

Archeology reveals that runes were more than likely used by noblemen to sign their names, to assert their identity, their status or their belongingness to a specific clan. Runes were also sometimes engraved to show who made the object or to whom it belonged. They were finally engraved in the memory of a dead person, as an offering or to bring into reality a magical and symbolic action.

Before the time corresponding to great migrations, the letters ALU were often engraved on various objects. No one knows exactly what these 3 letters mean. The meaning of the word ALE has however become to mean a sacred drink and then beer. My personal feeling is that these 3 letters combine symbols of "will power/action/creation" then "spiritual/magical power of faith/sacredness" and then "condensing into matter/joy". From that, one could write a magic formula that would go as follows: "My creative power becoming sacred makes me attain my goals" or "May what brings me joy come through thanks to by will and my faith".

Because the Germans burned their dead, almost all objects from that time disappeared with their owners. There is no written information giving us the names, the meaning or the pronunciation of the runes that make up the old runic alphabet.

Comment: Historians and seekers have made deductions from sources and objects that are dated more than 800 years after the invention of runes. To be fully aware of how things were then, one should access life memories from that time or somehow go back in time during an out of body experience. Very few people on Earth can do that and they probably would not have the will to do this.

Second time-space: The Anglo-Saxon Futhork: Year 500 AD to about year 1100 AD and much letter in some remote places.

German tribes, mainly Angles and Saxons, who settled in present day England, created 5 new runes and later 4 others, which makes a total of 9 new runes. This new 33 runic alphabet is called the Anglo-Saxon Futhork because the fourth rune A has become an O. This alphabet was mainly used in England by specific scholars. Below are the 9 extra runes created in England. The fist 8 runes make up an additional family or Aett while the ninth rune if kind of apart.

Rune 25: Name: Ac. This rune is connected to the oak tree or to the oak's acorn that one day becomes a big oak tree.

Rune 26: Name: As or Os. This rune symbolizes expression of power though speech, information and emotion.

Rune 27: Name: Yr. This rune represents a bow made from a yew tree branch. It is connected to hunting to find food and with what nourishes.

Rune 28: Name: Ior. This rune represents the world snake and the weight or burden of handling this material world and its sufferings.

Rune 29: Name: Ear: This rune is connected to water from source to ocean, to the end of things and to the invisible worlds.

Rune 30: Name: Cweorth: This rune is connected to the apple tree but also to fire that symbolizes here fuel, a power that transforms and an eternal force that brings heat and light.

Rune 31: Name: Calc: This rune symbolizes a recipe, an attitude that enables one to attract something, an event or someone but also the action of ending, terminating and closing something.

Rune 32: Name: Stan. This rune symbolizes stone which is seen both as a long lasting raw material, as a means to be protected but also sometimes as an obstacle.

Rune 33: Name: Gar: This rune is kind of isolated from others, as if it had retreated from the rune group. It is used but make something or someone go away or retire and to put an end to the effects of a talisman.

At the end of this second time-space, all three alphabets co-existed and were used in a very wide geographical era from Iceland to Russia and from Finland to France. Various talismans and other wooden objects which were found from that time all over Europe, particularly in harbors and in bogs, prove what has just been said.

Source 1: A document called the Codex Sangallensis 878. It is kept at Saint Gall Abbey in Switzerland. It was written in the ninth century and shows various alphabets, including the runic alphabet existing at that time. The runes are not named.

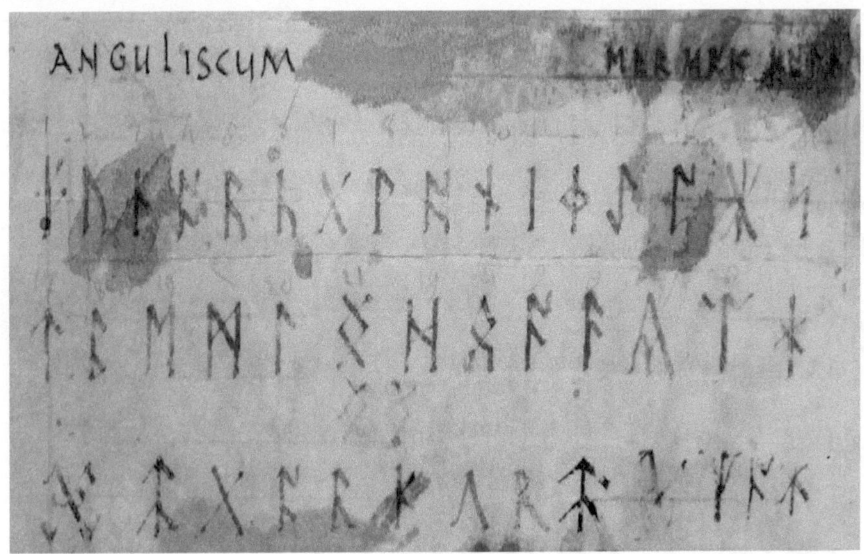

Source 2: A document called the Codex Vindobonensis 795. It is kept at the national Library in Vienna, Austria. It was written in the ninth century and shows the English runic alphabet with the name of the runes.

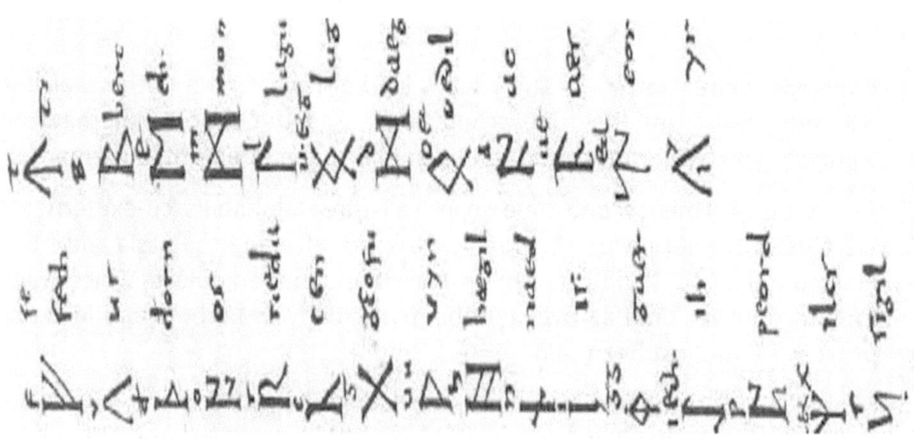

Source 3: A paper called "De Inventorum linguarum" written by the archbishop of the city of Mainz in Germany, Rabanus Maurus (780-856). This paper is about the origin of languages and it mentions the runic alphabet though in a quite strange and distorted manner.

1581   DE INVENTIONE LINGUARUM.   1582

Litteras quippe quibus utuntur Marcomanni, quos nos Nordmannos vocamus, infra scriptas habemus : a quibus originem, qui Theodiscam loquuntur linguam, trahunt. Cum quibus carmina sua incantationesque ac divinationes significare procurant qui adhuc paganis ritibus involvuntur.

asc. birith. chen. thorn. ech. fech. gibu. hagalc. his. gilc. lagu. man.

not. othil. perc. chon. rehir. sugil. tac. hur. halach. huyri. ziu.

Source 4: The English runic poem said to be from Cotton Otho. This manuscript is a copy of the original one which is said to be from the ninth century. The original manuscript was kept at the London Cotton Library and it burned during the great fire that destroyed part of the city in 1731. It was luckily copied by Humphrey Wanley (1672-1726) and published by George Hickes in 1705 under the name « Linguarum veterum septentrionalium thesaurus». The manuscript contains for each rune an enigma were the rune is the answer to the enigma. Mister Hickes added the name of each rune according to information he found elsewhere. You will find the texts of this poem in the chapter describing each runes.

Third space-time: The younger Futhark. It existed approximately between year 800 AD and year 1200 AD but until much later in remote parts of Iceland and Scandinavia.

This Futhark was created when changes in linguistics were implemented in German lands. It was created by the northern Germans, also called Viking, by reducing the number of runes from 24 to 16. This new alphabet gradually replaced the old one in northern lands. It was often called the Viking's alphabet as they carried it along with them on territories they looted and conquered. It was brought to Iceland, to Russia and to England.

It inspired various other alphabets like "the gothic alphabet" and the "Kok Turk alphabet" which were used during the eighth and ninth centuries in Asian countries surrounding the Caspian Sea. According to history, the time of the Vikings spans from year 793 when Lindesfarne abbey was looted to year 1263 when the Norwegian Vikings were kicked out of Scotland during the battle of Largs. Scandinavia was then converted to Christianity during the tenth and eleventh century.

Source 1: Part of a document called quarter 83. The document is called "Codex Leidensis Latinus". The interesting part of the document is a copy from a ninth century document. The 16 runes of the younger Futhark are named in Latin letters as follows: Fehu, úr, thurs, aus, ræidu, kaun, hagal, naud, ís, ár, sólu, tíu, biarkan, mann, laug and ír.

Source 2: This is a document called "Gesta Hammaburgensis ecclesiae pontificum" which means the deeds of the Abbots of the city of Hamburg. It was written by schoolmaster and historian Adam of Bremen (we know he died in 1082). It was last seen at Sorø Abbey in Denmark in the sixteenth century. It describes the life of Christians between year 792 AD and year 1182 AD but also the way of life of German people. It talks about a sacred temple located at Uppsala, that was very important for the German people and it mentions a very far away land called Vinland, discovered by the Vikings on the other side of the ocean!

Forth space-time: Year 1100 AD to about year 1500 AD: Medieval runes and Icelandic runes and sagas. In Scandinavia, the younger Futhark was gradually changed. New runes were added so that each sound could be matched by a rune. Europe was being Christianized and German culture gradually disappeared. German traditions existed only in Iceland and in some remote parts of Scandinavia.

Source 1: A document called "the codex runicus" which is kept at Copenhagen University in Denmark. This document is actually written using runic characters and is dated around year 1300 AD. It is mainly a guide that defines Danish laws, border between Denmark and Sweden and the kings that ruled Denmark. Someone added a song at the end of the document! I found this information on Wikipedia.

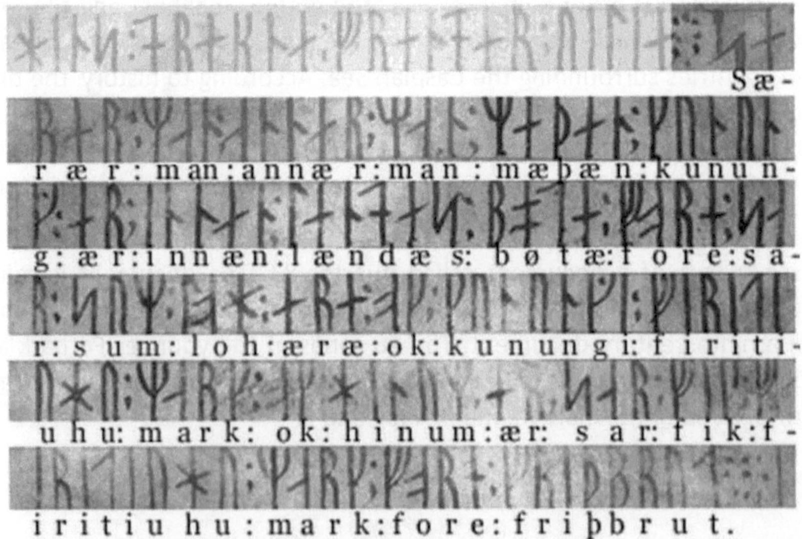

Source 2: A document called "Computus runicus" which was created in year 1328 AD. It was published in 1626 by Danish doctor Ole Worm. It reveals the Anglo-Saxon Futhork in a more or less accurate manner as seen below.

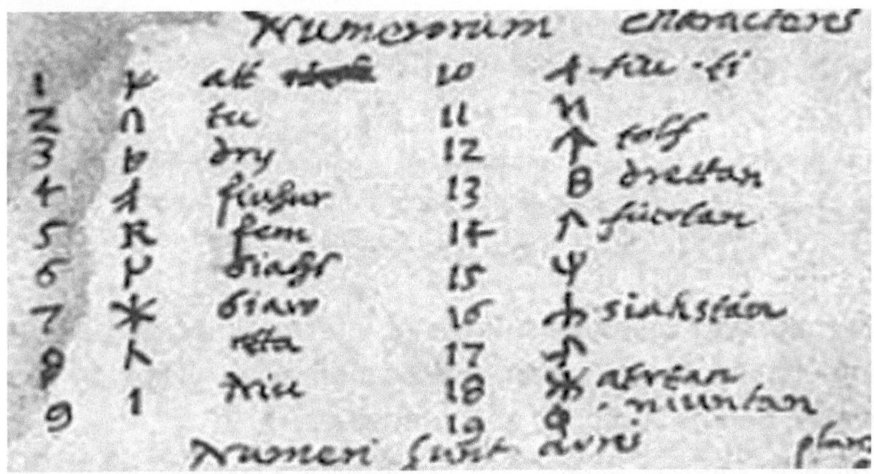

Source 3: A manuscript called "The Norwegian runic poem". This document is a copy of a document said to have been written in thirteenth century AD. The original document was destroyed in a fire in 1728 but two copies were made before that by Doctor Ole Worm and by Arni Magnússon and Jón Eggertson. A copy can be found at the library of Copenhagen University. Two phrases describe each rune. The verses of this poem are shown at the end of each text explaining the 24 runes.

Source 4: A manuscript called "The Icelandic runic poem". It is dated from the fifteenth century. There is a copy at the Copenhagen national library. Each rune is described by a sentence.

Source 5: Objects from excavations that took place in the Norwegian town of Bergen. In 1955, a fire destroyed part of the town. A huge building site was set to rebuild and in doing so, many objects engraved with runes and dated between year 1100 AD and year 1300 AD were found. Here are a few examples of what was engraved on various objects.

- Kiss me my love.
- Remember me as I remember you; love me as I love you.
- Love is above everything so submit yourself to love.
- Come back home.

Fifth space-time: From year 1500 AD to nowadays: Renewal of German traditions.

When Europe experienced what has been called "The Renaissance" which means renewal, German linguists started studying runes. Runes were then used by groups of people who were interested in magic and occult sciences. One of these groups called themselves "The Armanists". Rune number 16 of the old Futhark, "lightning from the sun", sadly became famous when it was used by the German Nazi regime who doubled it and fitted it in its corporate identity. Nowadays, one can see rune "h" written on ambulances where it symbolizes help from the sky. You can also see runes in the comic book series "Thorgal" and in certain movies or TV series like "The lord of the rings" and "Stargate".

German and Icelandic sources of information that help us understand the German and Scandinavian vision of the world, beliefs and gods and goddesses.

Icelandic sources: German and Scandinavian mythology, beliefs and rituals were only passed on orally. There are therefore very few sources that reveal Scandinavian mythology and most of these are only found in Iceland, country which officially became Christian in the year 1000 AD, i.e much latter than any other country. These sources reveal that the sacred and the secular are deeply connected and that the gods, natural elements and magic are intensively part of daily life. Two enlightened men have created or gathered the Icelandic sources in various groups of texts.

Snorri Sturluson, the younger Edda and the history of Norwegian kings. He was a poet, a writer, a historian but also a politician. He lived between year 1179 and the 24th of September 1241 when the king of Norway sent an agent to murder him. He wrote what is known as "Snorri's Edda", a history of Norwegian kings or Heimskringla and various sagas like for example Egill's saga. A Saga is a long story with many episodes and intrigues.

Brynjölfur Sveinsson and the older Edda. He was a Lutheran priest. In 1643, he discovered a bundle of poems written between the eighth and ninth century AD. He gathered most of them together and created a book called "the Codex Regius". These poems were originally written, according to Brynjölfur Sveinsson, by the sage and poet Sæmundr the wise.

All of these poems are today knows as "the ancient poetic Edda". Two of them are well known in Anglo-Saxon countries, the "Voluspa" which means the clairvoyant's predictions and the "Havamal" which means the Ode to the high one, the high one being in this case Odin himself. These poems were written between the year 900 AD and the year 1300 AD. Part of the Voluspa (verses 138-146 and 147-165) is called the "Runatal" and it contains a lot of information about the use of runes. This will be discussed further in the chapter dedicated to runic magic.

German sources: Jacob and Wilhelm Grimm. Another source which helps gain better knowledge of German mythology is to be found in the works of the German "Grimm brothers". Between 1816 and 1818, they gathered German tales and legends found in various European countries

Special ways of engraving runes: Combined or bind runes and Cryptic runes.

Combined runes: Two, three or four runes are engraved on one another, one after the other, while singing, to create a new symbol that has a specific meaning, a specific intention and that is filled with a specific energy related to the runes used. Combined runes can make up a sentence or are chosen to bring together similar energies that bring for example success, happiness, safety or a pleasant trip. Such runes were engraved on objects to make them magic, i.e. to turn them into talismans.

Example: Runes Raidh, Eih and Eh symbolize a successful passage ritual or shamanistic trip. Combining runes Fehu, Ken and Eh creates a very happy encounter. The runes As, Lagu and Ur make the word ALU which is often found on objects and which means something like "the power is magic is now working in the world of matter". Combining runes Gyfu and Wynn suggests a joyful gift or conquering joy.

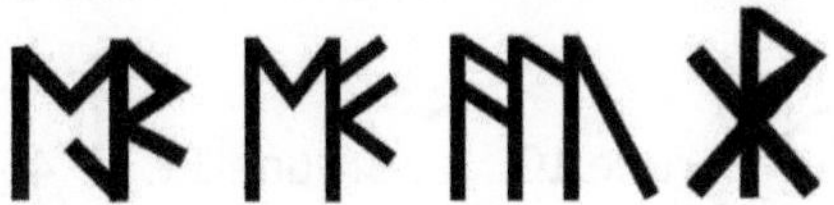

Creating bindrunes requires having a clear intention, a specific goal and a perfect intuitive knowledge of each rune.

Coded or cryptic runes and bind runes: The word rune itself means a secret as what occurs between a person and that person's magical soul is only that person's business, whatever may say journalists or people too intensively connected to their thinking monkey mind and who always want to know. Same thing when a person shares information with another person. A great deal of secrecy went along with rune practice. The men and wemen who turned simple objects into magical objects using runes or who used runes to pass on messages didn't want other people who find out what was going on, who engraved or what was written. Messages and magic formula were thus coded by for example writing runes backwards (wendruns), by writing one rune on top of another (bindruns), by moving each rune by one or two steps backwards or forwards or by coding the runes some other way. Below are some of the coding systems that were used.

1: Runes with bars or Eisrunes: This coding system uses rune eleven Isa or Eis. The rune is written in two different sizes, in a smaller size to designate one of the three Aetts or families and in larger size to pinpoint to the rune number within the family. Each rune could be coded as a set of 2 numbers, the first for the family and the second for the position within the family. This system, which is similar to Morse code, enabled the use of rhythmic sounds and so to pass messages during rituals using drums, sticks and in more recent times bells.

Example: If you want to tell someone that you love them and be romantic, you can for example write « I love you » in French (je t'aime) in the following manner.

Reminder of the original Futhark's three Aetts:

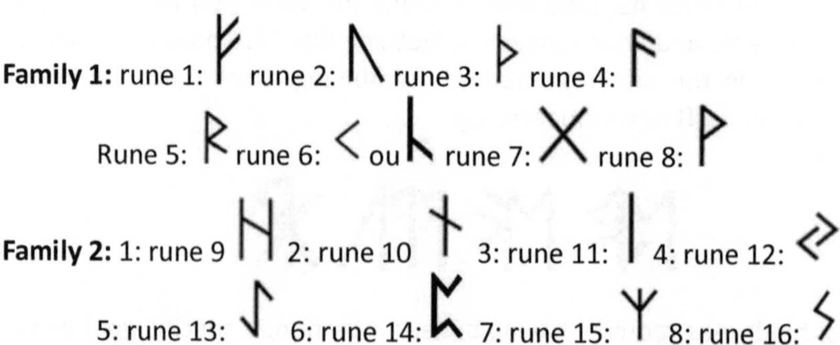

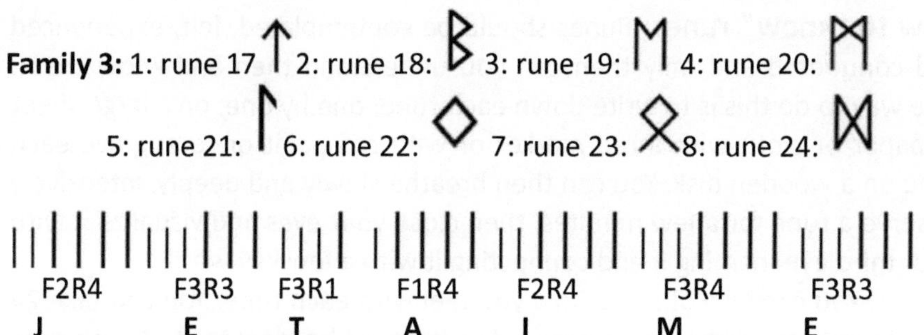

2: The branch rune system or Kvistruns: In this system, based on rune 15, Eohl, one first engraves a vertical line. One, two or three 45° angled lines are then engraved to join the vertical line, from the left hand side or from the right hand side, at regular intervals. This will define the family. Then from one to eight lines are engraved to pinpoint the rune within the already defined family.

Example: If you want to say yes to someone in French, you can do so by using cryptic runes and by engraving the following branch runes:

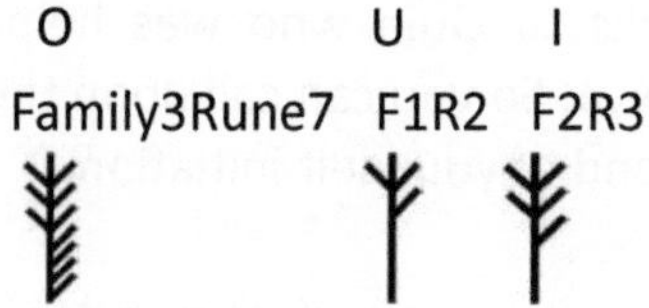

Example: A system similar to that of the branch rune system also existed using rune 21, Lagu. If you wanted to send a « yes » message in French using the Lagu cryptic system, you would then engrave the runes as follows:

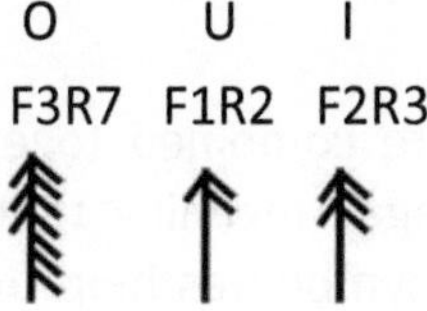

3: Other systems with other runes were also used, like for example with rune 7, Gyfu. This system was called the comb rune system or Tjaldrunar ou Tjaldruns. Runes were sometimes encrypted using two systems, an Isa/Eohl/Lagu system and a moving one, two or three runes backwards or forwards system. Finally, the name of the person who engraved runes and a date were sometimes coded within messages.

How to "know" runes: Runes should be contemplated, felt, experienced and conquered and only then can you understand then and know them. One way to do this is to write down each rune, one by one, on a large sheet of paper or cloth with a red marker or with red paint or to engrave each rune on a wooden disk. You can then breathe slowly and deeply, intensively observe a rune for a few minutes, then close your eyes and visualize it with your third eye, naming it and connecting it with a few key words.

You can also observe how you feel with each rune. You can take 24 days to initiate yourself, one rune a day. It would be ideal to start with rune 1 on the first of the month so that you are tuned to the numerical energy of the day. Each day, you can draw or paint your rune, take a few minutes to visualize it, to express what the rune is about, to feel it and to thank it.

You can also engrave each rune on something you eat or bake something that has the shape of the rune and eat it early in the morning while at the same time visualizing, expressing and thanking. You can also scratch each rune on your body with your nail, tattoo it or write it on yourself preferably with organic ink.

This initiation can also take place in 24 weeks, one rune per week. Runes exist, according to legend, thanks to Odin who was helped and inspired by both his wife Frigg and by Freya. So you can call upon them and thank them at the beginning and at the end of your self-initiation.

Two runic symbols existing in everyday modern life:

1: Ambulance rune:

Sometime ago in Denmark, runes 7 and 11 were combined together to create a new rune with replaced old rune 9, Hagal, meaning that which comes from the sky or hail. This rune therefore symbolizes help from the heavens and emergency relief brought by ambulance personnel.

2: Bluetooth rune: Blue tooth is a tooth that is blue. How did that come to symbolize a technology that enables connecting different machines that can work with one another like for example a computer, a mobile phone and a printer? Well, here is the story!

Once upon a time, there was a Scandinavian king called Harald Gormsson (940-981) or Harald Bluetooth because one of his teeth was blue for some medical reason. His initials were thus HB.

Over one thousand years later, a group of engineers from telecommunications corporations IBM, Nokia and Eriksson worked on a process that could make different technologies work together. The solution was found and the next step was to find a name and a symbol for this new technology.

The IBM team found a name (Pan) but it was not unique enough so it was rejected.

Scandinavian engineer Sven Mattisson, working for Eriksson, had a passion for history and he was reading a book about how king Harald managed to unite and Christianize most of Viking Scandinavia, uniting Danes, Swedes and Norwegians. He suggested to call the new unifying process bluetooth and to symbolize it with Harald Bluetooth's initials in Danish runic characters. A vote was organized and Sven Mattison's proposal was unanimously approved. That's how Viking runes travelled through history to create a modern technological logo!

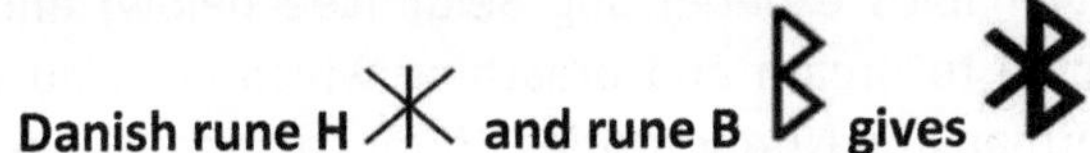

Chapter 2: Germans and Scandinavians

Germans didn't really have a religion as such but rather a belief system with rituals. Nowadays, this system of beliefs with its rituals tends to be referred to as Asatru or sometimes Odinism. Germans believed in three different main forces: the forces of destiny, those of gods and goddesses who express natural life forces and those of various beings who inhabit both visible and invisible worlds. They were keenly aware that everything is connected, that everything emits vibrations, that everything is a part of "Life" and that all Life is created by "The Source of all Life". They had a strong sense of sacredness and of magic which according to them springs out from the invisible world and has direct effects on the visible world. In their world, magic and the influence of an invisible reality is part of daily life, along with ancestors who can be of great help or of great bother.

The human being and its bodies: Germans were aware that a human being is made up of different parts.

Lik: This is the visible physical body, made of flesh and bones.

Hamr: This is the body which creates form. We nowadays call this the astral body. It accompanies a person all lifelong and gives the physical body the shape it has. It enables experiencing Seidr (see below) and magic. It is strongly connected to breath and breathing which is called Ond or Ondr. According to German and Nordic stories, Hamr can enable one to see in the invisible world (Ofreskir), to seem invisible to someone else's eyes, to travel to different places, to teleport, to travel in time, to accomplish remote actions, to deeply connect with animals, to travel in an animal body (Hamfarir) and even to change oneself into an animal (Hamrrammr). So now you know what inspired Harry Potter movies!

Likhamr ou Likamr: It is the guardian of physical life, of survival and of the physical body's life processes. We nowadays call this the etheric body. Life energy or life force is called Ond (when it is grammatically an object) or Ondr (when it is grammatically a subject).

Ond ou Ondr: This is life energy (Chinese Qi pronounced Tchee or Hindu prana). It penetrates all bodies when breathing occurs and it can also be moved using sound, postures, attention and concentration. It exists in air, in the sky, on land in plants and trees, in water and underground.

It can be stocked within objects made of organic matter, within certain shapes, within religious images or within talismans and it can be released when necessary.

Seidr: It is experiencing travel in the invisible world, what we would call in modern times astral travel or shamanistic travel. It is an inner experience where one can get access to required information, heal, see one's deep memories, know oneself, gather within oneself the different parts that live within of free oneself from something. This experience can include awakened dreams and conscious out of body experiences. This activity was mainly done by wemen in the German world.

Hamrrammr: This world means the ability to change into an animal. This may sound like science fiction but according to sagas, some people had to ability to change into animal or to influence other people's perception so that they were seen as an animal. On the other side of the Atlantic Ocean, writer Carlos Castaneda described how Mexican shaman Don Juan Mathus could do this.

Munr: This is the body that carries tastes, envies, desires, choices, feelings, sensations and emotions.

Hugr: This is intelligent awareness that can understand, know and adapt. It defines an ideal, a direction, a purpose and shows were to go.

Minni: This is technical intelligence that can think, analyze, find solutions and create tools to adapt.

Fylgja: This is a life form that accompanies every human being all along its life on earth, like a double, a guide, a protective being that attracts help and luck. Germans believed that if a person's Fylgja died, then the person also died. Fylgja could be a totem animal or a person. The word Fylgja is sometimes connected to the word soul. Most people discover it when they are about to die while shamans use it consciously for "out of body experiences" in the world hereafter.

Hamingja: This is part of family inheritance or to be more precise luck that accompanies a specific family and therefore a person from that family. It thus has come to mean personal inherited luck.

Destiny and law:

According to Germans, every effect has its cause even if one does not see the influence or the law that lies behind the observed effect. There is order behind life or rather a system of natural laws. This order that makes the world go round and the life form that created it was called Orlog. The idea of fatalism, of chance or of absolute freedom does therefore not exist according to the German way of thinking. There are laws, rules and influences due to family inheritance and to the way a person is structured. The path of the soul towards enlightenment and total unity with "The Source of all life" was called Wyrd. This word therefore meant destiny and sometimes fatality. Etymologically speaking, it comes from the word "wurt" meaning turning around or going back to where one came from or from the word wirth which is what must be done.

Supernatural beings called Norns imprinted a structure or a destiny pattern that is like an inner sky or an inner landscape. This structure gives people certain gifts, abilities and talents that the person should express as best as he can. The more a person does what she or he is good at, the more luck that person has. A person's gifts and his individual luck are called "gaefa". Norns regularly made prophecies called "Skop".

The use of personal power, self assertion and the practice of magic could then change one's destiny according to one's will, beliefs and certainties. What seemed to be written could therefore be re-written or written differently. The more a person understands the laws of life and takes them into account and the freer he becomes. Everyone should do his or her best to become a freer person and to accomplish one's destiny. Personal honor that results from accomplishing one's destiny and family honor were very important values for German people.

If personal, family or even national honor was attacked or spoiled, some Germans believed they had the right to punish, to ask for a compensating payment or even to murder whoever did that. This belief unfortunately nourished a spirit of vengeance that one often finds in German mythology and culture, even though German lands became Christian. This spirit of vengeance caused many wars, including WW2 and much suffering. Christian religion tends to bring to light the behavior of accepting what is, forgiveness, the power of love and firmness in doing what seems right.

How the German world is structured:

The three levels of existence: Asgard, Midgard and Utgard: The universe is divided into three areas. The visible, physical and more or less civilized world in which men live is in the middle and it is called Midgard. Above Midgard is the sky world Ljossalfheim which is inhabited by light elves and at the very top is Asgard the world of Ases or Gods. Below Midgard is the land down under, called Utgard and sometimes Hel. A rainbow bridge called Bifrost connects Midgard and Asgard.

The tree of life at the center of the world and the nine worlds: The whole universe is structured by a gigantic central life tree called Yggdrasil. It bears none worlds and exists thanks to the well of destiny, an enormous well called Wyrd. The well nourishes the tree and in return, the tree produces dew that fills up the well thus creating a complete life and water cycle. The word Yggdrasil either means Odin's vehicle or Ygg's battle horse, Ygg being Odin as creator or father of all life, or "the yew pillar or column". On the very top of the tree lives the eagle Hresvelg and on his head lives a falcon called Vedrfolnir. In a Nordic poem called Fjölsvinnsmál, a rooster called Vidofnir also lives in the tree. He takes care of cosmic order. At the bottom of the tree where the roots are lives a huge dragon snake called Nidhogg and many other snakes. Nidhogg lives under the third root of the tree and it is said that he devours the dead and turns them into nothingness, especially oath breakers, those who commit adultery and murderers.

A squirrel called Ratatosk runs up and down the tree to deliver messages between eagle and snake. All life and all souls are born from this tree of life. In many ancient cultures, eagle and snake symbolize male and female energy. Yggdrasil has three roots that plunge into three different worlds. One root reaches Niflheim (the world of fog) and below it is a source called Hvergelmir which is guarded by the dragon snake Nidhogg who constantly chews the root. From that source emerge all rivers as waves of ice that give birth to 12 rivers called Elivagar. The fog is created by fire and ice mingling together. The second root reaches a world called Jottunheim and under this root is a source, a fountain and also a well called Mimirsbrun. It is guarded by a giant. This is also where the giant Mimir's head lives. Whoever drinks from this fountain gets access to complete wisdom, to absolute knowledge and to all of the secrets of the universe.

This is where Odin sacrificed one of his physical eyes in exchange for wisdom and knowledge. Under the third root which goes right up to the world of Asgard is Urd's well also called the magician's well. Urd is one of the three Norns. The Norns engrave men and wemen's destinies but also the destinies of the Gods. This is the place where the Gods gather and meet. Somewhere in Yggdrasil also lives a goat called Heidhrun. She eats small branches to feed herself and she produces a special honey from which a magic drink called Hydromel is made. A deer also lives somewhere in the tree and feeds on the trees branches. It gathers huge amounts of rainwater and pours it into Hvergelmir, under the first root of Yggdrasil. Four smaller deers also live in the tree, upside down and feed on its spines. Their names are Dain, Dvalin, Duneyr and Durathnor and they symbolize the four directions. Just below Asgard is the world of The Vaenir Gods, Vanaheim and the world of the light elves, Alfheim. Men live in Manheim, the home of men, within Midgard.

The underworld is divided into various different worlds. In the southern regions is the fire world Muspelheim and in the northern region is the ice world Niflheim, also called Helheim as it is the world of the dead. Manheim, the world of the living, is separated from the world of the dead by a massive gate or door called Helgrind. Finally, a world was created specifically for giants, another, called Svartalfheim for dark elves and another called Nidavellir for dwarfs.

Creation of the world and giants: At the very beginning existed a huge empty space called Ginnumgagap. The physical world was then created and one day it will be destroyed during what is referred to as Ragnarok or the end of the world, event which will be preceded by an endless winter called Fimbulwinter. After that, it is said that a new world will arise.

So, after the very beginning of time when there was nothing, salted ice and fire were created. From these two elements were created the first two beings, a giant called Ymir and a cow called Audhumbla. The cow fed on salted ice and nourished Ymir with her milk. Audhumbla liked a block of salted ice and from it created the very first human giant called Bori and then another called Bolthorn. They are often called the first frost giants as they were created from frosty salted ice. In the part of the Icelandic story called Voluspa, it is written that the first human giant Bori had a son called Borr, that Borr married Bestia who was Bolthorn's daughter and that they had three sons, Odin the governor of Midgard, Villi the conscious will and

Vé the sacred faith. That was how the world of the frost giants, the Jotnar, was created. It was called Jotunheim and was one of nine worlds created in the universe. The three sons killed Ymir and used the different parts of his body to create earth, the salted sea, forests and clouds that all together make up Midgard, meaning the land in the middle, where men now live. They created other life forms like the dwarfs and latter, using two trees; they created the first human beings.

Aesir and Vaenir gods and goddesses: A group of gods and goddesses is called a pantheon. The German pantheon is made up of two groups of gods and goddesses who were at first at war one with the other and who then made peace and joined together. These are the Aesir and Vaenir Gods and goddesses. Vaenir Gods are a heritage from a period of time called the Neolithic (11 000 BC to 3000 BC) when the way of life changed from hunting and gathering to agriculture and livestock breeding.

The word "Ase", singular of Aesir, has the same etymology as Asura, the Sanskrit word that means "a god". It is said that Aesir gods and goddesses were brought to Europe by indo-European tribes migrating eastwards from Asia sometime around 3000 BC. Asia or Ase-ia actually means the "land of the Gods" because that is where they come from and because a few of them still live in the highest mountain of the world.

Distribution of activities into three categories: Long long ago and for a very long time, human societies, in Asia but also in Europe and more specifically in Greece, were organized into three groups, the group made up of leaders and priests, a group made up of warriors and organizers and a third group of farmers, craftsmen and small traders. Everyone knew which group they belonged too and each group had its gods and goddesses, who were often consulted using specific rituals so that requests could be answered and favors granted. The first group (rulers and priests) was at first governed by sky god Tyr or Tiw who was the king of the kings, the guardian of all laws and the supreme judge of harmony with the sky's will. Requests were made to him to create or bring back order, for legal matters and to obtain harmony and victory. Odin, who was a High Priest and Master Magician, also governed the first group. He was consulted to obtain answers, to gain more wisdom and to increase the effectiveness of magic rituals. The second group of people was governed by Thor. He took care of daily matters, of the world's businesses, of safety and of the weather.

He was consulted for protection and safety, for appropriate weather, for freedom and for victory. The third group was governed by twins Frey or Freyr and Freya, who brought adaptability, smartness, fertility, health, beauty, abundance and joy. Requests concerning love, richness, giving birth and happiness were made to them.

The Aesir: They have the responsibility of ruling the world and thus of war and peace. The first three Aesir are Odin, Villi and Vé. Odin marries the goddess Frigg (etymology friggu=love), earth goddess, life goddess and goddess of motherly love. They have many children including Thor and Baldr or Balder. Odin also has a son called Vidar with one of his mistresses, the giantess Grid or Gridr. Vidar becomes very famous for killing the giant wolf Fenrir. Amongst Odin and Frigg's other children are Meili, Nep, Vali, Ali, Hildolf, Hermod, Sigi, Saeming, Skjold and Itreksjod et possibly Heimdal, Hod et Bragi.

Odin: He was also called Wotan or Wodan amongst German people. The etymology of the word Odin seems to come from Od, which means divine breath. Odin means something like "inner fire from the divine source of all awareness" or "the fury to live and thrive" or "divine magical inspiration" or "the intelligent soul that lives here below and in the world hereafter". The world hereafter is called Walhalla and Odin's female assistants, the Walkyries, escort warriors who died on the battlefield to Odin's big hall where they continued to live. Icelandic sagas give Odin more than 160 names. He can suddenly appear under various nicknames or usernames. The goddess Freya thought him all about magic, rituals, how to get into a state of trance and how to create events and objects using the power of the verb through words and faith. He can turn himself into many animals and he sometimes becomes an eagle to travel. Odin has great curiosity and so he gave himself the means to acquire great knowledge. He travelled to the very source of wisdom, one of the three sources hidden under Yggdrasil, Mimirsbrun, that was guarded by the giant Mimir. There, he sacrificed one of his eyes in exchange for unlimited access to knowledge, magic and wisdom. He therefore became one-eyed. He then wounded himself with his spear and hung himself up a tree upside down during nine days and that's when he received the symbolic information system called the runes. Before Christianity arrived in German lands, people were sometimes sacrificed to honor Odin by piecing them with a spear and by hanging them to a tree! This was later in history considered barbarian, criminal and forbidden.

Odin finally succeeded in snatching the magic drink, Hydromel, which inspires people to write poetry. The two dwarfs Fjalarr and Galarr created this drink from the blood of the wisest and most inspired of all giants, Kvasir, whom they murdered. The recipe was transferred to the land of the giants were Odin, changing himself into a snake to get in and into an eagle to get out, was able to return to the land of the gods, Asgard, with the precious drink. It was then drunk by the gods, giving them access to intuitive knowledge and poetry.

Odin regularly questions Mimir's head which he maintains alive using herbs and magical spells. He uses it to gain knowledge about all that is hidden. He also tamed two crows or ravens called Huginn and Muninn (thoughts and memory), who travel to the various worlds and bring him back fresh news. He is thus very well informed. He has a long grey beard and is wears a dark blue coat. He travels riding his eight legged horse Sleipnir or by changing himself into a bird. He is sometimes escorted by two wolves, Geri and Freki. He also has a magic ring called Draupnir which can duplicate itself eight times and so create eight new rings every nine days. Odin invented writing and poetry. He sometimes conceals his identity when he travels using various disguises. He takes care of souls that pass over between this world down below and the world hereafter. For these reasons, when the Romans heard about Odin, they compared it to their god Mercury.

Odin helps bring success in all undertakings. He can see every person's destiny. He can bring victory on battlefields and help a person to cleverly adapt when difficulties arise. He can heal wounded horses and wounded people. He travels a lot, giving wise advice and intuitive inspiration to those who seek them. He is seen as a High Priest, as a Magician and as the Father of the Gods. Some people however said that he sometimes made them feel insecure because he can be cunning, totally unpredictable, deceitful and unreliable. He rules a day of the week named after him, Wotan's day which became Wednesday.

Goddess Frigg: She is Odin's wife and the mother of his children. She lives in Asgard, the land of the Gods. She is the only one, with, Odin, to have to right to sit on Throne of Gods, which is called Hlidskjalf and to take care of life in the universe. She takes care of households, of families and of the house. She can see what is invisible and she can see the future but she seldom reveals what she sees. It is said that she can weave clouds!

When Odin is away, she lives with her two brothers in law, Villi and Vé. She rules over Monday. She tends to overprotect her son Baldr because she feels that is not going to live for very long. When Baldr was murdered, she was deeply grieved and distressed and had to learn to live without him.

Thor: He was called Dunor, Dunat, Thunor or Thunar in ancient German languages. The word thunder is derived from his name. He is Odin and Frigg's first son. He protects humanity. He has red hair, a red beard and an incredible strength. He governs the world of men and does his best to bring order where there is chaos. He is a symbol of power and authority. He is nearly always traveling on his chariot, holding the reins in one hand and a magic hammer called Mjolnir in the other. With his hammer, he can make rain fall and lightning strike in a specific place. The giantess Grid, a word meaning impetuosity, gave him various magical objects like a magic belt called Megingjord which greatly increases Thor's strength, a magic glove called Jarngreip which allows him to hold and use his magic hammer and a magic spear called Gridarvol. Two magical goats called Tangrisnir and Tanngrjostr pull his chariot. He can feed on them as they regenerate themselves after each of Thor's meals. Thor fights many battles against giants. He is married to Sif with whom he has a daughter called Trud, who became a Walkyrie. He also has a mistress called Jarnsaxa, with whom he had a son called Magni and another called Modi. Romans compared him to Jupiter and to Hercules. He rules over Thursday which means Thor's day. He spends a lot of time solving the numerous problems and mischiefs created by the god Loki and by Loki's son, the Midgard snake called Jormungand. The rest of the time, he uses his power to serve humanity and to make the world go round.

Goddess Sif: She is Thor's wife. The word means an official and legal relationship. Sif was incredibly beautiful and she had golden hair. She was renowned for her great wisdom, for her inner peace and for her ability to see the future. She brought order and fertility to both land and families. Her golden hair symbolized wheat and barley fields. Many of the gifts made by dwarfs to the Gods were actually designed by her. Eddas (Nordic tales) say that Loki cut off Sif's braided hair as a joke. Thor was about to strangle Loki when Loki promised to help dwarfs make golden hair. And so it happened. Dwarfs then made many other objects for Sif, Thor and Odin. Thor and Sif symbolize unity between sky and earth and this unity was celebrated through rituals before Christian times.

Baldr: A tenth century manuscript resting in Merseburg cathedral mentions his name. Son of Odin and Frigg, he married a woman called Nanna and had a son called Forseti. The word Baldr means either lord, king, goodness, noble heart, whiteness or light. Baldr is a light god. He enhances and promotes people and objects. Icelandic poet Snorri Sturluson says he built the biggest and the most beautiful ship, called Hringhorni, ever built. One of the poems in the Edda is called "Baldr's dream". It actually describes Baldr's nightmares as he sees himself die. The other gods had a debate over these nightmares. They decided to build a special armor for Baldr and had all objects swear that they would not harm the light god. All objects swore except mistletoe. Loki heard about this, made a special arrow out of mistletoe and had Baldr's blind brother Hod fire it, thus killing Baldr. Hod was killed and Loki chained up for eternity. Following tradition, Baldr's body was placed on his ship. The ship was set on fire and a giantess pushed the ship far into the ocean. Eddas say that after Ragnarok, i.e. after the end of the world occurs, Baldr will revive and rule over the world with other gods.

Heimdal: Heimdal is Asgard's sentinel. He guards and protects Asgard. He is said to be an enigmatic god. He is described in very different ways in the various sources of information previously mentioned so we don't really know who he is. It is said that he has extraordinarily sharp eyesight that can see even in the dark, a very strong sense of smell and that she shines even in daylight because he is so white. He is sometimes compared with a ram or with the sun. Legends say he is the son of nine mothers but we don't know who his father is. He carries with him a magic spear and a special trumpet called Gjallarhorn, which he is supposed to use to warn the gods when the end of the world comes. It is him who will kill Loki when the end of the world comes. According to Snorri Sturluson, he lives just beside Bifrost, the rainbow bridge that connects Asgard with Midgard. He travelled all over the world and had three children who gave rise to the three social groups previously mentioned. He is therefore the father of humanity. He knows all about runes and though some of his children how to make and use them.

Loki: The etymological origin of the word is unknown. He is the son giants Laufey and Farbauti. He is both a giant and one of the Aesir gods. He is extremely intelligent but also jealous, sardonic, sarcastic, facetious, malicious, perfidious, treacherous, vicious and always creating problems. He loves disguising himself and he can change into any animal. Many tales relate his numerous mischiefs. He cut off Frigg's braid and ran away with it.

He stole Thor's gloves and belt and also the sacred apples that give eternal youth. His worst crime was the murdering Baldr. When Baldr died, the gods asked the goddess of death to bring Baldr back. She only agreed to do so if no one disagreed. But as Loki disguised himself into someone who did disagree, Baldr had to stay amongst the dead. The gods chained Loki up to three enormous rocks and place a venomous snake on top of him. Poison often dripped from the snake and burned Loki, making him scream out with pain. According to Nordic tales, this is what causes earthquakes all over the world. Loki did sometimes help the gods however. He recovered Thor's hammer which was stolen by a giant. He also got Freya out of trouble when a giant made a bet that would have obliged Freya to go live with the giants if he won. Giant's bet they could build an enormous wall around Asgard in a relatively short time, thanks to a magical horse that could carry stones extremely quickly. Loki turned himself into a beautiful mare that distracted the horse and so the giant lost his bet.

Loki was married to Sigyn and had two sons called Vali and Narfi. One of his sons was changed into a wolf by the gods and he killed his brother due to jealousy. He had a mistress called Angrboda with whom he created a daughter called Hel, a giant wolf called Fenrir and a snake called Jormungandr. When he disguised himself into a mare to help Freya, an eight legged horse called Sleipnir, who became Thor's horse, was born. One of the Icelandic poems called Lokasenna talks about Loki's critics made towards the other gods during a feast organized by the giant Aegir, the god of oceans. It is said that when the end of the world comes, he will lead the giants to fight the gods and will get killed by Heimdal.

Tyr or Tiw also spelled Tiew and Tiwaz: He is one of the most ancient gods. Tiew is a very old word meaning God. It was written Ju and gave rise to the word Jupiter meaning the father of gods. At dawn of humanity, he was the supreme sky god and the light of god or the Star of God. He then became the god of cosmic justice and of victory in battle. He was renowned for his bravery and wisdom. Eddas say he accepted sacrificing his hand in Fenrir's mouth so that the other gods could then tie the wolf up. He chaired the Thing, the assembly where gods met and he dealt with order, law and justice. Romans curiously compared him to the god Mars. A day was named after him, Tiew's day and so he rules over Tuesday.

Vidarr or Vitharr: Son of Odin, he is often called « the silent God » as he seldom talks. It is said in Icelandic Poems that it is he who will kill the giant wolf Fenrir when the end of the world comes, after Fenrir kills Odin. He kills the wolf by putting one of his feet in the wolf's mouth, by opening the wolf's mouth with one hand and by stabbing Fenrir with the other hand. French expert in mythology Georges Dumézil (1898-1986) says that Vitharr is the god who creates space so that people, events and life can exist.

Other Aesir gods: Amongst them is Aegir, God of Oceans and also of beer. He was nine daughters who are responsible for creating waves in the ocean. The other Nordic gods are Bragi, Hod, Vidar, Valli or Ali, Ull, Forseti son of Baldr, Villi and Ve, Modi and Magni, Mimir, Meili, Hoenir, Hermod and Delring.

Other Aesir goddesses: Eir, Fulla, Gefjun, Gna, Hlin, Lofn, Sjofn, Snotra and Syn are the other Aesir goddesses.

Vaenir gods: Little is known about them. They were created when life was created. They rule over wildlife, fertility, luck, health, youth, love, joy of being alive, farming, crafting and abundance. They live in the land of the Vaenir, Vanaheim. They are masters in Seid or Seidr, i.e. magic and witchcraft. At the beginning of time, tem and Aesir were enemies but as no one could win, they finally made peace and exchanged hostages. That's how Vaenir god Kwasir and also Njord, with his children Freyr and Freya immigrated to the land of the Aesir while Vaenir gods Hosir and Mimir immigrated to Vanaheim. From a historical point of view, the war that took place between Aesir and Vaenir gods symbolizes what happened in Europe, where farming communities (Vaenir) were overruled by nomadic hords of hunters, gatherers and warriors (Aesir) coming from the east. Some people suggest that the Aesir/Vaenir issue also symbolizes social class conflicts because the first ever existing two social classes made of rulers/priests and organizers/business people got together to fight the third social class made up of farmers, craftsmen and small traders. Another point of view deserves attention. Aesir gods symbolized the power to create, to have goals and to fight to make them come through while Vaenir gods symbolize the power to master the world of matter and to live a happy and healthy life. The word Vaenir is very similar to the word Venus which actually is the goddess of nature, pleasure, happiness, craftsmanship, love and artistic abilities. Both words seem to come from the Sanskrit word "vanas" which means nature, forests, desire and physical love.

The god Njord or Njordr sometimes written Nierdh: According to Eddas, he was created by the powers of wisdom. A poem called Solarljod says he had nine daughters, that the eldest was called Radhveig and the youngest Kreppvor. He is Freyr and Freya's father. His home is somewhere in the heavens. He rules over wind. He can create life and abundance on both land and sea. He has abundant wealth. Due to a combination of circumstances, he married Aesir goddess Skadi, who had to choose a husband just by looking at his feet. Njord wanted to live by the sea while Skadi wanted to live in the mountains. They were at first able to compromise, living half time near the sea and half time in the mountains but they eventually separated because neither was truly happy about the situation. Skadi then went out with Odin with whom she had many children. Sailors and fishermen prey to Njord to get favorable winds and great amounts of fish. He is often linked with a Goddess called Nerthus, who is the Goddess of abundance and who seems to be either his spiritual sister but also possibly the companion with whom he had his children.

Frey or Freyr: Roman historian and writer said Germans believed to come from an original ancestor named Mannus, the first man, who was himself created by an androgynous god called Tuisto. Mannus gave rise to three German tribes called the Ingvaevones, the Herminones and the Istvaeones. Ing meant "lord of the light" and at first Freyr was called Ingvifreyr. He symbolized the sun and the life it brought. Freyr travels around on a huge boar called Gullinbursti. He is the son or Njord and the brother of Freya. He married giantess Gerdhr and to do so, he had to give her his magic sword. This symbolizes using and sharing one's strength and creative power. He is sometimes represented by statuettes with big penises to show his power to fertilize. He rules over good weather, sunshine, rain and the growth of trees, fruit and vegetables. He brings success, peace, prosperity and abundance. It is written that he will be killed by the god of fire from the sky at the end of time, during Ragnarok. This is an old way of saying that all life in the solar system and on earth will eventually be destroyed when galaxy Andromeda collides with our own, in some 4 or 5 billion years.

Freya: Her name comes from ancient German languages and meant female goddess (Frau+Ase), princess or woman (fraujaz, fraujo). She may be the Scandinavian version of German Goddess Frigg although Frigg symbolizes the moon (the mother of life) while Freya symbolizes Venus (wife and woman). She is Njord's daughter and Freyr's sister.

She is incredibly beautiful. She is the goddess of love, beauty, sensuality, sexual pleasure, joy and sacred connection with nature but also of magic, seeing what is invisible and creating forms and events. During special ceremonial acts, she helps people find the right partner and is consulted for issues concerning weddings and prosperity. She helps wemen to give birth and also sometimes accompanies warriors to the battlefield. She married the god Odh, who travelled a lot and was often away. She sometimes cried because her beloved husband was not with her and it is said that her tears changed into pearls of gold. She sometimes went out looking for him under different names. She was sometimes called Gefn, she who brings happiness, Syr the lady boar who nourishes all and also the Vaenir dise or Vanadis, dise meaning fairy, goddess, lady, woman, spirit or ghost. She had two daughters called Hnoss and Gersemi.

Many a giant tried to kidnap her because he wanted her at his side but every attempt failed. Her most precious possession is a magic necklace made by four dwarfs after Freya spent a night which each one of them. She also has a falcon feathered coat can allows her to change into a bird, a chariot pulled by two cats who can fly and a huge boar called Hildesvini. She lives in a beautiful palace called Folkvang where beautiful music is played. Half of all warriors and all wemen that die on the battlefield arrive at her estate while the other half go to Odin's estate. Loki accused her of doing witchcraft and of sleeping out with anybody to get what she wants. She is the goddess of Life, of Mother-Earth and of Mother Nature.

Dark forces and the end of the world:

Midgard's snake, the world snake also called Jormungandr which means giant snake:

He is Loki's second child. When Odin leaned about his existence, he went out for him, grabbed him and threw him in the ocean. He became so long and big that he was able to wrap himself around the entire planet by biting his own tail. That is actually how the world of matter, Midgard, can actually continue to exist. In one tale that gave rise to many theater shows, Thor goes out fishing with the giant Hymir. He cuts an enormous cow's head, clips it on a fishing hook and throws it into the ocean. The snake bites the hook and Odin is about to cut its head when Hymir cuts the rope just in time. In Icelandic poems, it is written that when Ragnarok, the end of the world comes, the snake will unravel his tail causing the world to break up into pieces.

Fenrir: He is a giant wolf created by Loki. After having failed twice to tie up the wolf, the Aesir gods asked the dwarfs to create a very special rope. The wolf only accepted to be tied up if someone put one of their hands in his mouth. Tiw was the only one who accepted. As the wolf could not free himself before the end of time, he bit off Tiw's hand. Some Icelandic poems say he will devour the sun and the moon at the end of time and then get killed by Vidhar. Various Nordic artistic creations show episodes of Fenrir's story.

Ragnarok, the end of the world: Nordic legends say that when the end of the world will occur, almost everything will be destroyed by fire. Fenrir will eat up the sun and the moon and kill Odin and then die. World order will collapse when the Midgard snake frees himself. Thor will kill him but die by being poisoned. Most gods and living creatures will get killed but not all. Then, after a while, a new earth and a new world, ruled by the light god Baldr, will rise from the ashes of the past. Later, two new human beings called Lif and Liftraser, who hid somewhere inside Yggdrasil, will allow humanity to slowly but steadily exist again.

Other life forms:

Elves: Etymologically speaking, the world Elf means the first one as the elves where the first beings created on planet Earth. They came from the east and they mostly live in forests but also in the heavens. They are supernatural beings who are amazingly beautiful and intelligent. They mostly help men when their help is asked for but they also sometimes punish people.

Dwarfs: They were created at the beginning of time to help and support life on Earth. They live underground or in the mountains. They are described as beings that are small, often ugly but very strong and gifted with great practical and creative skills. They have an amazing talent for working with metal and for creating magical objects. All of the fantastic objects and tools used by the gods were created by dwarfs. They also sometimes guard sacred places.

Norns: Under one of Yggdrasil's roots, there is a well called the well of destiny or Udharbrunn also called « the Well of Urdh ». Three giantesses called Norns live and work near the well. They take water from the well and water the tree with it, thus keeping the tree healthy. They are master of destiny and so they know all there is to be known about men's destinies.

It is they who weave people's destinies. This means that that create, nourish, maintain and they destroy men and wemen's destinies. They decide what is and what will be. They are the guardians of fate. The first Norn is called Urdh or Wyrd (what happened in the past). She is the Gran mother. She creates by taking into account what has been and so she symbolizes fatality or karma. The second Norn is called Verdandi (what is happening now). She rules over the present moment. She is the mother that nourishes life. The third Norn is called Skuld (what should be and what will be). She puts an end to life on earth in a physical body. She is the daughter who can make promises for the future, for life in the world hereafter. Norns are sometimes caring and benevolent and sometimes harsh and malicious. According to Nordic stories, they were often accused when a problem arose and gratefully thanked when a lucky event occurred.

Dises: This word means something like "wemen who can do magic". Dises are sacred wemen, goddesses, female spirits who can bring about fertility, good harvests, harmony, luck and life on earth but also in the world hereafter. Before the coming of Christianity, they were worshiped during special feasts and rituals called "disablot". They protect warriors, wemen and also families.

Walkyries: The word itself means something like "those who choose the dead". Walkyries are often king's or noblemen's daughters. They are warriors and often wear armor. They bring about victory in the battlefields and so carry out Odin's will as to who will win a battle. They choose which warriors will die and then accompany them to their new dwelling place in the world hereafter. They travel on flying horses. Sometimes, they protect people, act as lovers and bring hydromel to heroes and to the gods.

Vaetirs: They are a special group of life forms that are part of nature's elemental forces. They create and maintain life in the world of matter. Amongst the different Vaetirs are the Landvaetir or earth spirits who tend to stay connected with a specific place, the water spirits called Sjovaettir, elves, dwarfs and giants. It is said that Viking warriors who landed on an unknown lands took off the dragon heads on their ships front so as not to frighten and stir up the local Vaetirs.

If you want to learn more about everyday Nordic mythology, the comics who tell the saga of Thorgal Aegirsson will greatly satisfy your curiosity and delight your imagination.

Odin's matrix: If you combine runes 7 and 11, you get Danish rune 9. If you multiply this new rune by three, you get the matrix below from which all runes are created. With this matrix, you can see how existing runes were created and you can also create new ones! Such a matrix can be created on a square wooden board using small nails, a ruler and fishing thread. It can be used as a talisman, for magic or to visualize a rune.

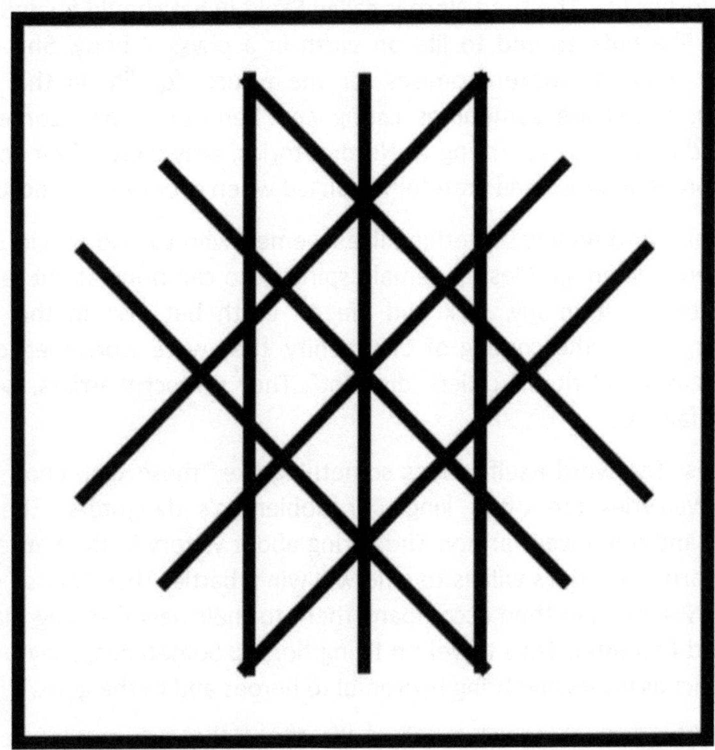

Chapter 3: The 24 true and original runes

The knowledge about how to use the runes and what each rune means was only passed on orally. German shamans spoke about how they experienced each rune and invited the apprentice to observe how he personally feels about each rune, to experience the runes and to move along his personal path towards his or her deep inner truth. And so that's what I invite you to do if you want to.

800 years then went by before anybody wrote anything about runes so we don't know if the information system was changed and if so how. "Reality" however is what it is so that one can suppose that men living at that time described it in a practical and meaningful manner and they were able to put aside personal beliefs that tend to filter information. Runes were created to be a communication tool between men and the gods or between men and secret forces of nature, life and soul but also as a tool to influence reality by being magical symbols or forms. One of nature's laws is that every form vibrates in a specific way and emits waves of energy. Runes are forms so they emit specific waves of energy.

Below is a vision both ancient and modern of the 24 runic symbols.

Runes were organized into three families, called Aetts, of eight runes each and each family is ruled the god represented by the first rune of that family. Freyr rules over the first family, which is called Frey's Aett, Heimdall over the second and Tiw over the third.

In this book, we will observe the name of the rune in the various Germanic languages, its graphical form, its number in the 24 runic suite, its meaning, it's sound, its key words and the oldest sources we have which are the English, Norwegian and Icelandic runic poems so as to describe how each rune vibrates and what energy it emits. We will then connect each rune to various things that are a part of life on Earth. We will finally see what god each rune is connected to, how to use each rune to do magic and how every rune can be compared to other information systems.

Rune 1: FEHU

Various names given to this rune:

Name and meaning in Old Norse: Fe. The herd. Creating wealth.
Name and meaning in Old German: Fehu. Livestock, ownership, property.
Name and meaning in Old English: Feoh or Fee. Livestock, market value, money, price or fee, personal property, what belongs to you and only you.

Its graphic design and form: 19 out of the 24 runes are built with a vertical line. This line symbolizes energy moving upwards from earth to sky but also from the sky down to the earth. It both embeds things into matter and allows one to see the appropriate spiritual meaning of what is. Diagonal lines symbolize the soul in action and motion across land and sky. Here, the two upward small moving lines symbolize both a powerful thrust of creative power and duality, or at least action in a world full of duality. If you reproduce the rune's form with your body standing up, your two arms will be raised towards the sky one above the other. You can then feel the rune's energy. You may also observe that rune Feoh has similarities and therefore connections with rune 4, "As" but that the two energies are different.

Its number: Because Fehu is the first rune within the Futhark, it logically symbolizes beginnings, the origin of things, the birth of something, new events, someone young and with little or no experience and making things start so that they get on as they should and so that what must be done is done.

Summary and essence of this rune: I am, I act and I create wealth! I am the source of all energy, life's fire, the fire of creation that enables people to experience and use their creative power. This fire is expressed by the ability to have an intention and to focus attention towards attaining a specific and defined goal. It implies being connected with your heart, deciding, being motivated and acting spontaneously, confidently, with enthusiasm, energy and joy. So what is at stake with this rune is creating an event, a situation, an object or wealth, either from scratch or by using available resources, abilities and tools.

Putting energy into motion has consequences and a price to pay. It all starts with this rune. Each person is responsible for his or her actions and creations. When correctly used, Fehu is an energy rune and a success rune.

The dark side of the rune: When the dark side of Fehu is expressed, fire energy is used in an unbalanced way. There is a lack of clear vision, bad intentions, a problem at the source of things, a loss, a goal that is not achieved, illusions, lack of care leading to lack of efficiency and something that is just not balanced. It is then necessary to straighten things out, to define what is really important, what is really motivating and what must really be done.

Its sound: The f sound is the sound made when one blows on a fire to light it up, to make it grow and to keep it burning. You can experience this if you light up a fire in a recipe, in a chimney or a campfire. Fire brings heat, light and confidence. It is a source of energy that allows creating and transforming food, objects and wealth. It must however be channeled, managed and controlled.

Key words: Action, using creative power, beginning something, newness, wealth, resources, prosperity, a positive answer, financial power and what is earned through action.

People and jobs connected to this rune: A new born baby, a young and active person, a debutant, a creator, a workman, a craftsman, a salesman, an apprentice.

Gods connected to this rune: This rune is linked with Freyr who symbolizes life-force and also to Vidarr who create space so that life forms can thrive and so that events can take place.

Places and objects connected to this rune: Workshops, companies, sports halls, public sites, streets, markets, fairs and a place where something is going on.

Colors connected to this rune: Red, red and white, white.

Animals connected to this rune: Horses, rams, monkeys, dragons, otters, crows and salamanders.

English, Norwegian and Icelandic poems: They use figurative language, imagery and metaphors called "kennings" which often refer to elements of Nordic mythology.

The English poem:
Wealth brings comfort to all men
But everyone should use it and share it freely
To gain the approval of the lord

This poem firstly says that one must have the freedom to act and create wealth. It then says that whatever wealth is created, it does not belong to the person who created it but to life. The person is just the temporary owner of whatever material wealth he created. It finally says that goods created through activity should move around and be shared. Only so does a person horror his self (his lord) and express the best of who he or she is.

The Norwegian poem:
Wealth is a source of discord amongst kinsmen
The wolf lives in the forest

The first sentence refers to the story of Hreimarr the Dwarf who demanded other people to give him their wealth and yet who refused to share his own. He had two sons, Fafnir and Reginn. His son Fafnir murdered him to have all the family wealth for himself. Fafnir had the ability to change into a dragon and he was killed by warrior and hero Sigurd with a sword made by Reginn, Fafnir's brother. The second phrase is about the wolf Fenrir who was finally tied up by the gods after two unsuccessful attempts. The wolf represents the wild side of creative power. Creating something has consequences and any wealth that is not managed wisely and rightly can potentially be dangerous, like a wolf living in a forest.

The Icelandic poem:
Source of discord amongst kinsmen
And fire from the sea
And a path for the snake

Fire from the sea symbolizes life energy that gives rise to creative power and creation. The meaning is similar to that suggested by the wolf in the Norwegian poem but here, the phrase is about the world serpent, who allows the world of matter (Midgard) to exist but who can also bring about temptation and many problems. The giant snake also represents survival abilities and sexual instincts. It suggests that everything has consequences and that every impulse of energy is once born, lives and one day dies.

Using this rune to do magic: Fehu is used to successfully start something, to feel confident and to have the energy and motivation it takes to make decisions, to take action and to succeed. It is also used to optimize resources and to acquire or create wealth.

Links with other information systems:

I Ching: This rune is connected with the I Ching's first hexagram, "Creative Power".

Mayan Astrology: The first of the 20 Mayan glyphs, called the dragon, is very similar to what Fehu represents.

Tarot: Rune Fehu is connected to the first tarot card, the Juggler also called the Magician. Because it is also connected to the Nordic God Freyr who symbolizes life force seeking to thrive, Fehu can be also be connected with the Greek God Pan and thus with card 15.

Astrology: Fehu can be related to the astrological sign of Aries and to a mix of planets Mars, Sun, Mercury and Venus (planets as defined using astrology where the moon and the sun are considered to be planets or moving bodies).

Rune 2: UR or URUZ

then sometimes became

Various names given to this rune:
Name and meaning in Old Norse: Ur or Uruz. Water, rain, drizzle.
Name and meaning in Old German: Uruz. Auroch, cash cow, milk cow.
Name and meaning in Old English: Ur. Ox.

Comment on endings az, iz or uz: These letters were sometimes added at the end of a rune's name. They mean something like "something sacred, divine or magical".

Its graphic design and form: The first symbol shown is the original rune symbol when the 24 runes were created. If, looking at the first symbol, you go from ground level to up above, then you can say that two lines meet in the heavens, one completing and supporting the other. If you go from heavens downwards, then you can say that from one source emerge two lines that go in two different directions but both arrive on a same ground level invisible horizontal line. The vertical line stays as it is. It is the axis of life. One can also say that something leaves the top of the axis without the axis itself being changed. It connects with something else to create a new form. Now if you sit on a stool and milk a cow with your hands, you will be is a similar position to the form sketched by the rune Uruz. The rune's graphic can also suggest a tipi, a tent or a shelter.

Its number: Second rune within the Futhark, it logically symbolizes life starting to manifest itself, forms being created, preparation, things in a gestation period, the birth or delivery of something and taking care of what has just being created. Number two symbolizes female energy but also making a difference between two elements, separating something in two, combining two things and a life giving force.

Summary and essence of this rune: I am life expressing itself and the happy intuitive connection between the Source of all life and I. The source of all life naturally flows through me so that I can nourish, take care and support where necessary. I am the matrix, the reservoir or the chamber where life is created.

I am the structure of life that is made of energy and information and that acts as a mould from where everything is created. I am water who carries information so that new forms can be created. I am the Eternal Feminine who embodies in the material world and who creates and supports life. So, Ur represents a female power that nourishes life, that prepares what needs to be prepared and that gives birth to what is ready to be born. It represents intuitive knowledge of life and of the human soul, the ability to memorize and to see what has been memorized, faith that life always finds its right way through at the right rhythm and an ability to select and pass on required information. Just as Earth channels the flow of a river, Ur channels and organizes the flow of information. When it is well used, Ur is a powerful birth giving, slow, peaceful, happiness building, happy and persevering rune. It brings humbleness and the will to be of service to life.

If strong male runes or violent runes (example runes 7, 13, 15, 16) are close by in a spread however, it can then sometimes turn into a raging bull.

The dark side of the rune: It manifests as heaviness and passivity and also either as the slowness cows and bulls express or on the opposite as sudden moments of rage. In its dark aspects, this rune can symbolize a difficulty to give birth to something, excessive slowness, things lagging behind, inner confusion, lack of depth and vision, hidden things impacting the situation negatively, incorrect information or a difficulty in seeing invisible trends correctly.

Its sound: This rune is connected to the "oo" sound.

Key words: life force, physical or material strength, as strong as a bull, listen to what is, receptivity, motherly love and protection, refuge, shelter, nourishment, wellness, rest and undergo renewal, a slow process, natural and slow evolution, producing something, data media, handling an information system, preparing something, finding appropriate information, giving birth to, feeling happy because of connection to life.

People and jobs related to this rune : a calm and smooth person, a woman, a mother, a Granma, a cook, a nutritionist, a midwife, a schoolteacher, a babysitter, a trainer, a wet-nurse, a pediatrician, a therapist, a librarian, someone who created data media, a printer, someone producing objects, a psychic, a fortuneteller, a guardian.

Gods connected to this rune: This rune represents the mythological cow Audhumla. She was created from nothingness at the beginning of time along with hermaphrodite giant Ymir. She feeds herself by licking salty frost and gives rise to 4 milk rivers that nourish all the giants. As she licks a specific block of salty frost, she creates the giant called Buri who has a son called Borr. Borr marries Bestia and so he is the Grandfather of the gods who created the material world, Odin, Villi and Vé.

Places and objects connected to this rune: Hidden places, secret places, sacred places, mirrors, a therapist's office, a fortuneteller's office, a hospital, a clinic, a monastery, a temple, a library, a book store, a server room, a publishing house, any place where one experiments nourishment, resourcing, relaxation and renewal.

Colors connected to this rune: lavender or milk color.

Animals connected to this rune: a cow, an Auroch, a reindeer, a turtle, an owl, a cat, a beetle.

English, Norwegian and Icelandic poems:

The English poem: The Auroch is brave and has powerful horns. It is a wild beast who fights with its horns. It is a tough, resolute and courageous creature who roams across the land.
This poem is clearly about wild oxen or Aurochs who existed in great numbers before being wiped out, probably by hunting and global warming. The power and abundance of life is what is put forward here, whether it is symbolized by the milk giving cow or by the wild ox that can be either very peaceful or furious.

The Norwegian poem: Dross comes from bad iron. Reindeers often race over frozen snow.
The first sentence is about producing domestic objects and weapons made out of iron. At the time, this was a very complex process as the quality iron could be good or bad. Objects were produced with stone or wooden molds. What was produced often lasted a whole lifetime. So this is about producing something that requires time but that has long term effects. The second sentence is about running reindeers. They can only run because they are healthy and full of life but also because the ground they run on is solid due to dense layers of snow.

A reindeer is a symbol of life, of nourishment and of well being as it brought to North men milk, meat and also clothing and equipment to built housing.

The Icelandic poem: Shower is lamentation of the clouds and ruin of hay-harvest and loathing of the shepherd.

This poem is about water. Where the first rune was connected to fire, this one is connected with water. It says that if water can bring wellness and life, it can also bring about emotional stress if harvested crops rot because there is too much water or if rain prevents shepherds from taking good care of their sheep.

Using this rune to do magic: Rune Uruz is used to be healthy and full of life, to have the necessary strength to heal, to be inspired, to be connected to one's intuition and to feminine energy, to have faith in life and to use the magical power of faith, to correctly prepare what must be and to be psychologically prepared for what is to come, to produce something, to find the right keys and the appropriate information and to create strong emotional bonds with someone.

Links with other information systems:

I Ching: This rune is symbolically connected with the second hexagram of the I Ching, receptivity or the Eternal Feminine.

Mayan Astrology: Uruz can be linked with the third Mayan glyph which is called night or the dwelling place.

Tarot: Rune Ur is connected to the second tarot card, the High Priestess. Because this rune is connected to Vaenir god Freyr, pure natural material life force, represented by the God Pan in the tarot, it can also be liked with card 15 called the devil (too much water or fire).

Astrology: Rune Uruz is obviously connected with the second astrological sign, Taurus, with the Taurus-Scorpio axis and with a planetary mix of Moon, Venus and a bit of Mars and Pluto.

Rune 3: THURS ou THORN

Various names given to this rune:
Name and meaning in Old Norse: Thurs. A giant.
Name and meaning in Old German: Thurisaz. A strong man.
Name and meaning in Old English: Thorn. A thorn.

Its graphic design and form: The vertical line shows as always a connection between earth and sky, between reality and goals. A specific energy is then directed towards earth so as to dominate matter while another energy is directed towards heavens so as to nourish the sky and what the sky symbolizes (a higher vision, goals, will power and so on). The two energies meet in a central zone, halfway between sky and earth. From this encounter arises a new third energy which is always in motion. He or she who uses it can use it as a weapon for protection but also to adapt to surroundings. What is this weapon? It is the power of intelligence, of smartness, of being clever! It can force events into being and make a person adapt. It can however be double-edged! How so? Well, it can be like a thorn planted in your feet and a burden that hinders any progress. One can easily imagine a hatchet that can be thrown when looking at the icon. One can also imagine either a pregnant woman or a man holding his erect penis. It can finally represent a tongue coming out of a mouth. All of these images are clues to understand this rune. So rune Thorn helps protect against chaos. It brings life and connection to life and nature. It is a tool one can use to adapt by using one's intelligence and one's ability to communicate. But speech and sexual desires can also create discord and cause havoc when they are used in an aggressive and violent manner. Thorn can therefore be tricky and well, thorny. It is in its essence both a sexual conquering life energy and a mental intelligent always in motion energy that is created though unity between oneness and duality.

Its number: Thorn is rune number three and is created by uniting 1 and 2. It is a synthesis of 1 and 2, of two complementary male and female forces like for example will and faith, courage and joy, fatherly and motherly love, human nature and animal nature, spirit and soul, soul and matter. Three is a new unity, a new intention and the means to create new forms from two different but complementary elements.

Summary and essence of this rune: I am life's intelligence that is always in motion and life's organizational power. These forces can overcome chaos, obstacles and any hostile force. They can protect what needs to be protected, create new forms, objects or events and make me instinctively adapt where ever I am.

The dark side of the rune: It manifests as disharmony, lies, conflict, violence, perversity and misery brought about when rough sexual energy and the monkey like thinking mind express themselves in a stupid and wild manner, when they are not connected to the heart and properly channeled.

Its sound: This rune is liked with the « th » sound as in thorn or thank you.

Key words: a moving impulse, a force channeled by intention, organizational power, instinctive intelligence that is struggling to make life thrive, intensive use of a weapon, of the mind or of sexual energy to create something, adapting smartly to a changing environment, mastering energy, protecting what needs to be protected.

People and jobs connected to this rune: someone with lots of energy and with a fighting spirit, someone who adapts, a smart person, a sales person, a sales assistant, a press agent, a task officer, an executive secretary, a journalist, a writer, drafter or editor, an office clerk, a business woman, jobs implying providing and coordinating information, jobs were there is a lot of moving around, were there is contact with the public or were the use of numbers or communication techniques is required, white collar occupations, postman, footballer, psycho-motor therapist or speech therapist, physiotherapist, language expert.

Gods connected to this rune: This rune is related to Thor's fist tool. Before he got his famous hammer, he has a special ax, which he still has. This ax allowed him to chop off illusions so as to clearly analyze what is here and now but also to build a shelter and to protect himself. By symbolically going from ax to hammer, he goes from intelligence to power. This rune is also related to mistletoe and to the deadly weapon made by Loki to kill Baldr, who symbolizes beauty, eternal joy and grace. The Gods forgot to ask mistletoe not to harm Baldr as they thought mistletoe could cause no farm. So Loki made a mistletoe arrow as asked his blind brother to throw it at Baldr. Baldr was killed and that lead to the end of the world. Thorn can cause a lot of harm, be double edged and underestimating its power can be fatal.

Places and objects connected to this rune: Places where people share information and where there is a lot of movement, meeting rooms, conference rooms, offices, a communications agency, a shop, office equipment, quotations, sales documents and all objects that enable communicating, writing and adapting.

Colors connected to this rune: Light green.

Animals connected to this rune: A dog, Le chien, a magpie, a falcon, a crane, a stork, a lynx or bobcat, a butterfly, a rabbit.

English, Norwegian and Icelandic poems:

The English poem:
A thorn is extremely sharp, painful and deadly,
Something any knight must avoid touching
and fierce to anyone that sits amongst them.
The poem refers to the mistletoe arrow that caused Baldr's death. It is about sexual energy and how devastating it can be when it is expressed in a wild and chaotic manner. It is also about the sharp thinking mind that can cut reality into pieces and analyze clearly what is but that can also be painful and lead to loss of joy and to paralysis of the soul when it is wrongly used or when it takes the place that should be occupied by one's awareness connected to the heart. Sitting amongst thorns is symbolically using one's tongue or intelligence wrongly.

The Norwegian poem:
Giants make wemen anguished and even sick
Misfortune makes no one cheerful

Giants symbolize primitive female forces, chaotic subconscious impulses and also thoughts and words that made all creation possible. In the beginning lived giants. In the beginning was the verb. From giants everything was created. The first is about the power of sexual energy and the ability to think, which both make wemen anguished and sometimes unhappy. Using these forces wrongly leads to misery and takes away joy and cheerfulness which are of divine essence.

The icelandic poem:
Giant is torture of wemen and of cliff dweller and of the man from Vardhruna (husband of a giantess).

The meaning of the first sentence is very similar to that of the Norwegian poem but here attention is placed on female menstrual cycles, on female desires that are not easily shared, on giving birth to children that could in old times be deadly and on the thinking mind that takes place over intuition and faith. All that can be torture! The second and third sentences I'm not sure about and it seems some mythological data is missing here. Vardhruna means a secret that helps preventing something from happening or that protects against something. If the word "giant" is replaced by sexual impulses or the always thinking monkey mind, then the poem could be translated as follows: "wild instincts and thinking processes make people think that they are right, that they know everything or that they know the truth". That can lead to some people committing suicide by jumping off a cliff. Mind and instincts can prevent a person from being protected. Bad ideas, using one's intelligence wrongly or chaotic instincts can lead to mischief and trouble.

Using this rune to do magic: Thorn can be used to bring about change, to adapt efficiently, to make successful sales, to conquer whatever or whoever is desired, to have a partner respond positively to an offer, a request or a demand and to force love or desire upon a partner (not a good idea but it was used for that!). It can also be used to be protected, to put down or remove an obstacle, to overcome an opponent and to wipe out an enemy.

Links with other information systems:

I Ching: This rune relates to hexagram number three, "Adapting to one's environment" also called "Difficult beginnings".

Mayan Astrology: This rune is a mix of the second (wind), third (night), fourth (seed) and fifth (snake) glyphs. (See the book I wrote called Practical Mayan Astrology)

Tarot: Thorn is a mix of Empress (card 3), Emperor (card 4), Force (card 11) and Devil (card 15).

Astrology: This rune is a mix of Mercury, the Moon, Mars, Jupiter and Pluto.

Rune 4 : ASS ou AS

Various names given to this rune:

Name and meaning in Old Norse: Ass. A god. One of the Aesir gods.
Name and meaning in Old German: Ansuz. A god. Wotan or Odin.
Name and meaning in Old English: Os. A god. A mouth, an estuary.

Its graphic design and form: The vertical line underlines connection between sky and earth, between an ideal and live situation. From this axe sprout two downward going lines that seem to act together. The upper line takes off from heavens (the head and the mind) and heads towards earth so as to influence the world of matter. It is followed by a second line sprouting from the middle (heart and arms) to help dominate life on earth. So here, mind and heart act together to handle Midgard, the world of matter. The power of heart and mind is expressed through speech, speech that is backed up by awareness. It is also expressed through faith, authority, confidence and organization. We are therefore talking about words that support, organize and enhance life and also about magic through speech. The rune can visually represent two jawbones and thus an open mouth. If the second line starting off at the center of the vertical line didn't exist, then Rune Ass would turn into rune 21, Lagu. The two runes are therefore connected. Lagu is the ocean, what is complete. Rune Ass is the very first amongst a group to have a Lagu rune in its structure and each of these runes is therefore an important key or a pillar to get access to Lagu, to become complete

Its number: Fourth rune within the Futhark, Ass represents a combination of 3 and 1, in other words of intelligence acting efficiently, of life always in motion to organize things smartly and of the power of organized creation using tools and magic through speech. The purpose of this combination is to manage life as a whole and to organize things efficiently so that everything and everyone are where they should be when they should be. Number four symbolizes unity of earth and sky, of divine and human, of the horizontal axis and the vertical axis.

Summary and essence of this rune: I am the structure, in a human being, capable of receiving divine power, divine awareness and divine intuition emerging from "The Source of all life" so that they may be embodied into matter and used to handle and manage life on earth.

I also am the power that brings order to the world through speech and the use of authority, though knowledge and well organized magic. With this rune, what seemed impossible becomes possible and happens thanks to highly concentrated focus and a strongly determined will. I express within the world of matter "The Word" and "divine power" by using speech very efficiently. I represent the power of life that is passed on from generation to generation through genes and the expression of that power within a defined space like for example at home or at work.

The dark side of the rune: This is mainly seen as uncontrolled fury, as anger caused by past events that have not being accepted, as pure obstinacy or as abuse of power as when a person wants to take control of a situation or of someone's life. An unbalanced rune 4 can also manifest as a lack of ability to takes one's place due to refusal to express one's authority and power or as misuse of speech (lies, promises not kept or bad advice). Things must then be organized differently here.

Its sound: This rune is linked with letter "A" as in the word hat.

Key words: Using one's voice and personal power to control and handle a situation. Expressing oneself with great authority in a very official manner through demands, prayers, counseling, trade and negotiation. Divine inspiration. Agreement and favor of the gods. Strategic intelligence and efficient communication. Using one's ability to structure and organize. Being well anchored. Making one's dreams and ideas come true in real life. Occupying one's place within a structure. Putting goals and ideas into practice. Organizing life and events. Managing an empire.

People and jobs connected to this rune: The head of the household, a manager, a boss. Someone with great awareness, authority and power when dealing with people and events. Someone who can give great practical advice on how to handle the situation. A businessman, a builder, a leader, a politician, a real or symbolic emperor, a company director, a project manager, a supervisor, a monarch, a ruler, a soldier, a policeman, a prefect, a minister, a president. An enlightened person who understands the secrets of life and death.

Gods connected to this rune: This rune is connected with the father of the Gods, Odin but also with Thor, his son. Odin represents the power to create within the world, awareness of all that is invisible, divine intuition, divine breath, magical incantations, being in a state of trance, power expressed though words and magic expressed through speech. He also symbolizes knowledge of the runes, adaptability, smartness, travelling, using secret magic, communication between the world here down below and the world hereafter and going from this world to the next. Thor represents ruling over world affairs with authority and using one's power to play one's role in the world and to make sure that the economy is working as it should.

Places and objects related to this rune: Structures, big buildings, large estates, big patrician houses, executive committees, management boards, the empire's headquarters, government or parliament headquarters, decision-making centers, government agencies, trade centers, law books, legislative texts, anything that brings comfort, objects that symbolize power, armors, chairs and seats, building site equipment and building materials.

Colors connected to this rune: Green and dark green.

Animals connected to this rune: a crow or blackbird, an eagle, a wolf and a beaver because of his building abilities.

English, Norwegian and Icelandic poems:

The English poem:
The mouth is the Source where words come from
It is wisdom's support and brings good counseling to the wise
And blessing, joy and delight to all knights and noblemen
　　　The first sentence is about "The Source of all life" that creates and expresses itself in the world of matter through sound and language. It then points to the use of speech as a means to organize life in the world of matter. When well used, speech helps a lot and leads to wisdom. It enables people to adapt in a practical manner. It brings joy and success. It is also used to express authority as that expressed by knights serving their king.

The Norwegian poem:
Most journeys begin by leaving behind an estuary but the scabbard is where the sword should be.
　　　An estuary is a transitional zone filled with water and small islands where life thrives. It is a place where water dwells temporarily before returning to the ocean. It can be seen as a structure that helps the river get back to the ocean. The estuary can then symbolize the non-permanent world of matter, Midgard, where men and wemen just dwell before going back to the world hereafter and where life flows along.

This may suggest the necessity to make appropriate use of speech so that things flow the right way, to structure what needs to be structured and to organize things efficiently in the world of matter. Going from land to sea can also symbolize travelling from the world of matter into the invisible worlds, out of body experiences and shamanic travel. The second sentence suggests that everything has a place where it should be. A sword's normal place is in the scabbard which means a sword should only be taken out of it in extreme situations, where speech had no effect. A sward is a weapon used to make war and also a phallic symbol. Both Odin and Thor were called upon to enhance courage, furry in battle and striking force so as to bring about victory on battlefields.

The icelandic poem:
God, old Gaut and ruler of Asgard and lord of Vallhalla. Odin went about with different names and Gaut was one of these names, so this poem is about Odin in his various aspects (as creator of Midgard, magician and inventor of runes and poetry). The poem specifies that Odin is the ruler of the Gods, of Asgard and of Valhalla were the dead arrive after they die.

Using this rune to do magic: Rune As can be used to connect head and heart, to connect or disconnect two things or people, to increase one's personal power, one's confidence and one's authority, to gain awareness about how things are structured, how things fit together or were the right place for things and people to be is. It can be used to efficiently implement order and the appropriate organization, to connect to life force inherited from ancestors and to use speech efficiently for managing people, for negotiating, doing business, being successful during an appointment or an exam, for giving the right orders and to be obeyed.

Links with other information systems:

I Ching: This rune can be related to Hexagram 4, "Youthful folly" and to Hexagram 34 which is called "Handling power".

Mayan Astrology: Rune "As" has connections with the Mayan glyph called "Jaguar" and also with the "Wind" Glyph.

Tarot: Rune As can be related to card 1, the Magician, to card 4, the Emperor, to card 12, the Hanged Man and to card 20 which is called Judgment

Astrology: This rune is a mix of Mercury, Jupiter, Moon, Mars and Pluto.

Rune 5 : RAIDH

Various names given to this rune:

Name and meaning in Old Norse: Reidh. A chariot. To ride.
Name and meaning in Old German: Radha. A chariot, traveling by horse.
Name and meaning in Old English: Raidh. A trip, a raid, a ride.

Its graphic design and form: The vertical line shows as usual that sky and earth are connected. A first line springs out from the top of the vertical line and heads down towards the world of matter so as to exert an influence on it. Combining the vertical line and the first line gives rise to rune 21, Lagu. A second line springs out from the middle, from the heart and moves upwards to join with the first line. A third line also springs out from the heart and goes downwards. The second and third lines give rise to rune number 6, Ken which is firmly connected to the vertical line. Two lines depart from the heart and head both towards sky and earth. One's heart must take care of both daily earthly matters and celestial affairs. Travelling can take place on land or in the sky. It can be celestial or earthly. One can also say that earth forces and sky forces join within the heart, bringing awareness and connection with the Source of all life. The rune can be seen as made up of a stationary part ⌐ and a movable part ⟨ that can clip away from the mainframe, just like the astral body can move away from the physical body. Just as in rune 3 Thorn ⊳, there is an enclosed space but there is also an open space brought by rune Ken ⟨. Finally, when looking at the rune, one can also see it as the icon of someone about to lift his leg to take a step forward or to climb on horseback.

Its number: Fifth rune within the Futhark, Raidh symbolizes an organized motion of body and consciousness, expressing the Self and unity of the four elements (fire, earth, air and water) brought together so as to achieve a goal. Will, because it is connected to the Source of all life, is filled here with love and power. It can then dominate the four elements and be expressed in a positive manner. Number 5 is often represented as a five star branch or by a pentagram which symbolize unity and harmony of body, soul and spiritual body. It is also sometimes seen as a cross surrounded by a wheel.

It then symbolizes the sun, i.e. awareness in motion and more specifically awareness of the links between inner life and outer events. Number 5 is about expressing what lies within one's heart and one's light. It is about unity in diversity and about connecting head and feet so as to act according to divine law. It is about royalty, knowledge of the meaning of what is taking place and knowledge of the laws of life. It brings about progress and something new and it enables creative power to be expressed within a specific space. It is finally connected to understanding information systems and to training, teaching and education.

Summary and essence of this rune: I am life's motion, expressed through rhythm, numbers and movement in space thanks to unity between sky and earth, between divine will and personal will. Life itself is a long long ride. This life force in motion allows me to express myself, to move forward and to guide me towards my right destination. I am the journey of both body and consciousness at many different levels of existence. Through body and mind and by using landmarks and values, I ride along an initiatory journey. I get access to understanding of divine laws, of religious laws, of official standards and rules and to the way in which all information systems are organized and hence get a first glimpse of the underlying order that supports life. I am a strong and keen sense of observation, the right vision, the correct judgment and the guiding system that enables people to find their way around. I value ethics, positive rules and a code of honor. I can therefore give a meaning to all that happens to me and express myself in many different manners as a life form created by the Source of all life. I can also use prayer and blessings to request what is in harmony with my evolution. I also symbolize health of body and mind. Rune Raidh represents the German Asatru religion and the great journey that leads to experiencing once again total inner unity with the "Source of all life".

The dark side of the rune: It manifests as a lack of awareness, as a meaningless life, by being astray, as a tendency to keep turning around in circles due to wrong beliefs or bad advice, as an issue when travelling, as a tumultuous journey, as a delay in delivery, as complicated negotiations or as a situation that seems stuck, that is getting nowhere or that is not evolving at the right rhythm.

Its sound: Rune Raidh is linked with the "r" sound as in ride ou right.

Key words: Find the right means or vehicle to move forward in life, to reach one's destination, to play one's role in life and to act in a meaningful manner and in full awareness. A trip, ride, adventure, transfer from one place to another, a physical or soul journey, a pleasant journey, an initiation trip or in-depth journey. A course, training session, teachings or an educational process that enables to achieve a specific goal and be better off. A clear vision guided by one's heart. Guiding or being guided. Ritual to be performed alone or within a group so as to achieve results, create order or give a deeper meaning to life or to a specific situation. Making a situation legal. Controlling wisely body and mind. Doing the right thing at the right time. Discovering new perspectives. Experiencing unity of sky and earth within one's heart. Uniting two different elements. A change, something new, negotiations, talks and a situation that is evolving. Arrival of a messenger or of a message.

People and jobs related to this rune: Someone who is playing an active part in the world, a very open minded person, a traveler, someone in transit, a rider, someone with legal, religious or medical knowledge and doing a ritual or a process, a guide or a teacher, an expert or a master, a counselor, an adviser, a consultant, a lecturer, a doctor, a priest or a bishop, a healer, a lawyer, a notary, a psychologist, a therapist or a coach. Activities implying the use or cars or trucks or that require travelling.

Gods related to this rune: This rune is actually about the many trips and journeys undertaken by the gods. Each journey had a specific goal. The rune that symbolizes horses is actually rune 19 and as chariot and horses go together, these two runes have a strong connection. Raidh can represent Odin's eight legged horse called Sleipnir but also the tree of life who brings structure and meaning to reality and who is called Yggdrasil. One of the meanings of Yggdrasil is actually Odin's horse i.e. Odin's mean of transportation. There is also a legend of two horses carrying the sun and the moon across the sky to their right place and then across space. They were called Skinfaxi or bright horse and Hrimfaxi ou frost horse. Some gods travelled using chariots. A chariot was considered to be a vehicle for body, mind and spirit, as a means to travel but also as a tool for religious rituals (celebrating birth, marriage, victory, departure on a journey or returning from a ride). A chariot, when you consider it, is a technological marvel and this rune has a strong connection with it.

In Nordic mythology, Thor's chariot was pulled by two goats while Freya's chariot was pulled by two cats and Freyr's chariot by a boar.

Places and objects related to this rune:

A positive workplace, a place where people express themselves, a training center, a conference room or hall, a university, a sacred and peaceful place, a vibrant place, a temple, a church, objects and equipment used to travel or to teach.

Colors connected to this rune: Purple, violet.

Animals connected with this rune : An elephant, a hippopotamus, a buffalo, an elk, a deer.

English, Norwegian and Icelandic poems:

The english poem:
Ridding is easy for a warrior when he is inside the hall
It is more difficult when sitting on a strong and powerful horse
Who races along land paths for miles and miles

This poem shows that there is a difference between inside and outside, between our inner world and the outside world. A hall can from a certain point of view be seen as your inside and more specifically as your heart. When you are inside your heart, riding, i.e. getting along, is easy. Travelling in the outside world on the other hand requires effort, getting away from one's comfort zone, focusing, overcoming difficult situations, facing the unknown and experiencing adventure.

The Norwegian poem:
Ridding is the worst thing for horses. Reginn forged the finest sword

The poem says here that travelling and getting a rider to reach his destination is a difficult task from a horse's point of view. As with rune 1 Fehu, the second line is about the sword that the Dwarf Reginn forged for the hero Sigurd so that Sigurd could kill Reginn's brother, who had the ability to change into a dragon. Reginn was Sigurd instructor and spiritual or adoptive father. Sigurd did kill the dragon but when he found out that Reginn planned to kill him so as to have the Andvari treasure all for himself, then Sigurd killed Reginn. This story is found in the Volsunga saga. Reginn helped Sigurd choose a horse and the chosen one was named Grani, with whom he travelled all over the world.

This story tells us that a bad intention turns against the person who created it and that when a person has the right vision, then his actions are right and evil has no grip on him.

The icelandic poem:
Ridding is joy for the horseman
And a speedy journey
And hard work (toil) for the steed

This poem enhances the joy of travelling, the time it takes and the work done by the horse. It may suggest a sexual relationship but also astral travel or shamanic travel. As specified in numerous sagas, shamanistic travel was part of daily life for German and Viking people and it can be an exhausting experience.

Using this rune to do magic: Raidh can be used to put one's awareness into motion, to implement motion, to find the right direction, to get things moving the right way, to live one's true purpose in life, to make sure that a journey runs smoothly, to transfer a person or an object from one place to another, to act according to divine law, to legalize a situation smoothly, to understand the meaning of what is happening, to get or give good advice, to master teachings and to evolve in full awareness.

Links with other information systems:
I Ching: This rune can be related to Hexagram 5, "Waiting" and to Hexagram 56 which is called "The Traveller".
Mayan Astrology: Rune "Raidh" has connections with the Mayan glyph called In Spanish "Caminante del cielo" which can be translated as "skywalker" or "sky traveler".
Tarot: Rune Raidh can be related to card 5, the High Priest and to card 7, the Chariot.
Astrology: This rune is a mix of Sun and Jupiter with a bit of Mercury, Pluto and Neptune

Rune 6: KEN

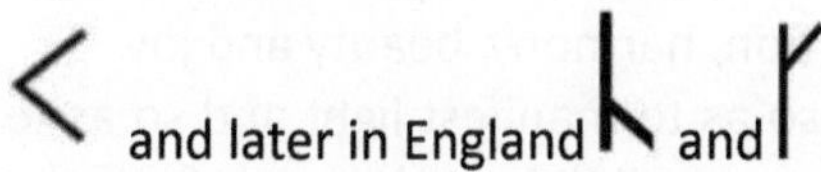

< and later in England ᚲ and ᚴ

Various names given to this rune:

Name and meaning in Old Norse: Kaun. A boil, a wound, an inflammation.
Name and meaning in Old German: Kenaz. A lump, a torch.
Name and meaning in Old English: Ken. A torch, a flame.

Its graphic design and form: Two streams of energy flow from a central point, from the heart. One goes to the sky (goals) and one goes towards the ground (live events). Another way to see this icon is to say that two streams of red and white energy emerging from earth (red) and sky (white) come together within the heart, producing a torch like effect and pinkish/greenish astral light, thus nourishing the flame of live within. So this icon is about energy moving and it symbolizes both the body and the soul in motion, with its male and female or masculine and feminine forces.
It is also about inner unity of male and female forces within and unity between man and woman in the outside world. The icon can also be seen as a mouth talking in order to create relationships between people. Rune Ken is graphically part of many other runes where connecting and uniting male and female energies is important. It is a part of runes 7, Gyfu, rune 12, Jera, rune 16, Sigl, rune 18, Berkano, rune 22, Ing, rune 23, Othala and rune 24 Daeg. In each case it reveals life in motion.

Its number: Ken is rune number six within the Futhark alphabet. Complementary male and female energy combine together to implement the flame of desire, life and motion. And where there is motion there is form. This motion is sometimes represented as a six star branch. Number 6 is obtained by adding 5+1, 4+2 or 2x3 and it symbolizes creating forms, commitment, choice, multiple possibilities and combinations, balance, sensitivity to beauty, desires and also necessary limits brought about by structure.

Summary and essence of this rune: I am a channeled, domesticated and mastered flame that is connected to earth and sky.

When I shine harmoniously, I bring about heat, light, the desire to create material forms and relationships and the ability to implement the right proportions, the most balanced organization, harmony, beauty and joy.

I am fire attached to the wooden torch so as to manifest light and so as to achieve a goal chosen amongst many possibilities. When I feel the connection to light, what I desire becomes obvious. I then make the right choices and can thus create harmony in my life. Sometimes, I am a flame of desires that pushes two complementary energies to come together so as to create something new. I am fire that transforms and that encourages a single unit to sacrifice itself so as to unite with someone else and create a new relationship. I am an enlightened person who masters an art. In ancient times, this rune was said to be linked with fire masters and iron masters.

The dark side of this rune: It manifests as ignorance, blindness, disharmony, health issues and also as conflict due to the fact that two wills are going in opposite directions because the right limits were not defined, because inner fire was not purified well enough or because if a person does not listen to his or her heart, feelings and true desires, he or she makes the wrong choices and that leads to conflict. An unhandled inner fire creates unbalance, wounds, inflammation, uncontrolled sexual desires and abuse of pleasure with all the loss of energy that comes with all that. It burns and devastates and then symbolizes destruction. Sometimes, the fire dies out or must be extinguished. Forms or relationships that no longer bring any joy must then disappear and be replaced by something new.

Its sound: This rune is connected with the "k" sound as in ski or king.

Key words: a light bringing fire, artistic inspiration, an encounter, a union, two complementary energies combine and unite, what you are attached too, what is lighting up, what is clearly visible, your fuel, what makes you run, someone says they love you, flame of desire, transmutation of matter by fire, a fire ritual, change of form, experiencing and expressing beauty, decoration, adornment, design, creation of form, art, joy of heart, sexual pleasure, many possibilities, a choice, seeing to what is in your heart and listening to it, listening to your true desires, artistic or craftsmanship abilities, a meeting in a well light place, social relationships, people sharing together, a wonderful encounter than enlightens your day.

People and jobs related to this rune: A young, happy, vibrant, sensual, loving, pleasant, in love, artistic, beautiful, enlightened and very social person. Someone with the ability to work with form (clothes, fashion, dressmaker, tailor, designer, jewelry, decoration, wooden objects, leather objects or metal objects), with art and beauty (beautician, make-up artist) or relationships (public relations officer, matrimonial officer).

Gods related to this rune: This rune is firstly linked with fire and water creating the world. When fire energy (coming from Muspellheim) and ice energy (coming from Niflheim) are balanced and correctly transformed, they nourish the world of men Midgard. Ken is secondly related to Goddess Freya, who embodies attraction power and sensuality, the ability to connect, to seduce, to create relationships, desire and pleasure. It is sometimes also related to the God Heimdall who guards the rainbow that connects Midgard the world of men and Asgard the world of gods. Ken is finally connected with dwarfs who are experts not only as craftsmen and smiths but also in the art of creating magical objects.

Places and objects related to this rune: Places where art and beauty are experienced and expressed, beautiful places, crossroads, places where lovers meet, meeting places, public parks and leisure parks.

Colors connected to this rune: Colors of the rainbow, pink, sky blue, light blue and orange.

Animals connected to this rune: a doe, a sheep, colored birds, a duck, a donkey, a rabbit, an Ibis.

English, Norwegian and Icelandic poems:

The English poem:
A torch is known by its fire
It brings light and enlightenment
Were princes and people seat inside gathered together.

At the time when the 24 runes were created, homes were lit up with pine resin spread around a branch or on a piece of cloth wrapped around a branch. This poem shows here how fire energy helps mankind when it is used with harmony, wisdom and greatness. It protects, enlightens, brings awareness and nourishes confidence, joy and happiness. It also says that one can recognize something by looking at its light and by the effects created.

The norwegian poem:
Ulcer is children's curse
Misfortune, misery, grief and death make a corpse go pale
The poem shows here how fire energy can create ulcers, fever and inflammation, especially with children or one's inner child, and how it can lead to misery, to great grief and even to destruction and death when things are not balanced, when a person does not listen to his heart and true desires or is not loving.

The Icelandic poem:

Ulcer is a disease fatal to children and a painful place
And a house of flesh that rots, where mortification takes place

The poem specifies that children find it very difficult to handle fire energy and that lack of control of it can easily lead to pain, unwellness, things rotting away and sometimes even to death. Mastering fire energy requires seeing the connections between things, listening to one's heart as well as a good amount of maturity and wisdom.

Using this rune to do magic: Rune Ken is used to connect, link and bind two people together, to bring artistic inspiration, to transform objects and forms, to attract and seduce, to create social or love relationships, to create harmony, joy and beauty, to become aware of one's true desires and one's feelings, to enliven sexual drives and to help feel pleasure and joy.

Links with other information systems:

I Ching: This rune is related to Hexagram 6, conflict.
Mayan Astrology: This rune can be linked with a Mayan glyph called « the star ».
Tarot: Rune Ken can be related to card number 6, the lovers but also to cards 13 and 15 who both master fire, passion and make metal objects.
Astrology: This rune is related to Venus but also to Mars and Pluto.

Rune 7 : GYFU

Various names given to this rune:

Name and meaning in Old Norse: Gipt. Gift, generosity, marriage, a present.
Name and meaning in Old German: Gebo. A gift.
Name and meaning in Old English: Gyfu. Generosity, a gift.

Its graphic design and form: Here one can either say that two energies come down from the sky and move towards earth or that two energies rise from the ground and reach the sky. In any case they meet at a central point. A central point gathers complementary energies. This central element can be a goal, a target, a location but also one's spiritual body where the "throne of God" is. Union of these complementary elements gives rise to a relatively stable structure and it is easy to see a cross when you look at the graphic of this rune. Such a cross can be used to strengthen a structure in the frame of a house or ship or on an antique chariot wheel for example. The very first wheels created for chariots actually had at first four spokes and then later five, six, eight or ten. The icon can also look like a person standing up and stretching his arms and legs, thus asserting his presence here and now. This rune can also be seen as previous rune Ken united with its mirror or complement and can thus be seem as the result of male and female energy mingling and working harmoniously together. Rune 7 is assertive and takes up its place in space. Finally, you may observe that rune Gyfu is embedded into runes 20, Mann ᛗ and 24 Daeg ᛞ.

Its number: Gyfu is rune number 7. Number seven can be obtained by adding 1 and 6, 2 and 5 or 3 and 7, i.e it includes all number that are before it. It is an all inclusive number. It can therefore symbolize union of sky and earth but at both an instinctual level and a mind level, fire (1) taking form (6), senses channeled in a specific direction, the greatness of female energy (2) expressed in full awareness (5), energy in motion, intelligence and ideas (3) manifesting in matter and structuring things (4) or structures (4) in motion (3). Number 7 has thus many times been considered as a sacred, mystical, magical and very powerful number as it combines instinct and organizational intelligence. It is related to the 7 colors of the rainbow, the 7 days of the week and the 7 musical notes.

Summary and essence of this rune: I am the result of male and female forces uniting together. I am an intention that is nourished by will power and by my senses. This intention is then channeled by organizational capabilities so as to get results and achieve a pre defined goal. I am a will that gives with great generosity the best of itself to life. I manifest and express those gifts, talents and abilities that life has given me. Connections and relationships are currently being structured and nourished by love and generosity. Exchange between two people or elements is now smooth and harmonious. Sharing is balanced. A rebalancing is occurring. I am the structure that can carry and support light, a torch. It is advisable to make an offering, to give, to receive or to accept a gift. There is a person who is giving, what is given and a person who is receiving. The act of giving can be considered as a positive sacrifice. Two elements (two people, the human and the divine, the world of men and the world of gods, past and present) are uniting so as to create a new structure.

The dark side of the rune: It can manifest as refusal to share, as difficulty in giving or receiving, as an unbalanced exchange or as an exchange that causes imbalance, as a tendency to give while expecting something in return or by an issues turning up during exchange. What is given or received can be like a poisoned gift or it can cause havoc.

Its sound: This rune is related to the « g » sound as in gift or great.

Key words: an opportunity requiring taking a decision, receiving a gift, it is necessary to give the best of who you are, a mission must be accomplished, a chance to experience a very beneficial encounter, lucky times, two complementary forces uniting, a sexual experience, harmonious sharing is taking place, organizational abilities must be used to obtain results, a relationship is being structured, stable bonds.

People and jobs related to this rune: a good and positive person, someone young, daring, bold, assertive, business like, very well organized, with well defined goals, efficient, generous and protective. Jobs related to organization, logistics and supplies, planners, jobs in companies, organizing events, sports people, ambassadors, conquerors, active people between 20 and 40 years old, coaches, counselors and consultants, taxi drivers, people working on cars or who travel a lot as part of their work.

Gods related to this rune: This rune is firstly related to unity between Mother Earth and Father Sky who gave us life. It is personified by Goddess Gefn who embodies abundance of nature and generosity of life. It is secondly related to the Dises who are life forces and female spirits that organize the destinies of men from birth to death.

Places and objects related to this rune: gifts, wheels, wheeled vehicles, roads, highways, the inside of a car, racing tracks, car factories and garages, places where decisions are taken, sports halls, driving schools.

Colors related to this rune: Red. The seven colors of the rainbow.

Animals related to this rune: tigers, cheetahs, jaguars and horses.

English, Norwegian and Icelandic poems:

The English poem:
Generosity brings value and honor to the person who gives
It brings help and joy to those who have nothing

This English poem may have been influenced by Christian religion. It shows that generosity is an important value as it brings help and joy, two divine qualities. Generosity leads to sharing, exchange and to a better distribution of wealth. At the time when runes were created, leaders were supposed to manifest the abundance and generosity of nature by sharing their wealth. Rune Gyfu can symbolize help received and a person's luck. Luck can be seen as help from the gods and as help from one's inner Living God.

This rune does not exist in the Viking Futhark so the Norwegian and Icelandic poems do not mention it.

Using this rune to do magic: Rune Gyfu can be used to be well centered in one's heart and in a state of awareness, to balance action of male and female forces, to organize something efficiently, to promote success of a campaign or of a project, to implement an agreement and a contract, to achieve a specific result, to reach a specific location, to express the best of one's self, to unite two complementary elements, to promote sharing and generosity, to facilitate and encourage wonderful encounters, love relationships and sexual relationships.

Links with other information systems:

I Ching: This rune is related to hexagram 7 called "The army".

Mayan Astrology: Rune Gyfu can't really be related to any specific Mayan glyph but is does have connections with two glyphs called "The seed" and "The earth".

Tarot: Rune Gyfu can be related to a mix of card 5 called "The high priest" and card 7 called "The chariot".

Astrology: This rune is a mix of Sun, Venus, Mars, Mercury, Jupiter and Saturn.

Rune 8 : WYNN

Various names given to this rune:

Name and meaning in Old Norse: Vend. Joy, felicity.
Name and meaning in Old German: Wunjo. Joy, prairie.
Name and meaning in Old English: Wynn. Pleasure, delight.

Its graphic design and form: As usual, the vertical line represents sky and earth being connected i.e. ideal and actions, goals and detailed organization. The two lines coming out of the central vertical line can symbolize the soul in motion. There are then two ways of seeing this icon. Two lines or forces are springing out of the vertical line.

One of them is going downwards from sky to earth while the other is rising from earth or from the heart and is going skywards. The two join together near the vertical line, in a place that is high up and so connected to consciousness, to being aware. Top and bottom join together and unite. This can symbolically suggest that when body, heart and mind are being expressed in a coordinated manner within civilization, within society, then everything that is done if done with "a will to feel joy" and with love. Sky and earth work in harmony, in agreement one with the other. And so then there is joy and happiness. The other way of seeing things is to consider that from a high up central point emerge two forces or energies that separate. One of them descends from the sky towards earth while the other rises upwards towards the sky. They join a vertical axis at two different places, at sky level and at heart level. This can symbolize, within civilization or society or within a group or a clan, life and experience that brings about joy and pleasure for body, heart, soul and spirit.

This rune's icon can represent a banner, a flag and as such a symbol. These banners exist since dawn of time. They were placed on flag-bearers at village entrances, on top of temples or of houses and also on ships, either at the front or on top of the vessel's central mast. The banner reveals the group or clan to which a place or a person belongs. Such a group can be a company, a firm, a clan, a sports team or a nation. Belonging to this group and acting in harmony with this group implies speaking a certain language, following certain rules and sacrificing part of one's personal will to nourish the energy and life of the group.

Rune Wynn can be found in the structure of runes 3 Thorn ᚦ, 5 Raed ᚱ , 18 Berkano ᛒ and 20 Mann ᛗ and each time a specific aspect of joy is revealed.

Its number: Wynn is rune number 8. Whereas number seven dealt with instinctual combination of male and female forces organized by reason, number 8 is about conscious unity between sky and earth, between what is above and what is below. It symbolizes awareness and understanding of firstly the underlying order of the world and secondly of the existence of "The Source of all life" that has created this "order of things" with love, joy and pleasure. Number 8 represents the great law of balance, of equilibrium, a sense of justice and of what is right, the spot where matter cycles and spiritual cycles meet one another creating causes and effects, an awareness that everything is interconnected and also social relationships between men. Rune number eight is the last rune within the first family (or Aett, Freyr's Aett in this case) of eight runes. It ends the first third of the 24 runic sequence. It does therefore suggest that is it the result of the first seven runes and how these first seven runes are handled.

Summary and essence of this rune: I am a force who gathers, organizes, puts into form and builds relationships and partnerships. I bring together and connect two or more components or people and stimulate them so that they act in a way that creates harmony and joy. Such forces can then work together so as to create and maintain a clan, a group, a club and a civilized structure that follows a set of predefined rules. I am the clan's banner. Such a banner brings unity within the group and ensures its integrity. I am every person's deep motivation, which is a will to feel joy, joy within heart, body and spirit. I am harmony, justice, what is right and the joy of sharing in a state of kindness and firmness. Such sharing connects heart and consciousness and brings people to do things together. Finally, I am the right action, the one that leads to joy and serenity and I am beauty that leads to grace.

The dark side of the rune: It manifests as imbalance, mismatch and distortion, as conflict within a group or with social services, as a refusal to connect with other people, as a disappointing situation, as a situation that is a burden, that is weighed down and deteriorated, as a lack of harmony, rightness, connections and joy or as false joy triggered artificially through alcohol, drugs or chemical substances.

Its sound: This rune is related to two different sounds, to the "v" sound as in vine or Venus and to the w sound as in wine or whisky.

Key words: the joy of being alive, the feeling of being in harmony with the environment, the group or clan or civilization to which one belongs, the right way, actions that are in harmony with the order of things, positive consequences of has been undertaken, a positive result, pleasure shared, sharing, creating social relationships, getting to know other people and to accept them as they are, sharing with others, community activities, a beneficial partnership, motivation that brings joy, a very pleasant evening, a party, grace, the opportunity to take advantage of a situation and to enjoy the fruit of previous labor.

People and jobs related to this rune: someone calm and serious, strict and yet joyful, serene and happy. People with stable jobs and who contribute to making society run smoothly. Jobs were human resources and the use of numbers play a key role (accountancy, managing supervisors, auditors and statistician). Jobs consisting of fixing physical or psychological imbalance, related to public relations, to dancing or art, to color and beauty, to law (judge, clerk, notary, bailiff, lawyer) and public administrations (mayor, administrative agent or officer).

Gods related to this rune: This rune is related to certain aspects of Goddess Freya but also to Tiw who embodies justice, rightness and appropriate actions that bring results and joy.

People and places related to this rune: a public building, the general government, public administrations, a law court, a bank, a place where people use numbers and count things or weigh things, places where decisions are taken and contacts signed, the rules of the game, laws, an examination hall, national constitutions and all legal documents.

Colors connected to this rune: Magenta. The seven colors of the rainbow.

Animals connected to this rune: beautiful birds, cranes, wading birds, herons, ants.

English, Norwegian and Icelandic poems:

The English poem: He who ignores suffering, sadness and misery can fully benefit from joy. And create prosperity, abundance, happiness and a lovely house. Another translation for the last sentence can be: He can enjoy his belonging to a strong group or to a fortified community.

This poem is about accomplishing a life cycle where what had to be done was accomplished and where what had to be shared has been so. It specifies how important it is to focus on what is right, to undertake with joy and to do what leads to joy. It suggest physical and psychological happiness, inner joy, harmony with one's environment, accomplishment of one's wishes and the achievement of one's goal, which leads to feeling joy. The last sentence suggests sharing with others and a pleasant social life.

This rune no longer exists in the Viking Futhark so the Norwegian and Icelandic poems do not mention it.

Using this rune to do magic: Rune Wynn is used to gather various different forces or people, to connect them together and to bind them together so as to make them work as a group in a coherent and civilized manner, so as to create balance and harmony and so as to achieve a specific goal. It facilitates sharing and good relationships. It brings joy and pleasure. It helps build long lasting and strong relationships.

Links with other information systems:

I Ching: This rune is related to Hexagram 8, civilization or Union and to Hexagram 58, the joy of sharing.

Mayan Astrology: This rune doesn't really match with any specific Mayan glyph though it can be partly related to the star, the sun and the dog glyphs.

Tarot: Rune Wynn can be related to a mix of cards 6, the lovers and card 8, Justice.
Astrology: Wynn is related to a mix of Venus, Saturn, Jupiter and Libra astrological sign.

Rune 9 : HAGL

ⴽ **Various names given to this rune:**

Name and meaning in Old Norse: Hagall. A snow flake, a crystal, hail.
Name and meaning in Old German: Hagl: Hail.
Name and meaning in Old English: Hagl: Hail.

A snow flake or an ice flake is a structured component that is complete and that falls down from the sky. It shows an unavoidable evolution of awareness, action and life in motion within a structure. It is finally a meteorological element that often appears very suddenly when it comes to hail.

Its graphic design and form: The vertical line, that symbolizes as previously in other runes a connection between sky (goals, ideals, conscious will) and earth (effective action and organization in real life), is here doubled. This suggests that there is an upward motion and a downward motion. What are these upward and downward motions? Well, if we see things from eternity's point of view, we are talking about what has been named since the very beginning of human presence on this planet « the fall into matter » and "the path back to light". The two lines are connected together by a third line that seems to be a bridge or a gateway. This third line can be seen is rune 4, Ass ᚠ. It symbolizes awareness and motion and it shows the path one must walk on and the building site one must start off with and take care of so as to evolve along the returning path to light. But what is this path? Well, before embodying into matter, each human being lived in invisible spiritual worlds as a complete being i.e. male and female and it was 100% connected to "the Source of all life". Some of these complete spiritual humans chose when they arrived in the worlds close by to this world of matter to experiment matter by embodying into a human mammal. The first consequence of this choice is firstly a splitting in two of the previously complete human being so that the male component embodies into a male mammal while the female component embodies into a female mammal. The second consequence s that each half human, so to say, is shattered into many more or less autonomous parts or personalities.

The third consequence is that most humans are totally disconnected from the Source that has created all life, located somewhere in the heavens, that has created them. And so the returning path to light then requires gathering all the different parts of the soul by experiencing them in full awareness and by mastering them. It requires balancing male and female, or masculine and feminine forces. And it requires dedicating one's life to this path by living in a manner that matches spiritual laws, by working on one's personal evolution and by becoming the best possible version of oneself so as to gradually reconnect one's self with "The Source of all life" or with "the tree of eternal life".

The Hagl icon also looks like a woodwork element where two beams are binded together by a third beam so as to create a stable structure. One can also imagine a door. It can also suggest the major energetical path within the human body where energy flows up from the grounds when one takes a deep breath. It then runs within the legs into the back of the vertebral column. When the tip of the tong touches the roof of the mouth, energy then flows through the throat and flows back down into the front of the vertebral column. Hagl then describes the architecture of energy and of life in motion, the structures of life and how energy moves about as time passes by i.e. the cosmic laws that rule the world make the world go round.

Hagl is sometimes represented as a snowflake or as a six branched star. It then symbolizes the original crystal-like seed from which material reality was created, the first atomic particle of life as physicists would say. At a human level, it then symbolizes the spiritual body that is the structure that carries and houses human awareness connected to the Source of all light. This spiritual body was called "the throne of God" at the time of Jesus-Christ.

Hagl is the first rune with two vertical lines. It will be followed by runes 19, Eh M, rune 20, Mann M and rune 24, Daeg M. These three runes are therefore key runes concerning the path towards light. Rune 19 is experiencing light and total unity with the Source of all life while rune 20 is the father of all angels and of all men who helps and supports while rune 24 is the returning of eternal daylight and recovering one's eternity on a permanent basis, which is the long term goal of every human soul.

Its number: Hagl is rune number 9 and number 9 was a key and sacred number for the Germans. According to them, reality was organized into nine worlds within the tree of life Yggdrasil. Odin hung himself nine days to receive the runic information system and Heimdall had nine mothers. Built from 1+8, 2+7, 3+6, 4+5 and especially 3x3, 9 includes all numbers, gathers them all and then transcends them. It symbolizes something complete, that inner silence and emptiness one must go through in order to access spiritual awakening, increasing awareness through meditation, returning to the source, what is eternal and never changes, the outcome, culmination or end point of something, the end of a cycle and the beginning or dawn of a new day. When nine is added to another number and deduced from it, it disappears just like a path one leave behind (example: 1+9=10=1, 2+9=11=2, 3+9=12=3 etc.). Number nine is finally related to the snake which is a symbol of "being aware of eternity" and "eternal cycles of souls being embodied in matter and going back to light". So number nine is a very deep and profound number!

Summary and essence of this rune: I am the depth and the essence of things. I am the structure or reality that bears life. I am the sadness that is as a consequence of the world of matter but also hope and the path that leads each person to their deep inner truth, back to light and therefore to serenity. This path tends to be structured with many small steps, with key points and with gateways that enable a person to go from one world to another or from one state of awareness to another. I am the ability to deal with structure, to organize things and to manage so as to help life thrive. I am the seed that contains all the necessary information to create a beautiful strong tree. Creating that tree is from a certain point of view a building site where a seed becomes a tree and it requires knowledge of processes and laws that enable changing a seed into a tree. Being an information structure, I represent schemes, archetypes but also time (the past, the present, the future and the present moment), History, causes and consequences of past events and destiny which is a force that organizes the lives of people according to their personal structure (birth diamond and astral chart). I finally symbolize the slow evolution of life in time and safety and protection (against bad weather) brought about by a structure. It is sometimes possible with this rune that a disturbing event looking like a cold shower or a hail shower arises suddenly and forces organized action so as to adapt and create a new situation.

The dark side of the rune: It manifests as difficulties, obstacles, blocks, lacks, frustrations, delays, disturbances, freezing cold atmospheres, rigidity, lack of love, solitude and loneliness (sometimes causes in northern countries by snow), unpleasing surprises and bad luck, as consequences of past events popping up and sometimes by havoc, chaos and destruction caused by a hail storm. A real or symbolic hail storm forces someone to stop and just wait till things get better or to organize things differently. A difficult challenge makes one grow stronger and evolve.

Its sound: This rune is related to the "h" sound as in the words hail or heat.

Key words: an upcoming event, a sudden and unforeseen event, something new and unexpected causes a temporary disruption in the normal flow of events, destinies' course, fate, influence of weather conditions, consequences of time, inner silence, winter time and its severe atmosphere, honestly observing what is, a structured element falling from the sky, awareness of structures and architecture, working on structures and on long term goals, seeing things from a deep point of view and seeing the essence of things, asking the right questions, a slow evolution through labor and effort, handling the situation so that it is safe, protecting one's self from cold or hail, getting to the point, preparing for change, growing and evolving.

People and jobs related to this rune: a person experiencing a building site like situation, a well organized person, someone who is aware of reality's structures, a calm, slow, deep, old and wise person, a retired person, someone evolving very slowly, a seeker, jobs were light must be brought to the past and were many questions are asked, loner jobs, explorers, difficult jobs were a lot of effort is required, jobs in the building industry, jobs in monasteries, plumbers, historians and history teachers, archeologists, archivists, gerontologists, architects, scientists, philosophers, builders, guides, therapists, farmers, geologists, dowsers, geobiologists, mountaineers and mountain guides.

Gods related to this rune: Hagl is related to the god Heimdall who was the son of nine ancestral lineages (son of nine mothers or of nine waves). Heimdall structures reality because he initiates action; he starts off the building site and then ends it when what has to be built is built. He guards the rainbow bridge that connects the world of men Midgard with the world of gods Asgard.

He uses his horn to warn the gods if something dangerous comes about and he is the one who will warns the gods when the end of the world Ragnarok will come.

Rune Hagl is also related to Goddess Mordgud who guards the gateway to the worlds down under, ruled by goddess Hella, guardian of Hell. It is finally related to Norn Urd, one of the three Norns or goddesses of destiny, who shows consequences of past actions in the present moment.

Places and people related to this rune: isolated places, a monastery cell, a research center, a laboratory, an old people's home, a cave, a cold-storage room, a building site, a cathedral, a gemstone shop, a mountain, a desert, an old house, a fridge, something very old, canes and walkers, stones.

Colors connected to this rune: Brown.

Animals connected to this rune : Goats, bears, camels and elephants.

English, Norwegian and Icelandic poems:

The English poem:
Hail is the whitest of grains, whirling from heaven's height,
Gusts of wind toss it about and then it becomes water.

A seed is a structured component that brings life. Whiteness suggests purity and truth. The poem shows that from hail originate all things (the first atomic particle from which this world was created is compared to a hail flake). The poem then describes a hail storm and how the situation then changes when ice becomes water again and flows back into earth and rivers.

The norwegian poem:
Hail is the coldest of grains
Christ created the ancient world

The first sentence is about the creation of the world as in the English poem and it enhances coldness i.e silence, meditation and inner peace which are like grains of evolution. In the second phrase, it is very likely that the word Christ actually at some stage replaced the word Ymir, who created the ancient world in Nordic mythology. This second sentence enhances ancient times, history, the beginning of time and the guardians of wisdom on earth.

The Icelandic poem:
Hail is a cold grain
And shower of hail
And a snake's illness or sickness of serpents

Matter was created from ice and fire so the first sentence is related to the creation of the world and to origin as in the two previous poems. The second sentence describes how hail can fall in sudden showers. This represents a factor, situation or upcoming event that cannot be controlled because it does not depend on personal will. One could call it fate or destiny. Serpent's illness symbolizes winter when snakes go underground and rest, recovering from the past and preparing the future. The snake symbolizes both life force flowing around but also the impact of evil. The idea suggested is that energy is here turned inwards and that evil forces have little or no impact because the situation is airtight. This rune was often used as protection against evil.

Using this rune to do magic: Rune Hagl is used to get access to structure and essence, to structure and to build, to deeply see and understand the past, destiny and what precisely caused the present situation so as to choose a different future, to move forward on the path that leads to one's deep inner truth and to experience and find inner peace. It was also used to seek protection against bad weather and so was often carved on houses.

Links with other information systems:

I Ching: This rune is related to hexagram 9, handling winter, to hexagram 33, strategic retreat and to hexagram 52, the mountain.
Mayan Astrology: This rune can be related to two glyphs, the flint or mirror and the storm.
Tarot: Rune Hagl can be related to card number 9, the Hermit but also to cards 14, the Angel, to card 16 the House of God and to card 20 called the Archangel or Sacred vision or more commonly Judgment.
Astrology: Rune Hagl is a mix of planets Saturn and Uranus and it can also suggest the long path that goes from the south lunar node to the north lunar node.

Rune 10: NYD

Various names given to this rune:

Name and meaning in Old Norse: Naudh. Necessity, obligations, limits, constraints, what is needed.
Name and meaning in Old German: Naudhiz. Necessity, a need.
Name and meaning in Old English: Nyd: A need and a feeling of distress because something is lacking.

Its graphic design and form: The vertical shows as usual a connection between sky and earth. It represents destiny and the axis or path of evolution. And something comes about that either disturbs this or either consciously controls things so that they go the right way. A force coming from upwards and going downwards from left to right encounters and crosses the vertical axis. One can say that it pierces the vertical line and interrupts the natural flow of life, just like an electrical switch or resistance slows down or prevents electricity from flowing in the vertical axis. One can also say that vertical forces are spreads horizontally due to active involvement of will power. If we compare this rune's icon to the previous rune, rune 9, the same oblique line connected two horizontal lines together while here, the two lines have become one.

The two lines can also be sticks and the two pieces of wood required to make fire when one is rubbed against the other with bits of moss placed where the two sticks come in contact. Moss is a symbol of service and sacrifice. This rune then represents a tool that can be used to make fire and this requires focusing, concentration, work and patience. It is also connected with using fire to survive, to protect oneself against cold weather, to keep animals away (rats, wolfs, bears and bats) and to cook food. This rune was therefore related to technical processes, rituals, spells and feasts celebrated with fire, as in Saint John's celebration or during winters solstice but also when burning the dead so that they could travel in the afterlife worlds thanks to the purifying effects of fire.

The icon also looks like a cross. It then symbolizes the heavy loads and burdens one carries, the necessary work on oneself through observation and self-knowledge and also adapting so as to change old habits, repeated patters and traumatic cycles.

In doing so one can then accomplish one's destiny and evolve along the path that leads to total unity within and to union of personal consciousness with the Source of all life. So rune Nyd is about an issue but also about the technical solutions to solve that issue so that in the end one has gained knowledge and evolved.

Its number: Nyd is rune number 10 and 10 is Necessity's number. Necessity was called "Ananké" in ancient Greece and it symbolizes the laws of evolution that show at every moment what it is best to do and how it is best to be so as to tune in with the present moment and adapt to the flow of life, so that things work out well and evolve positively. Necessity has to submit to cosmic order and thus to cycles and to repeated schemes that need to be transformed so that wellness and joy come about. This rune thus shows a need, something that is necessary and that must be satisfied.

As long as it is not then there is a feeling of lack and distress. To satisfy this need and to get out of this distress feeling, one must understand the order of things and cycles. One must be smart, handle data correctly and take action so as to take control of one's life, of one's destiny. It is also necessary to be well centered and that is symbolized by the point where the two lines meet. Rune 10 starts teaching a person how to become centered and how to go from the always thinking mind to the heart. It can both show discontent, distress and dissatisfaction because something needed is lacking and finding the appropriate strategic solution and implementing it so as to make things work out the right way.

The qualifications and abilities brought about by previous rune 9, such as depth, vision of truth, relevant questioning, simplicity and humbleness are here put into practice. It then becomes possible to end a cycle and to start a new one in the right way, on the right track.

Summary and essence of this rune: The harmonious evolution of the current situation is being disrupted. What is then required is adapting smartly to difficulties and constraints, seeing the meaning of things and the existing limitations and also patience. Difficulties force action in a certain way. This requires thinking, technical data and finding the efficient strategy so as to adapt. It may also require a sacrifice, getting to the bottom of an issue, experiencing chaos, a difficult trial or even a crisis that leads to change. Rune Nyd also symbolizes "life's intelligence".

This intelligence manifests firstly as a "health intelligence" that makes people do what is required to be in good health. It also manifests as an ability to see precisely what is required, as an ability to adapt very efficiently but also as a will and an ability to assist, to serve and to fulfill both physical and spiritual needs and constraints that come up in the present moment so that life can move on. Nyd then helps people free themselves from a bad habits and repeated schemes because they undertake what is needed to do so.

The dark side of the rune: The dark side of this rune was particularly feared because it manifested as bad luck, fate and chaotic events, as a situation where one is enslaved, as a burden that one cannot control but that one has to cope with, as instability, as inefficient organization leading to failure or technical problems and in any case to non adapting, as a lack of understanding concerning what is really needed and the true meaning of what is happening, as a health or hygiene issue, as a delay, a disruption, a malfunction, a breakdown or a collapse. When unbalanced, this rune can mean that the thinking mind and material things have far too great importance in a person's life or that a repeated pattern or a bad habit is maintaining an unhappy situation. It is then necessary to see what is not right, one's mistakes and to make the wheel of life turn the other way round. The difficulties encountered force a person to put everything on the table, to think things out, to find solutions, to fix what needs fixing and to start off a new cycle.

Specific historical landmarks for this rune: Because this rune can make things go either the right way or the wrong way, it has unfortunately been used to try and make things go the wrong way, to create imbalance and havoc, to attract bad luck and to strike people considered as enemies. Nordic sagas testify that some people thus made sticks called doom sticks or curse sticks, killed a horse, planted the stick in the horse's belly, carved a curse on the stick and poured their hatred on their enemies, ignoring that what they thus sent was doomed to come back to them and to create a cycle of unhappiness and misery. The Christian church forbid this and put an end to such practices.

Its sound: This rune is related to sound « n » as in the word need.

Key words: Il y a un besoin à satisfaire, une intervention du destin et de la nécessité, une contrainte et une difficulté à surmonter, une adaptation nécessaire grâce à une intelligence technique, à une analyse pertinente et à des actions stratégiques faisant appel aux bon outils. Il y a une nécessité de travailler, d'assister et de servir ou d'attacher et de contraindre une personne ou une habitude anarchique et source de désordre. Les contraintes nées du besoin.

People and jobs related to this rune: this rune can represent a servant, a person willing to serve, a smart person, people who have lost everything or won a lot of money, someone in distress, someone in need, people with great skills, handymen, financiers, techmen, precursors, people who take care of animals or plants or gardens and people who adapt. It can represent jobs requiring technical abilities, mastering technologies, handling and processing data, using numbers, having nerves, being very precise and moving around a lot. This rune can also represent shopkeepers and salesmen, accountants, inventors, mechanics, traders, clockmakers, professional players, people who use plants to heal, environmental caretakers, cleaners, school teachers, publishers and printers. It can finally represent jobs related to health and hygiene like physiotherapist, naturopath, pharmacist, respirologist, pulmonologist, neurologist and health technician.

Gods related to this rune: This rune is related to the three Norns, Urd, Verdandi and Skuld who weave men's destinies. It can also be related to specific events where people or animals are tied up as the wolf Fenrir or Fenris and Loki were.

Places and people related to this rune: woodlands, forests, Vaetirs or spirits of the elements, wooden objects, electrical devices, energy generators, a woodwork workshop, a workshop, a shop, a computer hall, a care unit with sophisticated machines and devices, a place where numbers are processed, a place where tools are built or used, a game room, a casino, a zoo, a roundabout, hub or crossroads.

Colors related to this rune: Light grey.

Animals related to this rune: clever animals, the monkey, the fox the coyote, termites, rodents, rats, mice, otters, squirrels and parrots.

English, Norwegian and Icelandic poems:

The English poem:
Need oppresses the heart
Yet it often becomes a source of help and salvation for the sons of men
If they take it into account it in time

This poem shows that if life's constraints and restrictions may be difficult to handle and to cope with, salvation comes from being aware of what is necessary and from accomplishing "necessity". An oppressed heart may suggest difficulties related to love or to the heart itself while doing what is necessary and what works helps and heals.

The Norwegian poem:
Constraint, need and necessity give no choice
A naked man is chilled by frost

In the first sentence, the poem puts on the table choice verses constraints, free will verses satisfaction of need. It shows that when facing necessity, what must be done is obvious and seeing this gives the required energy to do what must be done. A naked man freezes to death if he does not find what is needed for his safety, i.e. clothing and shelter. A very miserable scene with severe poverty and distress is shown here where what must be done is obvious.

The Icelandic poem:
Constraint is grief for the bond-maid
A state of oppression
And weary toilsome work

Here, the poem shows the very difficult living circumstances and conditions experienced by slaves, maids and hired workers in northern lands. They had to work hard and were often exhausted. It may be related to a saga, Volsunga Saga, were Princess Hjordas takes her servants place in order to stay alive.

Using this rune to do magic: This rune can be used to see what is required to feel well and to accept that what is cannot be any other way that how it is just now, to be aware of one's needs and of the obstacles impeding the satisfaction of those needs, to find the appropriate technical solutions, to organize things efficiently, to adapt smartly, to satisfy a need and to have needs satisfied, to get out of distress and repeated schemes, to slow things down if they are going too fast, to interrupt, disrupt, block or delay, to constraints and chain up, to protect against bursts of fever, from attacks or from people trying to influence one way or another and so that whatever is necessary comes about or happens.

Links with other information systems:

I Ching: This rune is symbolically related to Hexagrams 10, the right conduct, 47 Oppression, 50 the Cauldron, 60 the right limits and 62 the small crossing.

Mayan Astrology: This rune can be related to the glyph called « the hand ».

Tarot: Rune Nyd can be related to rune 10, the wheel of fortune and partly to cards 13, death and 15 the devil.

Astrology: This rune is a mix of astrological signs Virgo, Scorpio and Capricorn.

Rune 11 : ISS ou ISA

Various names given to this rune:

Name and meaning in Old Norse: Iss. Ice.
Name and meaning in Old German: Isa. Ice.
Name and meaning in Old English: Eis. Ice.

Its graphic design and form: seventeen out of the 24 runes are structured with or by a vertical line. Rune Isa is therefore like a central component or raw material with which most other runes are created, the raw material of life and of creation. At its highest level, the vertical line symbolizes the connection between sky and earth and a harmonious flow between what is above and what is below and a balance between top and bottom i.e. between human and animal. It also symbolizes the place in the body where sky energy and earth energy meet, i.e. the heart. When top and bottom are harmoniously connected and when they work together efficiently them awareness occurs, a powerful creative power is available and one can manifest the power of the heart, the power of love. This enables a person to set clear goals, to undertake efficient actions, to succeed and to become the best possible version of herself or himself. Rune Isa has a powerful centralizing effect. It allows a person to master whatever he or she is doing and develop autonomy. Unfortunately however, the bottom is disconnected from the top, disconnected with the self. The consequence of this situation is that ego (the feeling of being separated from everything other than oneself) continues to exist. This creates duality, a state where one is not natural, lack of being here and now, anger, coldness and harshness. If this is the case then action is disconnected from the heart and from consciousness and then manifests as chaos, disorder and disharmony, which is very much often the case on this planet.

Comment of the name of this rune: Even though Ice is frozen water, it was considered to be a special element in northern countries, apart from water, air, earth or fire. It is said in these countries that ice cuts and burns just as it freezes and preserves. Without heat it leads to rigidity and to death but it can also help build a shelter (an igloo) that protects from the cold. Ice can also be transparent, shining and dazzling.

It seems at first to be static yet it is always moving and changing though very slowly. It can break very suddenly and unpredictably. An iceberg, berg meaning mountain, brings about the idea that only a small part of reality is visible and that the rest exists within the depths and mysteries of life. Ice is also related to hidden dangers as one cannot always see the cracks on ice sheets. Some rune practitioners say that Isa is the opposite of Fehu (the first rune which represents fire in motion), of Ken the sixth rune which is a torch and which represents form and of the tenth rune Nyd which is centered in the thinking mind and not in the heart.

Its number: Eleven is two ones put side by side. This means creative power, energy, action, intention, focusing and conscious action is doubled. Where rune 1, Fehu symbolizes naturally efficient action, rune 11 symbolizes the use of power to fully master a situation. Where number 1 is a universal landmark and the origin of all life, number 11 is the personal landmark and the origin of personal success which means being the best possible version of oneself. Number 11 can therefore be related to the spiritual body located in the center of the heart and too spiritual energy. Numbers 1 and 11 can be related to two aspects of the all powerful strength of love, of which are made human beings, the gods and the "Source of all life". Number 11 can however also be related to duality, to inner conflicts, to struggling and to two opposite forces fighting against each other. These two forces can be the animal part and the soul or fire and ice. Rune Isa can then be related to the "dark matter" that keeps the cosmos into place, to antimatter that combines with life energy to create matter and the empty silent gateway that every person must cross in order to access their spiritual body deep within.

Summary and essence of this rune: I am Reality's structure, clear insight connected to the heart, the quest for total unity as it once existed, focused will that organizes efficiently what must be organized and that creates and masters. I also am potential energy, gathering components or forces around a central element, focusing on what is really important, harmonizing opposites (top and bottom, animal and soul, heart and mind and so on). I am purity, simplicity and transparency. I express what is unique in me. I create autonomy. I am what evolves slowly but steadily. I am able to enhance things and people, to bring about success and to make people become the best of who they are. I am intention, focus and awareness.

I am action with both the physical body in the world through boldness and through the spiritual body which manifests as creative power and as the power of love.

The dark side of the rune: It manifests as slowness, chillness, harshness, hardness, immobility, inertia, Nordic winter, ice, paralysis, difficulties in moving forward, obstacles, blocks, difficult crossings, selfishness, excessive self-importance, lack of love, isolation and loneliness, lack of vision and clarity, lack of will power and clear goals, lack of control and undertaking, lack of desire, hidden dangers and blindness. Ice can be dangerous and just like ice; this rune can have a cutting, wounding and freezing aspect. A tendency to want things to be as you want and to be stubborn tends to create conflicts. Anger can sometimes turn into violence with this rune. There can sometimes be an excess of structure and a lack of life, fluidity and help. Only the fire of love and a clear vision of truth can make ice melt. It is then necessary to do as best you can, without wanting more that what is possible.

Its sound: This rune is related to the sound "I" but as in fit, tip or sickle.

Key words: A clear and deep vision, listening to one's heart and body, focusing on a clearly defined goal, expression of heart and will, gathering and creating order, organizing things harmoniously, using will power to master something, undertakings so as to become autonomous, being centered on what is really important, asserting one's power, success though action, creating a better future, using creative power and personal abilities to enhance oneself and to become the best possible version of oneself.

People and jobs related to this rune: someone who is well centered, well connected, aware, awakened, completely involved and who lives in the present moment. Someone focusing on success. Someone calm, pure, with a generous heart. Someone vibrant, very active, bold and brave, with a fighting spirit and who struggles with a difficult situation. Someone truthful and seeking for the truth. Someone detached from the world or from everyday life. Freelancers, self-employed and liberal professions, managers, senor officers, supervisors, foremen and department overseers, jobs requiring self-control, inner strength, bravery or physical strength, sportsmen, sports coaches, firemen, rescuers, creators, organizers, people who maintain order, body guards and safety agents.

This rune can also sometimes represent someone sharp, aggressive, angry, violent, selfish, harsh, cold, weighed down or as rigid as ice.

Places and objects related to this rune: Places where one learns to master or to become a master, battlefields, places where sports competitions are held, places where people create things, head quarters, castles, zoos, circuses, training centers, sports halls, places where there is ice, sources of light and energy, sharp edged objects.

Colors related to this rune: Ice white and shiny yellow

Animals related to this rune: Polar bears, lion and wild cats.

Gods related to this rune: In Nordic mythology, ice is the raw material from which all life was created. This rune is related to the world of ice, Niflheim which is way up north compared to the world of fire which is way down south. From this ice world was born Ymir thanks to whom the creation of the world became possible. Ice is also related to the ice giants who also created life but who became the enemies of the Aesir Gods. Rune Isa is related to giantess Skadi who married the ocean god Njord because she chose him sort of by mistake. She then abandoned him and returned to her ice world. Rune Isa is also related to the Norns, Goddesses of destiny and more specifically to Norn Verdandi, who is the Goddess of present moment and of actions that create future consequences but also to Norn Skuld who rules over what will be in the future. Finally, rune Isa is also related to the guardian god Heimdall who protects Asgard from intruders.

English, Norwegian and Icelandic poems:

The English poem:
Ice is very cold and extremely slippery
It shines as bright as glass and gems
It is like a ground created by frost and beautiful to look at

This poem describes what ice is like. At a very deep level, it suggests the inner path that leads to the center of the heart and it invites you to let yourself be guided by the feeling of beauty and deep joy that are like solid ground you can safely walk on.

The Norwegian poem:
Ice is called the great broad bridge
A blind man must be guided

This poem is about a crossing from one world to another, from one state of being to another and it specifies how important it is to be guided and to accept guidance. The bridge concerned can either be Bifrost, the rainbow bridge that connects the world of Men Midgard with the God's world Asgard or Gjallarbru, the bridge that connects the world of men with the worlds down under. The blind man who needs to be led or guided could also be the blind God Hodr who let himself be misguided and fooled by Loki in throwing the mistletoe dart that killed the god Baldr. His ignorance and his lack of vision and consciousness created wrong or unharmonious beliefs. This may suggest that most human beings are blind, live in a world of illusions and can only find their way towards their deep inner truth by being rightly guided. If someone refuses to be guided and just does what he wants whenever he wants wherever he wants, then this sets into actions forces of destiny that create consequences, possibly disasters and to cause precisely what one wanted to avoid, just as it was so with Baldr.

The Icelandic poem:
Ice is the bark of rivers
The roof of waves
And destruction of the doomed

The first sentence compares life with a tree and says ice is the tree's dark. It thus describes ice as a structure of life that flows along. What structures life? Well, awareness of where one comes from, what and who we are and where we want to go or who we want to be and also what is the best version of oneself. A ware if life in motion connected to ancestral memories as the ocean symbolizes the invisible world where ancestors dwell. A roof symbolizes vision from high up and a vision that has meaning. In order to access one's heart and one's deep inner truth, one must ride or manage the waves of ancestral memories one bears. These memories produce consequences in the present and must be channeled the right way by expressing each one in the best possible form. The third line suggest that people who do not take care of their spiritual evolution are condemmed to wander about for ages until their illusions die down and until the find the path of evolution, change, joy and wisdom that leads them to their deep inner truth.

Using this rune to do magic: Rune Isa can be used to have a clear and correct vision, to define clear intentions, to focus one's will on a goal, to control and master what needs to be through appropriate organization and means, to succeed and also to slow down, calm, deter, neutralize, freeze or block off spoilers, aggressive energies or evil intentions or any unharmonious evolution. It can also be used to cut off past memories and to focus on the present moment. It can finally be used to experience a deep state of calm, clarity and stillness during meditation so as to go deep down into the heart.

Links with other information systems:

I Ching: This rune is related to hexagram 11, Strength of heart and to hexagram 45, Gathering. It has also connections with hexagram 50, the Cauldron and with hexagram 52, the mountain, where ice if often found.

Mayan Astrology: This rune can, be related to a glyph called Flint or Mirror.

Tarot: Rune Isa has connections with cards 8, Justice, car 9 the Hermit and card 11, Strength.

Astrology: This rune is a mix of Sun, Mars and Saturn with a bit of Uranus.

Rune 12: YER

 **Various names given to this rune:**

Name and meaning in Old Norse: Iar. A year, a cycle, a good season, a good harvest.
Name and meaning in Old German: Jera. A year, a good harvest.
Name and meaning in Old English: Yer. The year.

Its graphic design and form: This rune's icon is made up of rune 6, Ken, the torch and its mirror. Here is as a reminder what rune 6 is about. "From a central point emerge two flows of energy, one heading towards the sky and the other towards earth. We can also say that two flows of energy coming from sky and from earth join together in the center of the self, in the heart, thus nourishing the flame of life. Male and female forces uniting and dancing together create life, efficient action and a good harvest."

In rune 12, we have two double lines in motion. They are heading towards one another. They communicate. They meet. They move away from one another and one can easily imagine that they will meet again in the next cycle. Each double line represents a force in motion or one could say the soul in motion with its male and female forces. Two or four forces join, share, gather, mingle and create. They experience communion and community. Rune 12 icon therefore suggests completeness, a whole, life flowing in cycles, male and female forces joining and creating like for example will and faith but also the cycle of seasons and the annual earth-sun cycle. The Germans believed that there were two seasons, winter and summer. The icon suggests the summer solstice where the two seasons meet. We have been discussing cycles and thus things repeating over and over again and the rune does ask the question: what are you repeating over and over again in your life? It then says that a wise and efficient cycle management through a harmonious connection between man and nature or man and the gods brings a good harvest. This is what is at the heart of this rune. It also says that what you saw you will reap and if you want to reap and harvest then you must saw. The rune finally says that the present situation may be influenced by past actions and by memories coming from ancestors in the sense that you are reaping what has been sawed a very long time ago and that what is happening now is part of a cycle.

One harvests what ancestors sawed and that needs to be handled. A harvest can be good or not so good as that depends on many factors that one does not control like for example what's in the air. However, taking into account the four elements and managing time efficiently helps to get a good harvest. Fire means involvement and solar energy. Earth means efforts to labor the earth and to get organized efficiently. Air means adapting smartly and getting access to the right information or data while water represents rain and the water cycle that bears life. What is required here is to do your best and then to let go and to leave nature and life do its work. A good harvest is a plentiful one, one that can feed every one, one that enables moving from suffering to satisfaction and ecstasy. It brings a state of harmony and balance. This often requires helping, accepting help and compassion, being inspired and the ability to make sacrifices in terms of time and involvement. It also requires letting go of illusions and to see things deeply and clearly. Rune 12 is about all that. It should bring relief and joy after the harsh and difficult runes Hagal, Nyd and Isa.

Its number: Yer is rune number 12 within the Futhark. Number 12 represent the mystical uniting on numbers 1 and 2 so as to give birth to a new path, a new vision of things that take everything into account including soul cycles, ancestors and generations following one another. Number 12 is also about the two main forces that make this universe go round, i.e gravity and movement and the ability to balance and transcend them. 12 is a number that structures time in a cyclic manner through the 12 monthly new moons that organize daily life on earth. There are 12 astrological signs and two sets of 12 Nordic gods and goddesses. 12 is also the mirror one must cross to gain access to number 21 which is Lagu, the Ocean or completeness and self realization. This mirror is made of dreams one seeks to manifest, of unconditional love, compassion, faith, sacrificing what is inferior so that what is superior can emerge, spiritual vision, unity with the great wholeness of life and experiencing "God" and through it the "Source of all life".

Summary and essence of this rune: I am the magical cycles of life that bring good harvests, prosperity and even ecstasy when they are well managed. What has been sawing will soon be harvested. What is being done now will create consequences in the future. It is important to take into account the time factor, to accept that things take time and that every step of the cycle must be experienced.

What is due to come comes when it is time. Union between man and woman and between human and God takes place. This enables moving from suffering to relief, delight and transcendence. The situation flows and evolves with great harmony. Efforts that have been undertaken end up bringing excellent results. After entering into history one enters into legend.

The dark side of the rune: It manifests as a bad harvest, as illusions, as difficulties in seeing the spiritual meaning of what is happening, as a tendency to turn around in schemes, beliefs or situations that cause suffering, as a time where one feels lost, as meaningless chaos, as genealogical memories or past lives memories that cause despair and havoc or as a tendency to flee reality. One is going through a difficult phase of a life cycle. Collective events disrupt personal life and evolution.

Its sound: This rune is related to the « y » sound as in the words year, yes or yoyo. It has sometimes been related to the "j" sound as in joke.

Key words: What is being harvested from sea and land, what comes up in a cyclic manner, adapting to the flow of life, seeing things differently, seeing things the other way round, being aware of how cycles and past influences impact the present moment, the end of a cycle and the beginning of a new one, wait for results and harvest before drawing conclusions, sawing so as to be able to reap, getting the rewards of efforts undertaken, creating abundance and prosperity, prosperous times, summer time, summer solstice, managing what is being harvested, getting involved within a public service, going from suffering to relief , joy and ecstasy, living one's dreams, being inspired and following one's intuition, experiencing unity with life and God's presence.

People and jobs related to this rune: a loving person, a fairy-like person, a spell-binding person, a devoted person, an inspired person, someone full of compassion, someone who makes sacrifices, who saws and who reaps, someone receiving a reward, someone who brings relief to those who feels suffering and misery. This rune can also represent in its dark side someone experiencing suffering and chaos, someone who feels lost, someone having problems with ancestral memories, someone who drowned or who was sacrificed, victims, religious fanatics, martyrs, mad people and people complaining all the time. Otherwise, rune Yer can represent yogis, social workers, doctors and nurses, sailors and people working on boats, enlightened people, people living in communities and spiritual people.

Gods related to this rune: This rune was sometimes related to the eagle as the annual motion of the sun in the sky was compared to the flight of an eagle, which often flies making circles in the sky. Rune Yer is related to the Vaenir Gods Freyr and Freya who rule over prosperity within nature, to the God Njord and to goddess Nerthus and sea god Aegir who bring abundance from ocean and land.

Places and objects related to this rune: fields and harvests, ocean and goods coming from the ocean, petrol and goods made from petrol like plastic objects and resin components, collective unconscious, waiting rooms, a empty place where there is nothing to do but wait, monasteries and ashrams, meditation rooms, sacred objects and places, ladders, candles, places where one deals with ancestors and ancestral memories, places where one changes one's beliefs, places where people are relieved and healed, shelters, clinics and hospitals, temples and churches.

Colors related to this rune: Greenish blue and royal blue.

Animals related to this rune: Dolphins, whales, salmons, sea dogs, walruses, octopuses and jelly fish.

English, Norwegian and Icelandic poems:

The English poem:
Harvest brings joy to men
When God, heaven's holy king, causes the earth to produce bright fruits
For both the rich and the poor

This poem, which looks very "Christian", enhances not only joy resulting from achieving a great harvest but also blessings from Gods and Earth that enable such a good harvest. The bright fruits are probably apples which were the only existing fruits in Germany at the time when the runes where created. The poem says everyone can experience joy and abundance, regardless of social status. This gives rise to the idea that this rune is above worldly occupations and that it is related to the soul's eternal cycles i.e. when the soul looses contact with the Source of all life as it embodies into matter and then ends up walking along the long returning path to enlightenment and ends up being reunited, through hard work on oneself and through God, with this life form called "The Source of all life" or Heavens Holy King. It also shows that people's souls follow cycles and that it is important to take them into account and to manage them rightly.

The Norwegian poem:
A plentiful harvest is a blessing for all men
I say that Frothi was generous

This poem is talking about generosity, abundance and prosperity, about being blessed and about a good harvest. Frothi was a Nordic King. It is said that because of his spiritual unity with nature, with the gods and with the Source of all life, he was able to bring about in a magical way plentiful harvests all the time when he was king. It is said that he was in reality a manifestation of Freyr, who symbolizes fertility and the generosity of Mother Earth. In Nordic countries, the king's job and responsibility was to make sure that harvests were plentiful and if they were not, he could be fired and replaced so it was a very serious matter.

The Icelandic poem:
A good harvest is a blessing for men and a good summer and thriving crops

The poem enhances a lovely warm happy summer, healthy crops and a happy harvest.

Using this rune to do magic: Rune Yer is used to bring about change and motion, to undertake in an organized and efficient manner so as to create a plentiful harvest, to flow in harmony with life, to manage cycles efficiently, to make to power of faith work so as to produce a miracle or a great harvest, to become aware of past life or ancestral memories, to become disconnected from negative influences of past lives or difficult ancestral memories so that they return into the collective subconscious, to make unwanted things get lost and to experience a mystical unity with life. This rune is also connected with the ability of a shaman to return safely into his physical body after an out of body experience or a shamanic trip. It is finally used to help plants grow well and to create a plentiful harvest.

Links with other information systems:

I Ching: Rune 12 is related to hexagram 12, decline, to hexagram 55, abundance and to hexagram 59, dissolution.
Mayan Astrology: Rune Yer can be related to the seed and earth glyphs.
Tarot: This rune can be related to card 12, "the hanged man" and also to card 10 "the wheel of fortune".
Astrology: This rune can be related to astrological signs Taurus, Cancer, Virgo and Pisces and to the Sun, Venus, moon, mercury and Neptune.

Rune 13: EIH

Various names given to this rune:

Name and meaning in Old Norse: Ihwar. A yew tree.
Name and meaning in Old German: Eihwas. A yew tree.
Name and meaning in Old English: Eoh. A yew tree.

Its graphic design and form: The vertical line shows as always a connection between sky and earth. Two lines then join the central axis and make up a symbol that looks like a hook where one could hang a cauldron, food, weapons or clothes. From the top of the vertical line emerges a line or a force that moves towards earth so as to influence the world of matter. From the bottom left emerges a line or force that springs out seemingly from nowhere, from the past, from emptiness, from invisible worlds and it joins the central axis. This means here that the sky, the world of man and the invisible worlds down under are connected and work together. This rune can therefore be seen as a sort of bridge or crossing that connects the world of the dead or of the past, the world of life hereafter and the world of those living on earth in the present moment. It then symbolizes life and death, eternity, eternal life and its mysteries. It suggest that we men come from somewhere, that we are always changing life forms temporarily living in the world of matter and that we then go somewhere when we lose our physical body. Rune 13 was sometimes drawn as a reversed rune 15 ⅄, showing that the two rules are quite closely connected.

Its number: Eih is rune number 13. This number has always been special. Number 12 symbolizes wholeness and a complete cycle. And then what! Well nothing could be the answer but a nothingness that does finally turn into something! There is a break from the past and from past cycles, a questioning, a purification process, an emptiness, a halt of time, a dive into darkness and into emptiness, a first breakdown into many pieces, the end of something, a destruction of forms so that only essence remains and a crossing towards something new, towards becoming a new life form. Because this number is a powerful creator of change, it is often related to something becoming unbalanced, to lack of harmony, beauty and smoothness, to destruction and to bad luck.

It symbolizes death and renewal, going from one life form to another like a butterfly and thus the complete initiation process that every soul must go through so as to gain access to eternal life, to one's deep inner truth. Many souls resist and therefore experience pain. This initiation process leads to seeing what is invisible and thus subtle forces. It leads to seeing what is causing present events and also the consequences of past causes. Seeing the invisible aspects of life requires being intensively here and now and to coordinate simultaneous vision of different worlds, of different frequencies, the world of the dead and the world of the living, the visible world and the invisible one. And when doing so, it is possible to protect people and goods correctly and to balance what was previously unbalanced.

Summary and essence of this rune: Everything is changes all the time but certain things are eternal. I am a force that transforms by breaking down, dismantling and putting things apart and then putting things back together differently and reconstructing something new. I open up a bridge between the world of those living and the world of the dead. I bring people up to a specific threshold that must then be crossed. I open up a gateway into emptiness beyond which lies renewal, a new world or something new. I question, purify, eliminate toxic products or what must be eliminated and I put an end to what no longer needs to be there. I pinpoint painful zones, flaws and problems so as to fix and overcome them and in doing so, I bring about evolution, progress and something more genuine that gradually leads people to their deep inner truth and to awareness of the human soul's eternal nature. I bring about real or symbolic death and rebirth, an end and a new beginning. I enable deep vision and awareness of what lies beyond appearance. It is then auspicious to do what must be done even if it's not very pleasant, even if it's difficult or even painful.

The dark side of the rune: If what represents this rune is lacking, then there can be a lack of depth, of understanding the cause of existing issues, of truth, of insight, of structure and of perseverance. If what represents this rune is in excess, then there can be a tendency to be living like a dead person, to always see things the dark way and to turn around in circles in an unbalanced situation and to live in a situation of chronic insecurity.

Its sound: What I see and feel is that at first, when runes where created, this rune was related to the w sound as in the words was, wasp, war, wear as this sound fit perfectly with the strong emotional tension brought about by this rune. Then there was a change and the rune became related with the "i" sound as in the words kite, bright, night or knight.

Key words: a transition period, times of change, hook up or unhook something, an issue, the end of something, a collapse, the end of an era, the end of a relationship, take into account subtle forces and what is invisible, getting rid of what is toxic, taking into account the world here after, searching in the depths to find causes or raw materials, doing a checkup, seeing with great insight what is causing the present situation and how things are connected and work out together, seeing and understanding the secrets of life and death, handling safety, security and defense issues, regeneration, initiation, being persistent, crossing a bridge or a gateway or going through a vortex, undertaking a complete change, implementing a renewal.

People and jobs related to this rune: someone authentic and with great insight, a master who has learnt special skills, a samurai, someone experiencing great changes, someone having a seizure, someone in transition or in crisis, someone learning to master subtle forces, the dead, ancestors, widows, keepers, jobs related to death, to cleaning toxins, to safety, to change or to initiation. Butchers, funeral services, medical examiners, palliative care providers, ushers and bailiffs, waste recycling jobs, garbage collectors, archeologists, radiologists, osteopaths, psychics, psychoanalysts, change coaches, chemists, farmers, dentists, surgeons, safety personnel, criminologists, policemen or soldiers.

Gods related to this rune: Rune Eih is related the Yggdrasil life tree, to the very ancient archer god Ull or Ullr that symbolizes winter, true and right speech and awareness of the world hereafter and to his companion the goddess Skadi.

Places and objects related to this rune: hallways, passageways, corridors, vortexes, places where people change, gather themselves or are initiated to something, battlefields, cemeteries, mortuaries, foundries, fields, radioactive places, radiology services, places with high vibratory rates, electrical or power transformers, bones, skeletons, lawn mowers and trimmers, scythes and sickles, metal objects, fossil fuels and archeological objects.

Colors connected to this rune: Dark brown or orange and black.

Animals connected to this rune: Wolves, scavengers, vultures, snakes, lizards, salamanders, crocodiles, wasps, Scorpios, jelly fish, moths, spiders, crows and skunks.

English, Norwegian and Icelandic poems:

The English poem:
Yew is a tree with a rough bark
Hard and firm in the earth supported by its roots
A flame keeper and a joy when it is on the estate

The poem enhances the tree's structure with roots, trunk and leaves. This shows life's structure. Roots mean adapting to matter and finding one's place in life. Trunk means been healthy, connected to one's heart and fully in the present moment. Leaves symbolize being connected to the sky, to an ideal, to a goal and spreading amongst the surrounding space. The poem shows that the yew tree is firm and reliable, well grounded in the world of matter, useful to make fire and a source of joy. The poem thus shows how to symbolize being aware of eternity, the required path and changes to access this awareness and the intense joy that comes as a result.

Comments about the yew tree: The yew tree is said to defy time as its leaves are always green and it can live over 1000 years because of its strength and its ability to permanently regenerate itself. It becomes hollow and empty as it gets old which is precisely the state of being one needs to experience in order to access the spiritual body and thus to one's eternal identity. It secretes a special resin that is toxic and that brings about hallucinations. This resin was used to access new states of being during shamanic rituals. Bows, spears, dagger handles but also skis were often made out of yew. This tree therefore symbolizes safety, defense, death, regeneration but also the gateway towards life hereafter and the initiation path that leads to eternal life.

The Norwegian poem:
Yew is the greenest of all trees in winter.
It crackles when it burns.

The poem enhances here the yew tree as a symbol of eternity and the specific sound it makes when it burns. It is seen as fuel to heat, to protect people and goods and to cook food. It turns wood into ashes and therefore symbolizes all transformation processes.

The Icelandic poem:
Yew, a bent bow, brittle iron and giant Farbauti's arrow.

The poem first reminds us that yes is used to make bows and arrows. Faubuti was one of the original giants and father of the god Loki, who was the god that mostly messed things up and brough about misery but also change. This shows that weapons are potentially dangerous and that they can bring about destruction and misery. Brittle iron is said to be an homonym of yew and symbolizes an iron arrow head. Brittle iron was mentioned in the poem describing rune number 2, Ur, where it symbolized amongst other things producing metal objects. Here what is enhanced is transforming metal thanks to fire and therefore transforming hard cutting ego with the fire of love.

Using this rune to do magic: Rune Eih is used to anchor or hook up something somewhere but also to cut toxic emotional bonds linked with memories. Something disappears from somewhere and appears elsewhere as it is taken from where it was and put in a more appropriate place. It is used to be protected against negative forces, to make a place safe, to neutralize effects of poison and toxic things, to take away pain and to balance something unbalanced. If you feel pain somewhere, in a tooth for example, find a small sticking plaster, draw rune 13 alone if the pain is light and add one, two or three Isa runes if the pain is strong and stick it on your cheek. In most cases the pain will disappear after 20 minutes or so. Austrian doctor Erich Korbler found this out. I tried it and it worked for me! Rune 13 can be used to cross safely over a bridge or though a gateway, as a vortex to access higher levels of awareness and awareness of eternity or eternal life, to perceive subtle forces and what is invisible, to facilitate out of body experiences and undertake a shamanic trip, to become free from fear of death, to have visions of the past, of past lives or of time's memory, to implement important changes and to regenerate.

Links with other information systems:

I Ching: This rune is related to hexagram 13, "community with men", with hexagram 36 which is called "darkening of light" and with hexagram 49, "revolution".
Mayan Astrology: Rune 13 can be related to the bridge glyph called Cimi.
Tarot: Rune Eih can be related to card 13, the unnamed card also sometimes called death and to card 20 the Judgment.
Astrology: This rule is related to the astrological signs Scorpio and Capricorn.

Rune 14 : PERTH

ou **Various names given to this rune:**

Name and meaning in Old Norse: unknown.

Name and meaning in Old German: Perthra. Method for drawing lots, dice holding device.

Name and meaning in Old English: Peordh ou Perth. Object used to question destiny and to play together in small groups.

Its graphic design and form: As usual, the vertical live shows a vertical axis of evolution and involution flux and trends and also the natural and synchronized flow of energy and information existing between sky and earth. The vertical axis actually connects two double lines that join each other near the vertical axis. It's as if the two double lines from rune 12, Yer returned to the central axis of rune 11 Isa. The two double lines actually symbolize male and female forces working together in harmony. In this icon, what is above and what is below are firmly and clearly connected by the central axis but also in an invisible and more subtle manner, by the two angles facing each other and communicating from a certain distance. We are thus focusing on visible and invisible communication. This communication creates a new space and a new tool which makes life express itself in a new way. But who is communication with who and what for? What I feel as that firstly "The Source of all life" is communicating with men so as to help them find answers and solutions to fix what needs fixing and to help them see an alternative future, to help them see universal laws, cosmic laws, sky laws. Secondly men are communicating with men within a group so as to experiment community, teamwork, so as to build a network where people help each other and so as to try and build a better world. With this rune, what was unknown becomes known and what was hidden is now revealed, but very cleverly, in a global and multidimensional manner. This rune's icon and sound are very similar to those of rune 18 Berkano, as if the p sound was an opened b sound. It has also been said that this rune can symbolize a mother giving birth to a child with the help of other wemen as the shape of rune Perth suggest a space opening up so that something can come out of it. Finally, this rune was related to the apple tree because it was said that this fruit was a gift of the gods or angels, that it was of great help and that a remedy for all illnesses.

Its number: Perth is rune number 14. Rune 14 symbolizes a phase of a cycle and more specifically half of a woman's 28 day cycle. It connects sky and earth in a very active manner. It connects eternal fire that exists since the origin of time (number 1) with an intelligence capable of organizing this world of matter by organizing all the data required to make this world go round(number 4). It also brings awareness that one can flow in harmony with cosmic order and develop a sense of belongingness through teamwork. This connection between sky and earth, between action and highly intelligent organization gives rise to progress and evolution. On day 14 of a woman's life cycle, the ovule descends from the ovary and finds its place in the uterus. So for human beings, 14 symbolizes fertility, preparing to give birth to someone or something and transferring someone or something from one place to another.

Comments about the name Perth: a "perth" was a dice cup used to question fate i.e. a housing structure related to a questioning process. This process enabled the gods or angels to supply data and solutions that were used to make decisions and also to bring about a certain relief. A person who used a dice or dices to question the gods created a synchronicity between a question, the act of throwing one or more dices on the ground or on a table and the answer given through the dice. The dice then reveals a small portion of a person's destiny. Finally, rune Perth is related to Nordic games where luck has a lot to do with winning. One could see how lucky and smart a person was by observing whether he often won or not. These games which are still played today are called "tafl" games amongst which are the "hafltafl", the "henftafl" and the "tablut".

Here is a questioning process used here and there on this planet: It is first required to create a safe space that is protected from the surroundings forces. You throw a dice made with natural resources like wood, stone, amber or even baked clay. You can create your own system if you find this one unsuitable or use the following data questioning quantic system.

• Definitely yes, excellent and in perfect harmony with cosmic order.

•• The answer is obvious, you should feel it or wrong questioning

••• The answer is no and it's a very bad idea

•••• Not a very good idea, poor, low quality, the answer is no

••••• It's rather good but there are better options so it's good to wait and persevere.

•••••• Very good, definitely yes, you can more forward.

Summary and essence of this rune: I connect within me what is above and is below so as to be centered, fully focused and synchronized with necessity. I then become aware of my psychological structure and I question cosmic laws and chance so as put move forward on the tracks of my destiny. I use dices to find the appropriate solution. I use my psychological and technological intelligence to find solutions, to bring about progress, to fix what needs fixing, to relieve and to put things back on track. I implement within me a multidimensional, international and global vision. I ask my friends or my network for help. I help those who need it. I accept whatever help is offered. I get involved within a network or within a team. I organize my activities so that coincidences can take place and so that chance can manifest, like a catalyst that changes things without itself being changed. I keep an eye out to see connections between causes and effects, to observe consequences of past actions, to check out possible futures and to notice messages from the gods or from Angels. I take into account whatever hidden technical laws, spiritual laws or psychological laws put forward within the current situation so as to bring about solutions and progress. The result is then a crossing from one situation or from one state of being to another.

The dark side of the rune: It is symbolized by a disconnection with the sky or with earth, by false hopes, by a situation remaining virtual, uncertain and hypothetical, by deceit or an unpleasant surprise, by a non alignment with the will of the sky, by a lack of psychological or technological intelligence, by a difficulty with sharing or finding one's place within a group, by something going off track, by a technical issue or a bad solution, by bad advice, by help that brings out more problems and concern than solutions and relief and by a false vision of the future. You do not have freedom or action.

Its sound: This rune is related to the sound « p ».

Key words: unfolding your antennas to see opportunities and solutions, being a transparent and pure person, being connected, observing cause to effects relationships and coincidences, questioning and obtaining an answer though a divination process, distinguishing and prioritizing things, expressing one's uniqueness and free will so as to move forward on the track of one's destiny, helping and accepting help, asking for psychological or technical advice, undertaking a therapy or work within a group, gaining technical or psychological understanding of a situation, working within a team or a network, celebrate life amongst friends, finding an innovative solution so as to bring about progress. There is a manifestation of chance or of some effect whose cause goes back far in time. Healing, liberation and relief occur.

People and jobs related to this rune : a very intelligent person who knows how to adapt and how to help others or accept help from others, someone well connected and tuned in to what is going on, someone who helps others, who masters a technology, who is experiencing a transitional period, a short time resident, someone taking time off to rest or to take care of himself or herself, someone working in an international environment, a tourist or someone on holydays, a therapist, a psychologist, a social worker, a technical officer, a human resource officer, a human relationships adviser, a mediator or facilitator, someone who protects others, a special education teacher, a movie producer, someone working at a radio station, someone using alternative medical techniques, acupuncturists, magnetizer, healers, people working in the field of communication, telephone operators, people working in call centers, harp players, computer specialists, analysts and programmers, network technical staff, service technician, electrician, people who sell electrical devices, jobs related to the airplane and space industry, air hostess, ground control officer, air controller, flight checker, pilot, people who work in airports.

Gods related to this rune: This rune is related to the three Norns who implement cosmic laws, the laws of destiny. It is sometimes related to the goddess Frigg, Odin's wife and a shaman, therapist who can see the future and heal because she masters magic.

Places and objects related to this rune: a therapists' office, a technology center, an airport, a high speed train station, a place where people are on holydays, a leisure center, peaceful and serene places, a mountain or cold places, sports clubs, a pulsed magnetic field mattress and quantic technological devices, radios and televisions, mobile phones, computers and graphic tablets.

Colors connected to this rune: cyan and sky blue.

Animals connected to this rune: seagulls, albatrosses, wild geese, swans and unicorns.

English, Norwegian and Icelandic poems:

The English poem:
Perth brings recreation and laughter to the high spirited
Where proud warriors happily gather together in the mead hall (or hall where magic and divination are practiced)

This poem made many rune practitioners puzzled. It describes the state of mind with which divination and magic are done i.e a state of spontaneity, of joy and of amusement. The word proud refers here to one's self image, generosity of heart, achieving defined goals and being centered in one's heart. Laughter often dissipates tensions and liberates from emotional stress. Warriors sitting together in a great hall symbolizes a meeting concerning future plans, teamwork or discussing current affairs. Warriors could also be wemen warriors or wemen gathering together to share and to discuss daily matters. The hall may also have been a banquet hall where people gather to listen to music or sagas and to danse.

This rune does not exist in the Viking Futhark so the Norwegian and Icelandic poems don't mention it.

Using this rune to do magic: Rune Perth is used to get the right information, the right answer to a question or the right remedy to an illness or emotional stress, to get efficient help, to be synchronized and aligned with the will of the sky, of the gods, to succeed as a team within a project or to have a nice time with friends, to find a technical solution, to bring about healing, to find a lost objects and to make a specific event happen so that what is virtual is achieved in real life.

Links with other information systems:

I Ching: This rune is related to hexagram 13, "community with men", with hexagram 14, "Greatness succeeds" and with hexagram 35, "Progress".
Mayan Astrology: This rune can be related to a glyph called « The Human ».
Tarot: Rune Perth can be related to card 14, "Temperance" or "the angel".
Astrology: Rune Perth can de related with the astrological signs Gemini (dice games), Libra (social life) and especially Aquarius.

Rune 15: EOLH

Various names given to this rune:

Name and meaning in Old Norse: Ihwar. A yew bow.

Name and meaning in Old German: Algiz ou Elhaz. An elk.

Name and meaning in Old English: Eolh. An elk reed.

Its graphic design and form: The vertical line symbolizes as usual the connection between what is above and what is below, between sky and earth. Two lines emerge from the left hand side and the right hand side of the sky and join together at a spot located two thirds up of the vertical axis. These two lines look just like rune 6 ken rotated at a 90 degree angle i.e a ken rune but with a different vision. The two lines also represent an arrow head pointing downwards showing that it is auspicious to see and take care of what is down below, on earth. Rune Eohl can be seen as a combination of runes 11 Isa and a modified rune 6 Ken which means as a combination of ice and fire, of cold ice passion and of fiery burning torch-like passion. There is also a similarity between rune 15 Eohl Y and rune 17 Tiw↑. Here, with rune 15, one receives sky energy or awareness and this goes down to the ground while with rune 17, energy and consciousness return from ground to sky. Rune 15 icon can symbolize a reed stalk (marshland carex type reeds), a weapon to hunt and fish, a bird claw, a bird in flight, a human being stretching his arms out to the sky but also sexual intercourse where male penetrates female and where female is filled up with semen by male. This icon has also been related to elk horns and to a torch carrier.

Its number: Eolh is rune number fifteen. Number fifteen doesn't have any specific meaning on itself. It is a combination of number 1 and 5 put side by side., two very active and fiery like number who bring the fire of creation and the fire of awareness. This gives a powerfully active awareness as well as the ability to set a well defined goal and to focus intensively and act efficiently to achieve this goal in the world of matter.

Summary and essence of this rune: I am a survival instinct that can foresee danger or any perverseness and depravity and that can then fight through defensive action so as to protect goods and people, the surrounding space and whatever needs to be safe. I am the hunter who fears nothing so as to hunt its prey and protect his territory.

I am sexual energy and sexual drives that can bring life or excesses, exhaustion and misery. I am life wanting to take pleasure with the physical body and the world of matter. I am the blacksmith who is capable of creating metal objects from fire and earth. I am the soul's warrior like fighting spirit who can see with great insight what is here and now, what is coming, the dark side of things and the flaws within any situation or person. This fighting spirit allows me to express my personal power, to pursue my passions, to transform what needs to be changed to fight with great intensity and courage so as to get access to heaven's gate, to the realm of the gods and to divine light. Constant alertness and irreproachable conduct are the warrior's best weapons.

The dark side of the rune: Here, the rune is turned upside down. It then represents temptation, a flaw in one's defenses, an inner conflict, someone full of perversity that manipulates people, violent sexual drives, anguish bringing memories, human ignorance and stupidity, excesses, sabotage, destruction, something rotting, betrayal, reject, humiliation, unhealed wounds and physical or psychological pain and misery. Restoring harmony and healing are then here required to bring about change.

Its sound: This rune is related to the "z" sound.

Key words: remaining on constant alert, listening to one's instincts, one's intuition and one's feelings, being protected from temptation and danger, an effective defense system, fighting to change oneself or the situation, to settle an issue, to manage a crisis or to do what one passionately loves doing, to rise towards the light and to bring about safety, safety issues, an anti-virus, keen eyesight that can see what is invisible, causes and unsaid words, passion in action and in motion, force channeled through intention, power instinct, extremely smart and efficient mastery of energy and or metal, going beyond duality to see unity, healing old wounds, getting a powerful control of the situation, bringing light where the is ignorance and darkness.

People and jobs related to this rune: a master instructor, a well armed person, someone with great experience in combat, someone with complete understanding and mastery of something, a secret keeper, a psychic, someone with great passion, a very aggressive and threatening person, someone with great fighting spirit, someone extremely smart or with great personal power.

If the rune is negative then it can represent an unhealthy, wicked, pervert frightening, and depraved person, a thief or a crook, someone always overdoing things, a provocative person, someone experiencing great anxiety, misery and suffering, someone creating misery around them, an ignorant or stupid person, a dick and someone doing sabotage and creating an unbalanced situation. It can then represent people doing witchcraft and illegal, perverse and depraving activities such as terrorism, making horror movies, mafia, drugs and prostitution. Rune 15 can be related to work in industrial, chemical or financial companies, to jobs requiring the use of fire (smiths and metal industry) or where there is a certain amount of pressure and stress, to jobs requiring working in darkness or at night, to banking activities and tax collection, to politics and to secret organisations. It can also be related to jobs concerning security, safety and defense like for example security guards and officials, police officers, soldiers and military staff. It can finally be related to exorcism and to anti-criminal organisations.

Gods related to this rune: This rune is sometimes related to the life tree Yggdrasil because the shape of the icon does looks a little bit like a tree. But rune 15 is mostly related to the mischievous and malicious god Loki who creates havoc and misery wherever he goes and to the mistletoe dart that killed Baldr. It is finally sometimes related to the God Heimdall who guards the kingdom of Asgard.

Places and objects related to this rune: metal objects, weapons, talismans, foundries, extremely hot places, exiting places, dangerous places, chasms and pitfalls, frightening places, illegitimates places where one isn't supposed to be, places where people and changed, caves and volcanoes, nuclear power plants, war zones, battlefields and miserable places.

Colors connected to this rune: black, red and black together.

Animals connected to this rune: pigs, boars, goats and goatees, frogs and toads, lemurs, rats, snakes, scorpions, sharks, crocodiles, jelly-fish, salamanders, bats, skunks, badgers, birds of prey and eagles.

English, Norwegian and Icelandic poems:

The English Poem:

Elk-sedge grows in marshland, in water
It is grimly wounding, burning the blood of any warrior who grasps it.

In the first sentence, the poem symbolically puts forward the dark zones of life and the invisible realms emerging from the unconscious and from the unknown. It can be related to survival instincts, to urges or to unconscious impulses coming from deep down, from the reptilian brain. In many historical situations, people hid in marshes to survive and to protect themselves. The fact that this reed is capable of inflicting horrible wounds and damage means that it is a weapon capable of wounding either physically, emotionally and psychologically. It also suggest it can wake up the dark, ignorant, stupid and aggressive parts of people. The sentence "burning the blood of any warrior who grasps it" refers to the inner battle for light but also to the hatred that leads people to the dark side of human nature, dark side that sucks people's energy, blood and human values like vampires. The poem also suggests that with the help of this rune, any attack or aggression can be neutralized by the rune's defensive and protective power.

This rune does not exist in the Viking Futhark so the Norwegian and Icelandic poems don't mention it.

Using this rune to do magic: Rune Eohl is used to discover flaws and causes to existing issues and to protect someone of something from evil and negative forces. It was often used in architecture to protect a household through Eolh shaped beams. It can also be used to create financial abundance, to discover one's true passions, to fully enjoy sexual intercourse and the world of matter, to conquer what one desires, to obtain victory, to master one's inner fire and to gain access to an eagle like vision and to lucidity by intense focusing of attention. It can finally be used as a defensive combat tool when experiencing an inner conflict.

Links with other information systems:

I Ching: This rune can be related to Hexagram 15 called "Humility" and to Hexagram 44 called "Resisting to temptation".
Mayan Astrology: This rune can be related to the Snake and Eagle glyphs.
Tarot: Rune Eohl can be related to card 15 "The devil".
Astrology: This rune is a mix of planets Pluto and Jupiter.

Rune 16 : SIGL

Various names given to this rune:

Name and meaning in Old Norse: Sol. The sun, a sunray.
Name and meaning in Old German: Saugil or Sowil. The sun.
Name and meaning in Old English: Sigil or Sigl. The sun, sunlight.

Sigl is the last rune of the second family that of Hagl called Hagl's Aett. The next rune called Tiw or Tyr starts off a new family, the third and last one. So Sigl ends a phase of a cycle and prepares for the next step.

Its graphic design and form: We can firstly observe that the graphic design of this rune is made up of rune 6 $\langle$, Ken, the torch and its mirror binded together. We can also sse the graphic design of this rune as the two components of rune 12 $\diamond$ where the bottom double line of rune 12 moves upwards, where the top double line of rune 12 moves downwards and where the two double lines then join together.

What does rune Ken symbolize. "Two streams of energy flow from a central point, from the heart. One goes to the sky (goals) and one goes towards the ground (live events). Another way to see this icon is to say that two streams of red and white energy emerging from earth (red) and sky (white) come together within the heart, producing a torch like effect and pinkish/greenish astral light, thus nourishing the flame of live within. So this icon is about energy moving and it symbolizes both the body and the soul in motion, with its male and female or masculine and feminine forces. It is also about inner unity of male and female forces within and unity between man and woman in the outside world. The icon can also be seen as a mouth talking in order to create relationships between people."

Now lets have a look at rune 12, Yer." In rune 12, we have two double lines in motion. They are heading towards one another. They communicate. They meet. They move away from one another and one can easily imagine that they will meet again in the next cycle. Each double line represents a force in motion or one could say the soul in motion with its male and female forces. Two or four forces join, share, gather, mingle and create. They experience communion and community. Rune 12 icon therefore suggests completeness, a whole, life flowing in cycles, male and female forces joining and creating like for example will and faith but also the cycle of seasons and the annual earth-sun cycle. The Germans believed that there were two seasons, winter and summer. The icon suggests the summer solstice where the two seasons meet. We have been discussing cycles and thus things repeating over and over again and the rune does ask the question: what are you repeating over and over again in your life? It then says that a wise and efficient cycle management through a harmonious connection between man and nature or man and the gods brings a good harvest. This is what is at the heart of this rune. It also says that what you saw you will reap and if you want to reap and harvest then you must saw. The rune finally says that the present situation may be influenced by past actions and by memories coming from ancestors in the sense that you are reaping what has been sawed a very long time ago and that what is happening now is part of a cycle.

From that, Sigl, the Sun or more specifically sunrays, sunbeams and sunlight suggest a special divine connection between the divine source, "The Source of all life" symbolized by the sun and its rays and one's personal consciousness or another way to say this is that the ordinary "I" and one's luminous divine essence are connected or experience been connected together. The icon does also look like a park of light or like a stroke of lightning. Lightning strikes very suddenly, lights up fires and creates a shocking and surprising effect. It often causes dismay, awe and fear. If you do from the top of the icon to the very bottom, you change direction twice so the rune can suggest undoing something and then doing something else that can only take place after the first thing was undone. An example of this is demolishing a house and building another. This rune's graphic design is also related to half of a very old symbol called the solar wheel which represents the action and effects of the sun on mankind. Sigl is finally one of six runes with no central axis.

Its number: Sigl is rune number sixteen. This number doesn't have any specific meaning. It is made up of a 1 and a 6 put side by side, of 2 by 8 and of 4 by 4. Number 1 symbolizes the fire of creation, origin and destination or target and the final goal which to recover conscious unity with "The Source of all life". Number 6 symbolizes unity between male and female forces, creative power with form, commitment, balanced choices when one listens to ones true desires, multiple connections and relationships, sensitivity to beauty and limits that bring structure.

Number 16 can therefore symbolize a unifying fire that has a deconstructing and then a reconstructing effect. This fire creates a breach or an opening in one's consciousness so that it can become connected. It also brings a specific form of psychological, technological or building intelligence.

Summary and essence of this rune: I am the original luminous and creative will. I am an all powerful will and light that overcomes darkness and the dark side of human nature mentioned in the previous rune. I am the original Mind moving through space and magically expressing itself in the world of matter though data structures, data systems and though a code of honor. I am projected light, a spark of light and the power of light that enlightens, heats up, guides and gives landmarks wherever possible and necessary. I am a highly active connection between the world of Men, Midgard and the world of the gods, Asgard. I manifest myself as a sparkling connection with the divine, though opening of the crown chakra, by making people becoming aware of what is here and now and sometimes by true illumination. I retire within my own structure when necessary so as to go deep within and get access to my true essence at the center of my heart. When necessary, I improve thing, I find solutions, I change the structure of the situation and I bring about a new beginning. I then become an expression of the Sun on Earth thanks to the light that goes though me.

The dark side of the rune: It is symbolized by the small thinking mind and ego taking over, by a disconnection between mind and heart leading to creation of a psychological armor, by excessive inner tension and stress, by to much work and a burnout risk, by an accident, by an unpleasant, unforeseen and unexpected event, by a glare or a dazzle leading to blindness, by structure issues, by electrical or computer issues, by a tendency to seal oneself off in a fortress, by difficulties with understanding things or with being understood, by difficulties with self expression and with finding appropriate words, by tyranny and a tendency to make things or situation explode. This rune was used as a symbol by the Nazi regime during world war 2.

Its sound: This rune is related to the "s" sound as in the words sun.

Key words: the fire of awareness, a very relevant goal, a signal, a sign, an interpellation, a warning, a light or an energy discharge, a stroke of lightning, electrical energy, getting organized very efficiently so as to bring about success, expressing one's "sky's will power" and one's intelligence with structures, becoming aware of something very important, discovering something, awakening, illumination, success, victory, purification through awareness, things clearing up, liberation, enthusiasm in action, a change of structure or of direction, a new situation, a new beginning, a connection between the ordinary self and the higher self and being reconnected with "The Source of all light and of all life" which is feeling alive, joy, will power, efficiency, love and awareness.

People and jobs related to this rune: a bright person, a very intelligent person, a well connected person, someone capable of deconstructing and reconstructing, and someone capable of finding solutions and of fixing things, a liberator. Architect, estate agent, house builder, technical personnel, radiologist, fireman, emergency physician, wrecker, remover, psychologist, therapist, repairman, pyrotechnic technician, artificer, jobs using modern technology, astronauts, electrician, programmer, computer engineer, telephone salesman, cleaning agent and highly specialized jobs.

Gods related to this rune: This rune is related to the gods Sol and Sunna who symbolize both the manifestation on earth of "The Source of all life" and the structure within every human being that can connect to this Source. German people worshiped the sun as far back as the bronze age and it is still worshiped today. They believed that the sun was carried across the sky by a chariot pulled by two horses during the day and by a light ship called Nott during the night. They saw it as a turning around wheel of light subject to cycles.

Rune 16 is also related to the god of light Baldr who symbolizes purity, whiteness and light. It is finally related to the god Thor or rather to the lighting he triggers. When Ragnarok or the end of the world arises, when planet Earth ceases to exist, the Germans say that a gigantic wolf called Fenrir will devour the sun and then they say that a new world with a new sun will come to be. According to astronomers, a galaxy called Andromeda is heading right towards our own galaxy and will collide with it in some 4 or 5 billion years. It will then be the end of time for our solar system and a new super galaxy will come to be.

Places and objects related to this rune: public buildings, towers, fortified places, sky-scrappers, scaffoldings, jails, hospitals, laboratories, pits and quarries, commercial centers specialized in the building industry, places where scientific experiments are done, electrical power plants, places loaded with energy, technological research centers, data centers, therapist offices, places where people manage projects, modern electrical devices, highly specialized electrical or magnetic devices like magnetic mattresses, Pandora stars, quantic machines and free energy devices, lightning and laser beams and places where people become more aware or experience illumination.

Colors connected to this rune: electric yellow, sand color, red and metallic grey together.

Animals connected to this rune: roosters, gannets, seagulls and termites.

English, Norwegian and Icelandic poems:

The English poem:
The sun brings joy and hope to seamen
When they travel at sea over the fish's bath
Until their sea-horse brings them back to land

The poem show that is sun is an always existing landmark that brings awareness, joy and hope. It helps travelers to return safely home. This can be considered at a very down to earth level, as travelers and seamen sailing on their boats (sea horses) finding their way to and back using the sun and the stars (which are suns) but also at a deeper level meaning that by expressing one's inner sun one can return to a state of illumination and connection with the Source of all life.

The Norwegian poem:
The sun is the light of the world
I bow to its divine and sacred decree

Here, the poem shows that the sun brings light and therefore vision and awareness but also that the world is made up of light vibrating at various different frequencies. It explains that it is right to connect with the Source of all light/life and to sacrifice one's personal will or ego for The Source. This poem may have been Christianized, the words divine decree replacing the Source of all life.

The Icelandic poem:

The sun is the shield of the clouds
A shining ray or beam and the destroyer of ice

The meaning of the first sentence can be explained though symbolic language. Clouds and fog symbolizes lack of clarity, unconsciousness but also ancestral memories and past life memories. The sun brings landmarks, clear goal, efficient organization and a direction that centralizes everything around it. It therefore becomes a protective shield against any risk of getting lost in the fog of unconsciousness or memories. A ray goes from a point A to a point B, from a source to a destination. It lightens things up and therefore enables becoming aware of something. Ice reminds us of rune 11 Isa in its dark, cold, angry and selfish aspects. The sun brings the power of love, heart energy, awareness and heat that make ice (ego, coldness, fear) melt. It puts an end to old structures and reconstructs so as to bring about a new beginning.

Using this rune to do magic: Rune Sigl can be used to become connected with the Source of all life, the Source of joy and enthusiasm, to become more aware, to trigger a technical or psychological intelligence that can find the right solution and fix what needs fixing, to set the right targets and to find the means and the organization so get there, to liberate what needs to be liberated, to bring about a change of structure, to deconstruct and reconstruct, to increase will power and brightness, to chase away darkness though light, to guide along the narrow path that leads to illumination, to find light at the center of one's heart and to experience illumination, to manage efficiently, to set things or people back on track, on the track of their destiny, to be successful with customers, to succeed and to be well guided when traveling. It was and still is sometimes engraved on ships, chariots or luggage.

Links with other information systems:

I Ching: This rune can be related to Hexagram 16, Enthusiasm, to Hexagram 40, Liberation, to Hexagram 50, The Cauldron and especially to Hexagram 51, Storm.
Mayan Astrology: Rune 16 can be related to a glyph called Cauac meaning the storm.
Tarot: Rune Sigl can mostly de related to car 16, The House of God but also partly to card 19, The Sun.
Astrology: This rune is a mix of Sun, Mercury, Saturn and Uranus.

Rune 17 : TIW

Various names given to this rune:

Name and meaning in Old Norse: Tyr. The sky god Tiw/Tyr.
Name and meaning in Old German: Tiw/Teiw. The sky god Teiw or Tiw.
Name and meaning in Old English: Tir. The god of the sky and of victory.

This rune starts off the third and last runic family.

Its graphic design and form: The vertical line symbolizes the connection between earth and sky but also the path of consciousness towards the center of the self. Then, two lines emerge from a point in the sky, from left and right. They join together at the very top of the vertical line i.e at the final destination. (see further down : total inner freedom, reconnection with the Source of all life though a state of being called God within the spiritual body that lightens up and shines like a star, infinite joy).

These two lines look like a rune ken rotated at a right angle clockwise i.e. with a new vision which is the opposite of the vision brought about by the previous rune, rune 15.

The rune's icon also looks like a weapon and this suggests thriving for something and a specific and peculiar battle. It can be an arrow pointing towards the sky or a spear one can throw. So there is also a target. The target and battle are related here to elevation, beauty, harmony, eternal joy and life, against inertia and numbness that are often experienced in the world of matter. By pointing upwards, the arrow shows that and suggests that that's where you have to look and that's where you must symbolically go. And what's up there! Well, the sky which is either bright or sunny (this symbolizes success and happiness and clarity) or clouded (this symbolizes lack of clarity and problems with memories) and there are also birds (this symbolizes communication with the gods and life forms happily expressing themselves) in the sky. At night, there are stars and night living animals such as bats, insects but also birds. What is above symbolizes the final destination! And what does one find when one reaches the final destination of a human soul? Well, there is the spiritual body, a light structure that can house individual and personal consciousness. When one goes deep down within, this shining structure can at a certain stage be seen as a bright star and the rune then invites you to follow this inner divine star.

This rune could actually be called "follow the arrow pointing towards the sky" or even "follow the little white rabbit inside you"! Rune Tiw and be seen as a combination of rune 11, Isa and of a modified rune 6, Ken i.e. as Ice bearing fire in a totally balanced manner though a well mastered, orderly, harmonious, fairy-like and comfort bringing passion. It is by having one's two feet well placed on the ground that one can clearly see the sky which means that it is by fully living one's life in the world of matter that one can thrive spiritually. This rune was also related to the celestial sphere, to the entire night sky but also to one's inner night sky, i.e. to one numerological and astrological structure that can be seen in one's "astral chart" and "Birth Diamond" numerological chart. The rune's icon can also be seen as a man standing up with arms raised at 45 degrees. As said previously, there is a similarity between rune 17 ↑ and rune 15, Eohl ᛉ. One's awareness and energy goes downwards with rune 15 so as to master material life while it goes upwards, skywards with rune 17 after having been reconnected with the Source and after having experience a first illumination at the rune 16 stage. When dealing with rune 15, one learns to see and face the dark and miserable side of life so as to learn how to handle it and how to be safe and protected. Here at rune 17, the heavenly, luminous, joyful side is life is observed so that one can head towards it and recognize it as a genuine part of one's self and not as something foreign to whom we really are. Here, in rune 17, we take care of being in harmony with the sky with body and soul, of one's inner sky or astral chart and of one's joy and abundance. Here, one's joins one's will with "the will of the sky" and one's submits and kneels down to it, becoming "a sky agent", the sky's special fairy so as to bring hope, relief, joy, delight and love on Earth.

Its number: Number 17 doesn't have any specific meaning by itself. However, number 1 symbolizes the fire of creation while number 7 symbolizes action and organization to reach a well defined target, self expression, serious commitment and devotion to life, both to "Mother Earth" and to "Father Sky". Adding one and seven gives 8 which brings us to rune Wynn. Wynn is about joy, sharing but also civilization with its rules, its structures and its justice. So one can say we have here a disciplined expression of one's inner light so as to do what is right, so as to create more balance and a more harmonious organization but in a way that takes into account both the underlying order of thing, the divine order or in other words the laws of life and the rules of human civilization or society.

This requires the magical power of faith, being aware of what is sacred (a sense of sacredness) and a natural religion that links people with both the earth, their hearts and the sky. And this is what Asatru, Odinism and runes are all about. During dawn of History, the law of arms was often expressed as a means so as to bring back order and justice and unfortunately this often meant war. And so in ancient times, number 17 did also symbolize enforcing law with weapons or with "what it is necessary to do" so as to apply the rules and bring about justice.

Summary and essence of this rune: I am an awareness connected with earth, sky and with the natural order underlying life. This consciousness is like a park of celestial light within. It's allows me to be guided in the right direction with harmony, fluidity and grace. So guided by my inner sky and by my inner star, I express myself with great devotion and faith, rightly, with no fear, in a responsible and disciplined manner so as to create harmony, enhance beauty and bring about delight, joy and abundance in the world of man.

The dark side of the rune: It is symbolized by a lack of clear goals or by a goal that is not in harmony with the sky, by misunderstandings and confusion, by sweet lies and illusions, by useless sacrifices, by commitment towards a lost cause, by a lack of beauty, delight, order and harmony with the natural flow of things, by submitting to something or someone that puts you down on your knees, by seeking to many down to much earth pleasure (food, drugs, sex), by being half asleep all the time, by a lack of commitment, enthusiasm, bravery, boldness, action and discipline, by chaos and defeat. One may have an issue with joy, abundance and one's inner sky or astral chart.

Its sound: This rune is related to the « t » sound as in the word trust.

Key words: Two feet well placed on the ground and one's mind well connected to the sky, deep rootedness and elevation, being guided in the right direction, bringing back order, justice, beauty and harmony, managing life in an orderly manner, spiritual discipline so as to get closer to the sky and to one's inner star, channeling one's abilities to achieve a specific goal that brings great joy, intelligence of the human body, legal or artistic intelligence, reaching one's target, acting in harmony with the natural flow of life, balancing earth and sky within, devoting oneself to something, sacrificing what is inferior for what is superior, making sure rules are complied with, fighting for what is right, success and victory.

People and jobs related to this rune: a committed, responsible and devoted person who is smoothly and peacefully working for a legitimate cause so as to help and to bring about hope, beauty, harmony, balance, rightness, justice and elevation. Someone both well grounded in the material world and well connected to the sky. Someone mastering an art or wellness of body and mind. Someone capable of making things more beautiful and more joyful. Someone who can guide and enlighten so as to create a peaceful and joyful atmosphere, someone who can re-enchant the world and people and who can make the fantastic come to life. A wise and delightful fairy-like person. Someone who can read and interpret nature and the stars. If this rune is unbalanced, then it can represent someone on his or her knees, lost, without goals, filled with illusions, who makes useless sacrifices or who is just very lazy. Rune 17 can represent jobs related to creating abundance and managing the world of matter (supplies, purchasing, banking and production), to beauty, art, pleasure, fashion, hairdressing, painting, sculpture, singing, dancing, perfume industry and aesthetics but also to law and justice. Craftsmen, artists, decorators, aestheticians, massage practitioners, makeup artists, top models, « stars », landscape workers, gardeners, florists, complementary medicine practitioners, naturopaths, nature caretakers, ecology fans, biologists, organic farmers, people who work in the food industry, water management jobs, resource manager, capital manager, astronomers, astrologists.

Gods related to this rune: This rune is related to one of the oldest and most mysterious known German Gods, Ti, Tiw or Tiew who brings water, harmony, justice, rightness and victory in war and conflicts. The sound of Tiew is very close to that of the French word "Dieu" meaning God, word that comes from the Sanskrit "Deva" or "Dyaus" and quite often, Tiw meant what we now call God. Now God is defined as the state of being when reunified consciousness is brought back into one's spiritual body and thus reconnects with "The Source of all life". This state of being was called Zeus in Greek and dues in Latin. For Germans, Tiw ruled over meetings and assembly of Men (Thing) to decide what is right and apply the rules and laws so as to create the best possible future. He symbolizes the laws of the gods and of nature than men try to imitate. He represents such values as rightness, integrity and responsibility as well as the ability to make promises and keep them, to do what one says, to be impeccable with one's word and to be faithful.

According to Nordic mythology, when the giant wolf Fenrir, who symbolizes chaos and destruction, had to be chained, Tiw was the only god who accepted to place his hand in the wolf's mouth, condition demanded by the wolf to let himself be chained up. When the wolf realized that he could not break the chains, he bit Tiw's hand off and this is how the world, life's underlying order and the gods were saved. Tiw rules over Tuesday and the Romans related his to Mars when they first heard about him, which is only partially true.

Places and objects related to this rune: beautiful places, inspiring and wellness bringing landscapes, nature, the countryside, lakes, river banks, fields and gardens, animal parks and zoos, stars and planets, barber shops, hairdressing, massage and beauty salons, places where people sing, offices where the world of matter is managed.

Colors connected to this rune: sky blue, orange.

Animals connected to this rune: humming birds, doves, cows, giraffes, rabbits, squirrels, donkeys, frogs and peacocks.

English, Norwegian and Icelandic poems:

The English poem:
Tir is a sign or a star that guides, through faith it lead to the Prince
Set on its goal and track, it keeps advancing on its path beyond night fog
It never falters

Now this amazing poem was written by someone with a long and efficient practice of meditation! When a person dives deep down within, he or she first sees from far away his or her spiritual body which symbolically is his princess or her prince. This body shines like a star. By being guided by faith and love, by this inner star and by continuing on this journey in the very heart of himself or herself, beyond darkness, she will unavoidably at some stage reach his or her goal and gain access to the experience of God by placing her consciousness inside this spiritual body, sometimes referred to as "the throne of god" in a state of pure bliss! In the outside world, a symbolic match for this shining spiritual body that guides the soul is the Pole Star or some visible planet (Venus, Mars, Jupiter and Saturn are visible) that helps people find their way and to reach their destination

The norwegian poem:
Tiw is the one handed god
Often must the smith blow

The first sentence refers to Tiw's sacrifice made to chain up the wolf Fenrir. The second sentence show that to keep the flame alive, to accomplish what must be accomplished and to produce a work of art, one must make the necessary efforts and keep blowing or using the blower or air bellow. In other words one must be totally committed and devoted and persevere till victory is obtained.

The icelandic poem:
Tyr the god with only one hand and leavings of the wolf
And the prince of all temples

The meaning of the first sentence is similar to that of the Norwegian poem though the necessity to make a sacrifice (sacrificing what is inferior so that what is superior can exists) and to tame one's inner wolf is also enhanced here. The third sentence suggests that one's "spiritual body" is at this stage "only" one's Prince or Princess and that one day it will be permanently enlightened so that a person can then be Queen or King of one's own inner kingdom, fully reconnected with "The Source of all freedom and of life".

Using this rune to do magic: Rune Tyr/Tiw is used to see and embody the best possible future, to sacrifice what is low so as to gain access to what is high, to enable the will of the sky to express itself, to comply with rules and laws, to win a lawsuit, to enchant and delight, to experience paradise, to channel one's abilities to achieve a clear and joy-bringing goal, to make the power of faith triumph, to bring about joy, happiness and abundance, to get organized efficiently and to find the strength to do whatever is necessary to obtain victory. Rune 17 was often engraved on weapons.

Links with other information systems:

I Ching: Rune 17 can be related to hexagrams 7, "The army" and especially to hexagram 17, "Follow".
Mayan Astrology: Rune Tiw can be related to the Mayan star, seed and warrior glyphs.
Tarot: Rune Tiw can be related to cards 8 and 17, "Justice" and "The star".
Astrology: This rune is a mix of planets Venus, Mars, Jupiter, Uranus and Neptune.

Rune 18: BERKANO

Various names given to this rune:

Name and meaning in Old Norse: Bjarkan. The Birch tree spirit.
Name and meaning in Old German: Bairkan. The birch tree goddess.
Name and meaning in Old English: Beork or Berkana ou Berkano. The Birch and Mother goddess.

Its graphic design and form: As usual, the vertical line describes the connection between earth and sky through the central life axis. Four lines join the central axis here, just like a family joining a central character. They follow a zigzag pattern which suggests a path from top to bottom or from bottom to top, a bit like an alternative routing compared to the central main way axis. If you start from the very bottom of the icon, you can observe that the zigzag line begins at the central axis, goes away from it, goes back to it again, goes away again and finally joins it at the top of the axis. The lines go back and forth. But from where to where? Well, in the two previous runes 16 and 17, a human being has learnt how to connect with the Source of all life both within himself or herself and also with nature and with one's inner sky. A great victory was experienced. But the end of the path has not yet being reached! There are more than likely memories to clean up and fears to overcome. This new path enhanced in rune 18 is therefore a path that goes from a state of unwellness and emotional stress to a state of total well being. When looking at the icon, we can also say that there are two Ken runes (rune 6) rotated at 180° and gripped on the central axis or that the two elements of rune 12 join the central axis. And 6+12=18. So relationships (symbolism of rune 6), connection with life, awareness of cycles, seeking for wellness and for transcendence and total inner unity (symbolism of rune 12) are very important for rune 18. Rune 18 also looks a bit like rune 8, Wynn except that here, there are two closed up areas while there was only one at rune 8. Finally, the icon does look like a pregnant woman or like two breasts. They symbolize a mother giving birth to a new life form, motherly love that takes care of life and of the new born baby, a new life form thriving and also feeding or being nourished by the mother and by mother Earth.

This rune can therefore be related to motherhood but also to any safe and protected and more or less secret house like space where one can rest, decompress, recharge ones batteries and store food. It can also be related to one's physical "Home" and to ones "Spiritual Home" where the soul comes from.

Comment concerning the Birch tree: For Siberian Shamans, the Birch tree represents the ambassador of the subconscious or of the invisible worlds and it gives a step by step access to one's inner worlds. This journey in the invisible realms was symbolized by a birch tree branch with notches or cuts engraved in a ladder like manner so as to symbolically climb down deep within or climb up skywards. Birch tree branches and leaves were very often used during rituals dedicated to Mother Earth and for fertility rituals.

Its number: Berkano is rune number 18 within the Futhark. This number does not by itself have any specific meaning. Number 1 symbolizes creative power in action. Number 8 represents conscious unity of sky and earth, the point where spiritual cycles and material cycles meet and purification processes that follow, awareness of the natural order underlying life and of "The Source of all life" that has created this order though the power of love and joy and the joy of sharing within a given civilization or society. Number 18 is deeply connected with number 9 (1+8= 9, 2x9=18) and so with the 9 month/9 year life cycles and with rune 9 Hagl. It is also connected with numbers 3 and 6 as 3 times 6 gives 18. Number 18 can thus be related to the purification of the soul, to reuniting the different parts of one's soul together and the ability to make life flow naturally so as to adapt and so as to go one step beyond in the evolutionary path towards one's deep inner truth, towards one's total inner freedom, towards eternal life and towards unity with "The Source of all life". Here, memories are cleaned up. The past ends. One crosses over to a superior state of being where one gives birth to a new purified and reunited self. There is a new beginning in a new house.

Summary and essence of this rune: I bring life and makes things flow so as to bring about newness. With motherly love, I take care of life, of people and of situations. I follow a path, both in the visible and invisible worlds, that goes from a state of emotional stress to a state of wellness, purifying on the way whatever is corrupted, clearing up dark areas, souvenirs or hurt memories and recharging my batteries thanks to safe havens such as family, strong emotional bonds, home, music, water and food.

I learn how to nourish myself rightly at all levels. I express my emotions, my feelings and my imagination so as to make my dreams come though and so as to gather all of the different separate elements within me or within the current situation. Gathering myself so, I return to my true "Home" and to my true "Soul family".

The dark side of the rune: It is represented by fear, nightmares, emotional stress and psychic pollution, by absent-mindedness and forgetfulness, by illusions and disappointments, by emotional issues, by memory issues, by disturbing souvenirs, by child birth, delivery or maternity issues, by family issues, by water issues or lack of available resources or by a lack of fluidity as when things just don't flow right.

Its sound: This rune is related to the « b »sound as in birch.

Key words: a mother, a child, family, home, life, the flow of things, creating a new life, helping life emerge, purifying the soul, transforming the soul, cleaning up old memories, putting order in one's souvenirs, fertility, birth, nourrising oneself correctly at all levels, reconnecting with life, making things flow, intuition and inspiration, poetry and music, expressing one's emotions, finding a place where one can recharge one's batteries, a house, a home, taking care of life and creating well being in daily life.

People and jobs related to this rune : a very motherly person, someone expressing and using their emotions, intuition and imagination, a very nourishing person, someone who helps give birth to someone or to a situation, someone who takes care of others and who brings well being. If the rune is unbalanced then it can represent someone irresponsible, childlike and who does silly things. Rune 18 can be related to jobs in public spaces, to making and selling food or liquids (cooks, bakers, barmen), to jobs where one takes care of others and children (nannies, primary school teachers, pediatricians), to housing (estate agent, managing agents, housekeeper, mover, hotel personnel or cleaning personnel), to music, to writing and drawing (novels or children's books, tale telling, poetry, cartoonist, draughtsman), to animal caretaking, to night jobs and to jobs connected with social welfare, with the sea (sailor, lifeguards, bath attendants), with sleep, the past, relaxation, biology and feeling well.

Gods related to this rune: This rune is related to the Earth Goddess Nerthus, to Mother Earth but also to goddess Frigg and the Mani the Moon.

Places and objects related to this rune: a home, a family house, public places where there are lots of people, places where water is found, gardens with fountains, springs, ponds, rivers, lakes, marshes, swimming pools, beaches, drinks, thalassotherapy and balneotherapy centers, saunas, spas, public baths, places where emotions are expressed, memory halls, places with a high emotional charge and daily life objects.

Colors related to this rune: light grey and silver colour.

Animals related to this rune: cats, crabs, crayfish and lobsters, turtles, rabbits, wolves and meerkats.

English, Norwegian and Icelandic poems:

The English poem:
Birch bears no fruit but even without seeds it creates branches from which emerge leaves.
Its branches are splendid and it is beautifully decorated
Its noble crows rises high to the sky

The fact that the birch tree bears no fruit could suggest it is not fertile and yet there are shots and branches which implies birth of life at some other level. Branches symbolize the soul and all of the soul forces which are splendid when one takes care of them. The crows symbolizes the spiritual body which enables one to reconnect with the source of all life after a person has first gathered herself or himself together and after having cleaned up all memories.

The Norwegian poem:
Birch has the greenest leaves of all trees
Loki was fortunate in his deceit

The poem shows here two aspects of rune 18. The first aspect is about life flowing and renewing itself while the second aspect is about the glistening, illusionary and deceitful world of matter, of beliefs and of memories, which Loki represents quite well. Loki was a very handsome, fertile, imaginative and prolific God, (he gave birth to Fenrir the wolf, to Sleipnir the 8 legged horse, to Jormungand the snake and to Hel the witch). He was also very changing, tricky, unstable and emotionally disturbing. And yet his destiny could have been much more a disaster considering his numerous mischiefs. This is what the poem says.

The Icelandic poem:
Birch is a very leafy tree
And a little tree
And a young fresh scrub

The poem enhances the many leaves produced by the birch tree, it's smallness, its youthfull aspect and its freshness. This simply symbolizes the flow of life in motion.

Using this rune to do magic: Berkano can be used to bring about fertility or to recover it, to feel connected with life and with the flow of life, to access one's memories or memories of a place, to solve wemen's periodic cycles issues, to give birth harmoniously, to find a home or a place where one can recharge one's batteries, to find food or to be nourished, to clean up one's memories, to become free from any fear, to be protected and taken care of, To gather, connect, combine and bind a set of components together, to express one's imagination and creative power, to make a new life form evolve and thrive, to gather one's self together around a central home and to experience unity of soul and complete wellness.

Links with other information systems:

I Ching: This rune can be related to hexagram 18 « Fixing what is corrupted », to hexagram 17 "Nourishing" and to hexagram 48, "The Well".
Mayan Astrology: This rune can be related to the Night glyph, to the Seed glyph and to the Moon glyph
Tarot: Rune Berkano can be related to card 2, "The High Priestess" and to card 18, "The Moon".
Astrology: This rune can be related to the Moon with a bit of Neptune and Pluto.

Rune 19 : EH

M **Various names given to this rune:**

Name and meaning in Old Norse: Ior. A horse.
Name and meaning in Old German: Ehwo. Horses.
Name and meaning in Old English: Eh. Battle horses.

Its graphic design and form: The vertical line represents as always the central axis, with earth below, the heat in the middle and sky above. The two lines represent here the two poles of the soul, male and female. As seen in previous runes, each of the two 45 degree angled lines found here represents half of the soul. At the rune 19 stage, the two halves of the soul join together and reunite, each in its male or female axis. One can also say that a rune 6, Ken, ᐸ binds two runes 11, Isa, together and that it is rotated skywards while pointing towards the earth, suggesting it receives sky light and sends them down to earth. We can therefore say that two central male and female poles are brought together by the torch of awareness, joy and commitment. Rune Eh can also be seen as two Lagu runes (rune21) where one mirrors the other. To look a little bit deeper, we can say here that the soul has gathered itself together as one family in the previous rune and now, with rune 19, it totally balances male and female forces but also animal and human. Reunited consciousness now fits into the spiritual body at the very center of the self in a state of pure love, power and joy or bliss. Human personal consciousness unites with divine consciousness once and for all. The icon could look like two people kissing each other, two horses rubbing their snouts against one another. It can also represents two alternative situations repeating themselves over and over again.

What a horse symbolizes: Unity between Man and the Source of all life through the state of being called God, or to be more precise unity of Human consciousness and divine consciousness within the spiritual body that houses this reunited consciousness is the supreme goal of all souls living on Earth and elsewhere in the universe.

The Germans new this and compared this supreme goal, this symbiotic unity to the telepathic like relationship between man and horse. They also compared it to the Sun which was seen as a source of light and life. And they compared the power of God to a horse which was seen as a divine spark of life that can help consciousness set itself in motion though space and time. Horses were seen as sacred animals given by the gods. They were related to both the sun and the moon, to the sky and to the earth. Roman historian Tacitus wrote that Germans observed sacred horses and made predictions from their observations. Horses were often buried along kings, chiefs or noblemen so that they could help them travel in the world hereafter. Horses were sacrificed during magical rituals, either to crown a king, to honor the gods of fertility and make cereals grow or to make a wish happen in real life. In Siberia, drums are called Shaman's Horses as they create a structured life-force charged space enabling people to experience shamanic travel in the invisible worlds. People who nowadays work with horses are well aware of how there can be a beautiful love relationship between man and horse and of how man and horse can ride as one so that they almost become a new life form. Mastering horse ridding requires physical strength but especially spiritual strength and the power of love that horses feel very strongly. So the horse symbolizes mastering one's animal instincts, one's heart, one's emotions, one's power and one's awareness, intentions and focus of attention. It symbolizes a precious ally that can guide through space, the means to travel freely, to move forward, to be always in motion and also an evolution of consciousness towards one's supreme goal.

Its number: Eh is rune number 19 within the Futhark. This number by itself doesn't have any specific meaning. Number 1 is an energy spark, an inner fire that can create wealth, action and the beginning of something new. Number 9 is an orderly path towards inner peace, towards one's deep inner truth. It symbolizes gradual evolution, building sites and being aware of the great All. Nine was a sacred number for Germans as it includes all other numbers, gathers them and transcends them into a new unity. It symbolizes completeness, inner silence, the emptiness one must cross when going deep down within so as to access the awakening of one's spiritual body though true meditation and reconnection with the Source of all life as a long term goal.

When you add nine to many other numbers and reduce the sum, number nine disappears like a path left behind as you reach your destination. (Example: 1+9=10=1, 2+9=11=2, 3+9=12=3 etc.). So number 19 is about the beginning of the path that leads to reconnecting with the Source of all life, the end of the path when one actually experiences total unity in a state of pure bliss and what is in between beginning and end. It is the origin and destination. It is becoming a sun or a beautiful horse expressing the power of love and life on Earth. Finally 10+9=19 which suggests cycles of consciousness and evolution.

Summary and essence of this rune: I am an aware, positive, luminous, unified, noble, warm, creative and radiant power moving in a well defined direction. I bring vitality, set life in motion and go beyond frontiers. I bind together what needs to be binded. I work in pairs and do whatever is necessary to get appropriate help. I represent a balance between the freedom of a wild horse and the faithfulness of a tamed horse according to what is required. I create partnerships with respect, trust, loyalty and commitment so as to share and express my own light. I give the best of who I am within a protected space so that positive forces progress, thrive and evolve towards light and success. I am the power of love and of the sun who loves through me. I bring success, joy, delight and bliss wherever I am.

The dark side of the rune: It is described as a crazy horse that does not bring its rider where it should, by difficulties setting oneself or things in motion, by a lack of awareness and so self-control of one's love, feelings and of one's life, which leads to wondering here and there with no clear direction, by a conflict between one's animal nature and one's human nature or between two people and by issues related to love, vision, goals, unity and partnership. An unbalanced Eh rune can create imaginary bonds and nightmares (word made up of horse or mare and night). Too much uncontrolled light can lead to pride, arrogance or to a superiority complex. So either motion does not occur and that may sometimes be okay or either to much motion can lead to an unstable situation, to confusion, to inner restlessness, to wandering and sometimes to painfully falling off a horse. Too much power can lead to tyranny or lead to an issue when traveling.

Its sound: This rune is related to an "ay" sound as in the word day.

Key words: Two elements working together thanks to a special heart or love bond, union and marriage, working as a pair, a responsible relationship full of respect, trust, loyalty, commitment and sharing, a goal that guides though space and life, expressing one's creative power though a strong connection with one's heart, mastering a situation, one's instincts, one's heart and one's feelings and emotions, exploring faraway lands, going on a trip or a journey, adventure, traveling with body and spirit, setting something in motion, moving to another place and a positive change. A rider and his or her horse ride together with joy and harmony in the right direction.

People and jobs related to this rune: someone with a big heart, a bright, powerful and radiant person who has the ability to succeed, someone in motion, travelling, on a trip or a journey, the father, the boss, a manager, a director, a king, brilliant people, generous people, fatherly people with a natural authority, people who know how to get things go their way, group leaders, strongly bonded couples, celebrities and valuable people. Jobs related to children, teaching, education, management and entertainment, to animal taming, where creative abilities are required, where close one to one relationships are important, very demanding jobs, liberal professions, well established and clearly labeled jobs, cardiologists, jobs related to solar energy and to bringing light, heating installer, top models, actors and actresses, makeup artists, film directors and luxury goods traders.

Gods related to this rune: This rune is firstly related to the god of fertility Frey/Freyr who brings happy partnerships and unions, success and prosperity. It is related to Odin's eight legged horse Sleipnir but also to the dive pair of horses called Arvak and Alsvith who carry the sun across the sky. I can finally be related to Baldr, the shining god.

Places and objects related to this rune: Luminous or very well lit places, hot countries, places where the is a lot of sunshine, beautiful places, places where people gather so as to share, places where people express their creative power, their joy, places where people are happy, theater stages, highly valued places, well known international companies, places where people go on holidays, valuable objects, works of art, beautiful objects, glistening objects, lamps and objects made of gold.

Colors related to this rune: Lemon yellow, golden color and white.

Animals related to this rune: Horses, swans, prairie dogs and lions.

English, Norwegian and Icelandic poems:

The English poem:
Horse is joy for princes amongst noble warriors
A steed is proud of its hoofs when prosperous riders enhance their worth
And it is always a comfort for those who are restless

This poem may have been altered compared to its original version. It enhances the joyful connection between man and horse, awareness of what is valuable and prestige. It suggest that mastering one's impatience and ardor brings comfort, wellness and peace, as then a horse can give an appropriate direction and meaning to one's life.

This rune does not exist in the Viking Futhark so the Norwegian and Icelandic poems don't mention it.

Using this rune to do magic: Rune Eh is used to gain inner clarity, to set things in motion, to bind two elements, to increase one's joy, luminosity, creative power and confidence, to find one's sister soul and unite with her, to find one's life mission and achieve it, to find the right goal and find the means to accomplish it, to succeed though appropriate help, to express one's male and female forces in a balanced manner, to work in pairs efficiently, to protect frontiers, to increase one's power, to have a nice journey or trip, to experience shamanic travel and to be reunited within with God (state of being where the soul is gathered together in full awareness within all bodies, when male and female forces are completely balanced and when reconnection to the Source of all life with the help of Angels is achieved) and the Source of all life

Links with other information systems:
I Ching: This rune can be related to Hexagram 19, "Positive drive" and to Hexagram 56, "The Traveler".
Mayan Astrology: Rune 19 can be related to two glyphs called « The Skywalker » and "The Sun".
Tarot: Rune Eh can be related to card 7 « The Chariot » and to card 19 « The Sun ».
Astrology: This rune can be related to astrological signs Gemini, Leo and Sagittarius and to planets Mercury and Jupiter and to the Sun.

Rune 20 : MANN

Various names given to this rune:

Name and meaning in Old Norse: Madhr. Humanity, a human, a man.
Name and meaning in Old German: Manna. A human, a man..
Name and meaning in Old English: Mann. A human being, a man.

Its graphic design and form:

The icon of this multidimensional rune carries within it many other runes and there are many ways of looking at this rune. To start with, rune 20 can be seen as a Gyfu rune (rune 7) or two Ken ᚲ runes (rune 6) binding together two Isa runes ᛁ (rune 11). It can also be seen as a rune Wynn ᚹ (rune 8) and its mirror binded together. It can finally be seen as the previous rune Eh ᛖ (rune 19) with a rotated rune Ken now pointing upwards. We can actually almost say that rune 20 is the Mother/Father of almost all other runes. What did the creator of Rune, Odin and to say to us here? Well, we have here a mystery that words cannot describe very easily! When a person reaches the stage of the previous rune, rune 19, he experiences complete inner unity, both an "animal and human unity" and " Man-God" unity in a state of pure love, light, power and bliss. A man and his inner living God have become one. A person's consciousness is put back into the person's spiritual body at the center of the heart. The spiritual body is lit up and connected to all beings vibrating at the same frequency or to put that in other words to the True Humanity whose members live in the light worlds. We can say that in doing so a person experiences a totally new vision of reality, that he dies to what he was before and is reborn into a new life form in a new state of being. And this new state of being reconnects with someone very special called "The father of all humans" even is this very highly human life form or Archangel is androgynous or both male and female. He is called the Father of all Men because he is the direct representative of "The Source of all life" for the solar system and so for planet Earth, the big boss of all "human light beings" and Angels one could say. He is the original, cosmic and perfect first invisible Human life form, the supreme model from which all other human life forms of lesser luminosity and density were created. So "The Father" referred to as "Man" by the Germans created Humanity. He created you and me!

He exists everywhere and sees everything on every level of existence, on every vibrating frequency, from the lightest to the darkest. Now if you look again at rune 20's icon, it does look a bit like two eyes and in its highest meaning, rune 20 symbolizes a multidimensional, sacred and shamanistic vision of a situation or of life and a very special intelligence that can manage very complex projects and make life, people and situations emerge and thrive though the magic of will power, love, organization and faith.

Its number: Man is rune number 20. At first sight, this number doesn't have any specific meaning. It can be related to the 20 fingers a human being has on hands and feet and so to a complete set of something. Number two is about depth, memories, knowledge, wisdom, mystery, the ability to give birth and the beauty and power of feminine or female forces. Number zero is about the universe created by "The Source of all life". So the two put side by side can symbolize crossing through a new door or vortex so as to gain access to a new level of vision, awareness, enlightenment and life and so as to become someone new, a new life form emerging from its past thanks to being in this case permanently reconnected with "The Source of all life".

Summary and essence of this rune: This rune is about Human beings and what makes them so special. It is about communicating with signs, speech, images and sound or music. With Mann, thanks to a permanent connection with "The Source of all life", I develop a multidimensional vision of reality as it really is, awareness of what is sacred and awareness at a planetary and galactic level. I become completely aware. There is a message leading to an important change. A complex project is being achieved either alone or within a team though the use of a technological, organizational or psychological and human intelligence. I am he or she who moves forward on my evolutionary path by expressing my potential abilities and my human qualities. I am and express the best of what a human being can be because I am reconnected with "The Source of all life" and thus because I act according to "The will of The Father", Mann. I am he/she who brings the right tone, the right tune, the right sound, the right messages and the right information and the right organization to others so that they can bring about positive change, thrive, and evolve. I am he/she who handles complex projects, who expresses and coordinates all abilities in the best possible way in the world en men and who accomplishes my destiny.

The dark side of the rune: It is represented by relationships issues, by an environment full of conflicts, by wrong data or not getting the right message, by hostility from one or more groups of people or by a tendency to condemn humanity, religion or what is sacred. The dark side of this rune can manifest as a difficulty in seeing things deeply, in seeing and understanding signs and messages brought about by life, in understanding the current situation and adapting to it, in seeing and grasping opportunities, in getting out of one's tower or grave, in finding help and solutions, in accepting change and unforeseen events, in expressing one's potential abilities, in achieving one's destiny freely, in being autonomous, in handling projects efficiently, in being reborn and in becoming healed.

Its sound: This rune is related to the M sound as in the word Man.

Key words: Doing things within a group, being part of a large scale project or handling such a project, messages from life and coincidences, getting or giving good advice, accepting and experiencing a very important change, death and rebirth, going away into the unknown or something unexpected, seeing things in a multidimensional or sacred manner, important negotiations, making a speech or attending a conference, experiencing great success, succeeding in finding and understanding the right course or teachings, commitment to help out, experiencing shamanic initiation, seeing or being a therapist for both body and soul, recovering and accepting one's human nature, finding one's soul family, implementing a wise and practical interdependence, freely achieving one's destiny, efficient teamwork, expressing human values like solidarity, overcoming duality by seeing the deep meaning, finding solutions and fixing or healing what must be fixed or healed.

People and jobs related to this rune: An outstanding person with a very deep vision of life and people, a shaman, a musician, a therapist, an engineer, a guide, a teacher, a counselor, a project manager, anyone bringing a message, a speaker, stage technicians or engineers or people playing roles on stages, people who receive an important news coverage, people who make a diagnosis or who deliver a judgment (judges) , members of a jury, angels and archangels. Jobs related to media, radio, TV and internet, sound engineers, journalists, news casters, webmasters, jobs where one speaks to an audience, jobs related to advertisement, music, sound or vibration, highly qualified and specialized jobs, inventors, plane and space industry jobs, jobs related to giving birth, midwives and nurses,

Jobs related to cleaning, to tourism, to travelling in faraway places or dimensions, healers, prophets or those who awaken others to true Reality.

Gods related to this rune: Rune Mann is related to Ymir, the first being, to Borr and Bestia, the first couple, to the god Heimdall who created the three social groups and also to Ask and Embla, the very first man and woman who were created from two ash and elm trees.

Places and objects related to this rune: Places where one sends or receives messages, judgments, advice and data, where one plays music or listens to it, where one uses sound and vibrations, theater or TV stages, entertainment halls, podiums, tribunes, stadiums, conference halls, vibrant places, health centers, music instruments, shamanic plants (Peyote, San Pedro, Ayahuasca, Iboga, Kombo), futuristic objects, 3D printers, quantic healing devices, space suits, teleportation halls, food synthesizers, holosuites and holograms.

Colors connected to this rune: Night blue.

Animals connected to this rune: Phoenix and eagles.

English, Norwegian and Icelandic poems:

The English poem:
A rejoicing man is beloved by his kinsmen
Yet every man is someday condemned to falter and betray
Because the lord's judgment though decree
Will give his corpse back to earth

This poem, which may have been slightly altered, enhances joy, love and sharing with others. It suggests that all human bonds are fragile as one cannot always count on others and because physical bonds end when someone dies. It also suggests that what is important is life in the afterworld.

The Norwegian poem:
Man is an increase of dust
Powerful is the hawk's grip

The first sentence shows the impermanent aspect of this world of matter where everything ends up with time as dust. The second sentence symbolically suggests how important it is to take control of one's life, to express one's abilities, to achieve one's destiny and to reach one's celestial destination by traveling through different states of being.

This sentence could be referring to the saga where Loki changed himself into a hawk so as to bring to the gods the guardian of Love Apples which when eaten allow to gods to remain eternal.

The icelandic poem:
Man is delight for Man
And an increase of dust
And adorner of ships

The first is about love, sharing and joy and how delightful happy human relationships can be. The second sentence shows how short life on earth is compared to eternity and life in the afterworld. Dust can also be related to space, to galaxies and to the cosmos. The third sentence is about building ships and decorating them. This symbolizes handling complex projects requiring various technologies and the means to travel to other lands and dimensions and destinations. A ship or vessel can be compared to a person with their different physical, astral, mental, soul and divine bodies. Adorning means being the most beautiful version of one's self. This is the ultimate destination. The poem enhances that a true human being lives with joy in its heart and does what is required to achieve his or her destiny while knowing that one day he or she will die and go to the afterworld.

Using this rune to do magic: Rune Mann can be used to increase one's vision and psychic abilities, to clearly and deeply see what is here and now, to see things in a multidimensional manner, to be connected with the Source of all life, to successfully handle complex projects where modern technology or organizational procedures are used, for efficient teamwork, to implement great changes, to make a relevant speech, to bring about messages that lead to change, to be successful with a coarse or an exam, to find correct advice, the right guide or teacher, to balance what was unbalanced, to fix something and find the right solution, to heal and to move forward on the path of one's destiny.

Links with other information systems:

I Ching: This rune can be related to Hexagrams 20 and 61 , "Sacred vision" and "Total Synchronicity ».
Mayan Astrology: Rune 20 matches the « Human » and « Storm » glyphs.
Tarot: Rune Mann can be related to card 20, "Judgment".
Astrology: This complex rune is a mix of Mercury, Jupiter, Uranus, Neptune and Pluto.

Rune 21 : LAGU

Various names given to this rune:

Name and meaning in Old Norse: Logr, the ocean, water or laukr, an onion or a leek.
Name and meaning in Old German: Laguz. Water.
Name and meaning in Old English: Lagu. The sea, water.

Its graphic design and form: The vertical line symbolizes the vertical axis of life where sky and earth are connected. The small oblique line represents the soul in action descending from the heavens to earth to master the world of matter and then going back to its origin, to "The source of all life". This icon reveals the essence of the runic graphic system. 16 out of the 24 runes are made out of these vertical and oblique lines, which makes two of the 8 rune families out of three. It represents an accomplished person, who masters his or her life and who achieve his or her destiny to the very end. Rune 21 does look like rune 17 without the small left oblique line, as if it has become liberated from its left side, from its past and from ego so as to manifest on a daily basis "the will of the sky". It also looks like rune 19, Eh, the horseᛗ who has here evolved to duality to unity. This rune's icon can also represent an onion or a leek, tow vegetables considered sacred by Germans due to their antiseptic characteristics.

Comments on the name of the rune: Water symbolizes female energy in motion though time and space, individual and collective subconscious, the invisible worlds, sensitivity and intuition, movement and change, life forms in motion according to cycles but also the paths taken by life to go where it must, with the different steps and crossings along the way. Water symbolizes birth, spiritual evolution and death or rather going from world to another. Water exists coming from the Source or from springs, from dew, torrents, rivers, clouds, rain and the ocean. All water ends up flowing back to the ocean which is the ultimate destination for water but also a source of abundance and food. And from a certain point of view, all souls are like little drips or sparks of life that end up in the "Ocean of all Souls". All souls were created by "The Source of all life" and return to it someday.

Knowing this, Germans poured water on every new born baby during a ritual where the baby was given its name so as to connect him with his family, his group or clan and to Life itself. And when an important person died, they placed that person on a boat offshore and then set it on fire so that with fire and water, the person's soul could travel in the invisible worlds to "the world of the gods", into the flow of eternal life. Leeks and onions also represent the various layers of life and gathering the different parts of the soul so as to go on the great journey to the center of one's heart, to the spiritual body. These two vegetables also symbolize good health, healing, multidimensional awareness, traveling and mastering one's life within the outside world.

Its number: Lagu is rune number 21 within the Futhark alphabet. This number doesn't have any specific meaning by itself. 21 is three quarters of a monthly moon cycle. It is about going from 2 to 1 or from duality to inner unity. It can be obtained by multiplying 3 by 7 which suggests movement with great awareness, power and commitment, full self-realization, and complete achievement.

Summary and essence of this rune: I am a human being carried along by the flow of life and managed by my awareness, organization, intelligence and connections. I gather the different parts of me to achieve a sacred inner unity that then radiate in the outside world. I am the concentrated and highly organized power of life flowing step by step on an evolution path according to law, numbers, rhythm and cycles. I am the outer journey beyond the seas and the inner journey that leads to the Source of all life and that enables having a spiritual vision of everything. I am the synthesis, the final assembly, the end of a cycle and complete healing of the reunited, complete and reconnected soul. I finally am the water cycle who enables life to be constantly changing though space and time.

The dark side of the rune: It is symbolized by a lack of self-knowledge, by a lack of understanding of how life works, by a tendency to ignore one's intuition and feelings due to a lack of connection with one's inner life, by a tendency to get lost in the meanders of the outside world or in one own subconscious, and to be submerged by one's emotions and by an inner confusion. This rune may represent an issue with water or memory, a form of madness, dangers, disturbing elements, obstructions or blockages coming from the outside or from the inside world.

It may symbolize a lack of open-mindedness, of stature, of organization and or economic understanding, a tendency to accept a role or job above one's abilities, an issue with a woman or with one's mother, an issue during a journey or with foreigners or with managing the environment or with a large group or company, a tendency to find an easy way out that finally causes more problems than expected solutions and by a difficulty in finishing something, in reaching one's final destination and in ending a cycle.

Its sound: This rune is related to the « L » sound as in the word lake.

Key words: A very beneficial journey, a trip abroad, a great crossing, life in motion, mastering one's trajectory, fishing, being synchronized with what life has to offer, listening to one's feelings and intuition, going back to the source, expressing one's psychic abilities, experiencing an apprenticeship or teaching people, implementing change, growth and progress, supervising and mentoring, fulfilling great work or a masterpiece of art, efficient coordination of a complex project, implementing a process, an important company or organization, taking control of a situation, going a step further, a solution being found, support from a woman, help from the heavens.

People and jobs related to this rune: Someone well adapted to life and to the surrounding world, someone living his or her life at 100%, someone who masters an art, someone of great stature or who is in charge of an important group or organization, rich people, a traveler, a foreigner, someone on a business trip or coming from very far away, gifted people who succeed in their fields of activity, celebrities, people playing an important role in the world or with a high social status, clubs and club members, people with great cultural knowledge, ambassadors, diplomats, spiritual guides, cosmopolitan and worldly people. This rune can be related to jobs in management, banking, coaching, human resources, teaching, logistics, traveling, tourism, shipping, fishing and oil industry, business, international trade, purchasing (imports and exports), large scale distribution, engineering, industry, languages (translating and interpreting), environment and sports. It may also concern liberal activities, artistic activities like dancing, architecture, politics and any highly qualified jobs and jobs in international companies or organisations.

Gods related to this rune: This rune can be related to the sea god Njord who knows how to make beer and to the god of oceans Aegir who loves to gather the gods and to feast. It is also related to Odin's journey to Mimir's source where he sacrificed one of his eyes so as to gain access to the invisible worlds, to awareness of the underlying order behind life and to total knowledge, which enabled his to create the runic information system. Germans often did "gratitude rituals", thanking the god by throwing various objects in water, in marshes, rivers or in the sea. This rune can finally also be related to the god Thor who takes care of the world and of travelers and who protects the world's economy as best as he can.

Places and objects related to this rune: The outside world, foreign lands, faraway places, large buildings, shopping centers, training centers, universities, international schools, clubs, imported or exported objects, cultural or ethnic objects, tuning forks, works of art, masterpieces, diplomas and official documents, boats, ships and whatever comes from the sea.

Colors connected to this rune: Dark green or sea color.

Animals connected to this rune: Dolphins, whales, salmons, seals, sea lions, octopuses and jelly fish.

English, Norwegian and Icelandic poems:

The English poem:
Water seems unending to men
When they go sailing on their ships
Sea waves terrify them
When the steed from the depths does not heed the bridle

This poem shows how people must adapt as best as they can both to travelling in the chaotic outside world and to their inner journey towards their final destination where they become reconnected to "The Source of all life". It also enhances the art of bravery, of doing one's best and then of letting to so as to be guided deep within with faith that what needs to be found at the center of one's heart will be found. It shows how water has great stature, how it is always in motion and how unpredictable and uncontrollable it can be.

The Norwegian poem:
Water is a river falling from the mountain-side
But ornaments are made of gold

If we consider water, we can imagine it springing out of earth, becoming a torrent and then a river flowing in a fjord and into the ocean. But there are also waterfalls where water takes a leap of faith downwards in the flow of life so as to get back to the ocean. This symbolically describes deep meditation where one, after having gathered one's soul together and after having balanced male and female forces, takes a leap of faith down to one's spiritual body within one's heart. The poem enhances motion, the power of gravity and the water cycle i.e. the forces that make the universe work from stars and planets to atoms. Golden ornaments suggest that water is the most precious element on earth but also that water can also symbolize illusions as all that glisters, like the sun's reflection in water, is not gold. So clear intentions and focusing on the returning path to the ocean, like a telescope focusing on our inner star (the spiritual body), is crucial.

The Icelandic poem:
Water whirls out of the spring
And a large geyser and a land of fish

This poem enhances the origins of water, a specific expression of water and the fact that it is the natural media or field of expression where fish (symbol of the soul) and aquatic life can thrive and where mankind can find nourishment. Water therefore symbolizes life emerging and the places where it can express itself and where life can thrive.

Using this rune to do magic: Rune Lagu is used to make water magic, to implement growth and thriving, to make things flow smoothly in harmony with the flow of life, to move forward on the tracks of one's destiny, to overcome obstacles, to be protected from pollution, negative forces and poison, to gather and assemble different elements or people and make them work together, to control one's energy and vitality, to focus one's personal power so as to control a complex situation, to successfully implement processes and organizational procedures, to obtain a diploma, to persevere until the final destination is reached, to make rain fall, to get plentiful fishing and to experience a pleasant journey when travelling or when at sea.

Links with other information systems:

I Ching: This rune is related to Hexagram 21, «Law and punishment, to Hexagram 29, "Water", to Hexagram 46, "Pushing upwards", to Hexagram 53, "Step by step evolution", to Hexagram 57, "Socially adapting" and to Hexagram 63 "after completion".

Mayan Astrology: Rune 21 can be related to the "Skywalker", "Moon" and "Storm" glyphs.

Tarot: Rune Lagu can be related to card 21 "The World".

Astrology: This rune is a synthesis of the 10 planets. It has strong connections with the water astrological signs (Crab, Scorpio and Pisces). It can be seen as a mix of Sun (synthetising), Moon (giving birth to, life and making things flow), Venus (joy, abundance and dancing), Jupiter (mastering one's life and the outside world, travelling), Neptune (the great crossing, handling chaos and transcendence) and Pluto (struggling to navigate, protection against danger, managing one's dark aspects and accomplishing one's final transformation so as to become a new life form).

Rune 22 : ING

 **Various names given to this rune:**

Name and meaning in Old Norse: Yngvi. The god Ing.
Name and meaning in Old German: Ingwaz. The god Ing, a genius.
Name and meaning in Old English: Ing. The god Ing, a hero.

Its graphic design and form: This rune's icon has a specific and well recognizable diamond like shape made of four lines or of two double lines. It reveals a closed space where energy can be stored, isolated from outside influences and freely used at will to set oneself in motion through space and time and even beyond space and time. Just as rune 19, Eh ᛗ, looks like rune 21, Lagu ᛚ and its mirror or just as rune 20, Mann ᛗ, looks like rune 8, Wynn ᚹ and its mirror, well here, rune 22, Ing ◇, looks like rune 6, Ken ᚲ and its mirror. And rune 6 is about inner fire, the torch or desires that motivate people. It is about shaping form freely and beautifully and it is about creating wonderful relationships that make one feel free, great and happy. Rune Ing's icon also does look like an energy particle, a hole or female sexual organs.

Its number: Ing is rune number 22 within the Futhark alphabet. Number two is about Eternal Feminine forces, nourishing earth and water, fertility, the original matrix where life emerged, life flowing smoothly and giving birth to events, combining two elements but also seeing the difference between two elements and eventually separating them, finding appropriate nourishment and managing the world of matter and of form. Number 22 is therefore like a light particle full of life. The icon of this rune does however look like the conceptual number zero. Zero symbolizes the Source of all life, which creates all freely living life forms and the entire universe. It is the universal matrix where, from what looks like chaos, life emerges and then returns. Zero symbolizes nothingness, before the beginning, the "avant-première" and origin as where as the ultimate destination and the end of all temporal things. It also represents the absence of any specific value, potential energy and creative power and what has not yet being expressed and asserted with number 1. If you add zero or nothing to any number, well nothing happens so zero equals nothing. But if you multiply any number by zero well than your number disappears into nothingness as if it was devoured by it and you are just left with zero or nothing! The result is zero. And any number divided by zero gives you infinity, makes you go through the void, through emptiness, towards "The Source of all life". With that zero energy, rune Ing allows you to experience being hollow and empty and so to dive deep within and gain access to "the energy of the Source" and to the genius within you. It allows you to do a complete check-up, to reset and to start off with new goals, new instructions, new programs and so to create a new life in a new world.

Summary and essence of this rune: Rune Ing symbolizes "The Source of all life", of all creation and of all forms. It creates fire, water and Earth's fertility. It is the original and free particle, the zero point from where all life emerges, an unlimited source of free energy that allows for all possibilities. It is pure inspiration and a multidimensional vision that can lead either to chaos or to expressing one's inner genius. When energy from this source is channelled in full awareness, it enables all potentials to be achieved. It brings amazing results and thus makes people free and happy. It makes people step away from known and already beaten paths, from frameworks and currently used schemes and procedures, from usual limits and comfort zones so as to embody "Necessity" and so as to express a superior intelligence.

Rune 22 can also represent the vehicle or transportation means for genetic material that passes on from one generation to another, past life memories, ancestral memories or a psycho genealogical scheme. It is finally a marker revealing a new start, the end of an era, liberation and the upcoming of new times and of a new part or chapter in one's life.

The dark side of the rune: It is represented by a lack of respect for life, by a fertility issue, by an energy imbalance, by inner confusion, foolishness, stupidity and ignorance, by difficulties in finding one's place in life, in being well embodied or anchored in the world of matter or in getting through a difficult stage (end of a situation and creating a new one), by chaos and excesses, by a tendency to turn around in circles and getting nowhere, by troublesome genealogical memories and by strangeness, weirdness and bizarreness. Seeds and plants then do not emerge and blossom and things don't turn out as expected, go haywire or don't turn out at all.

Its sound: This rune is related to the "Ing" sound as in the word thing.

Key words: The Source of all life, unlimited potential energy, going beyond habits, current frames, usual schemes and forced organization, life force, a seed, creating new forms, fertility, expressing one's uniqueness and one's inner genius, growing and thriving, accomplishing one's potential, liberation, deliverance, abundance, departure from the old, a new step in one's life, the ending of a project and the beginning of something new, a new path and a new life.

People and jobs related to this rune: Someone with great potential, a genius with great creative abilities, multi-skilled individuals, jack of all trades (like Mac Ivor), people with great sense of humour who can laugh at almost everything, choking people who transgress rules and limits, wanderers, immigrants, exiles and travellers, illuminated people, revolutionaries, inventors, people who creates new ways of life, new procedures and futuristic solutions, unadapted or handicapped people, charlatans, tramps, mad or mentally sick people, people who are marginalized, prophets, avatars, spiritual guides, original people, living legends, great travellers and geniuses. This rune is related to strange and very special jobs that cannot be classified, jobs where creative abilities are required, jobs where the is a lot of travelling (sales or travelling agency representatives, postmen, delivery agent, taxi or ambulance driver), jobs where one has to find solutions, fix things or people and heal (psychiatrists, magnetizers, healers, specialized educator, handicapped person caretaker, quantic therapists) and some artistic activities like actor, clown, Biodanza facilitator or designer.

Gods related to this rune: This rune is related to a god called Ing or Ingvi. He was said to be the ancestor of all men, the Earth's companion or the male equivalent of Mother Earth, i.e. a sort of "Father Earth" or a "Sun-Earth", a source of energy and a life force gifted with great creative power, allowing life to thrive and all potentials to manifest. Ing is related to abundance, fertility, storing harvests and he rules over life processes like irrigation, plantations, harvests and distribution of goods.

Places and objects related to this rune: Markets, unusual places, unclassifiable places, places lost in the middle of nowhere, small countryside roads, by passes, an inventor's or special craftsman's workshop, a psychiatric clinic, a laboratory, caps and sneakers, strange objects, futuristic objects and objects with great design.

Colors connected to this rune: White with multicolored dots or stripes.

Blanc avec des points multicolores.

Animals connected to this rune: Cats.

English, Norwegian and Icelandic poems:

The English poem:
Ing was first seen amongst eastern Danes
Until, followed by his chariots
He went back eastwards beyond the waves
That is how warriors called this hero

A strange and unusual poem for a strange and unusual rune! It says Ing came from the East, from Asia and returned there at some stage. This may be about the sun rising east but also about one's of Earths spiritual guardians who lives on the highest mountains on Earth, the Himalayas or symbolically on the most spiritual worlds. Ing travelling with or on a chariot can be matched with the god Frey and Earth Goddess Nerthus, who were considered as heroes and celebrated during processions, where symbols of these gods were carried through villages and through the countryside to thank them for life, good harvests and abundance.

Rune 22 does not exist within the Viking Futhark so the Norwegian and Icelandic poems don't mention it.

Using this rune to do magic: Rune Ing is used to focus energy on a target, to accumulate energy, store it and use it when necessary, to control male sexual energy so as to avoid ejaculation, to plant good seeds that will give healthy plants, to organize and prepare a life cell, to see and express what is potentially there, to be connected with "The Source of all life", to store and preserve something so as to use it later, to make a talisman magical by storing energy in runes and by making sure that this energy is well preserved, to protect a house and to harmoniously and smoothly put an end to something or to a situation.

Links with other information systems:

I Ching: This rune can be related to Hexagram 22, "Form" or "Grace", with Hexagram 55, "Abundance", and with the last two Hexagrams, 63 and 63, "After completion" and "Before completion".
Mayan Astrology: Rune Ing can be related to the « Seed » glyph.
Tarot: Rune 22 can be related to card 22, « The Fool ».
Astrology: This rune is a mix of Moon, Mercury, Uranus, Neptune and Pluto.

Rune 23 : OTHALA

 **Various names given to this rune:**

Name and meaning in Old Norse: Odhal. Legacy, deep self, what is eternal within, one's dominion, ancestral house and land, sanctuary.
Name and meaning in Old German: Othala. Ancestral property.
Name and meaning in Old English: Othala or Ethel. Property, land of origin.

Its graphic design and form: This rune's icon can be seen as built from the previous rune Ing ◇ placed on a Ken rune ⟨ (rune 6) rotated 90 degrees rightwards or from a Gefu rune ✕ (rune 5) on which is placed a Ken rune ⟨ (rune 6) rotated 90 degrees. Ing is an energy particle that emerged from the Source of all life. Ken is a torch, a flame, fire getting into action. Gefu combines male and female forces to reach a target so as to express one's gifts. At this stage of evolution, the soul has been reunified, reunited. The soul's original male-female identity has been reestablished and the bond with the Source of all life has been reconstructed and stabilized, creating a state of total inner freedom and a superior intelligence enabling geniusness, conscious control of matter and a wise use of free unlimited energy extracted from the invisible. Now experiencing this happens only to very very few people on this planet and these people are true magicians capable of doing things that seem to most people like pure science fiction. That included controlling the elements, teleportation and space travel to the 10 or so other inhabited planets of this galaxy. The rune's icon can look like a mobile particle on its launching platform or on its landing zone, on a house-like structure created for it so as to recharge its batteries.

 Rune 23 icon is made up of a closed space above and an open space below and below symbolizes the past and the world of matter. It can therefore come and go as it wants, appear and disappear, split itself into smaller units and reassemble again elsewhere just like during teleportation, during a shamanic journey or when travelling through a vortex. There is a starting point, motion and a destination implying a conscious goal. There is dissembling and reassembling. Here one gives back to one's ancestors, with love and respect, what belongs to them so as to live one's own life freely.

Othala's icon finally looks like a fish and fish were often drawn by people all around the world both before the time period called the era of Pisces (vernal point located between the equinox and minus thirty degrees) the first Christians. It often represented Jesus Christ and focusing on reuniting through God to the Source of all life). Pisces represents the end of a cycle and the beginning of a new one. It represents ancestral memories, past life memories, life in the afterworld, the legacy left behind to those who stay, ghost that must raise their vibrations to evolve toward higher light worlds, unity with the great whole, the mystical journey in the invisible worlds towards transcendence, unity with "the will of the Father", the ability to relieve the sufferings and misery of the world but also the ability to do true magic and to enchant the world using the power of love, will, inspiration, faith and sense of sacredness. Rune Othala has a bit of all that.

Its number: Othala is rune number 23. Number two is about data structures and number three is about the organized motion of life. So number 23 is related to cells, places and information structures that make life go into motion. This can represent the genetic code i.e. what you come to Earth with, the places within you where the memories of humanity, of your ancestors and of your past lives that you carry are stored and the imprint which all of this has left within you. Rune 23 can also represent your "soul family" (souls were created in groups by the "Source") and the connections with your "spiritual family". Number two can also be about duality and number three about dispersion in space and time. Number 23 can therefore be about the splitting apart of human structures so as to gain access to new experiences and so as to create a new world.

Summary and essence of this rune: This rune is about understanding, integrating and making the best use of your genetic, genealogical and psychological inheritance given at birth but also of your life conditions existing at birth. How can you best use all these to accomplish your destiny and your life mission. It reveals what you are guarding and what you can give to future generations. At a deeper level, rune 23 can represent "the throne of God" which is your true "Home" and your most precious legacy. It symbolizes a very particular state of awareness, knowledge, richness, prosperity, joy and wellness resulting from an optimized management of your past, of your global legacy and of your destiny and the ability to express all that in a new and more authentic manner. With this rune one reaps what one has sown and what one sows will bear fruits when a new cycle comes about. Rune Othala can represent the spitting apart of something, the end of a cycle, transmitting a legacy, abandoning what no longer needs to be and the arrival of a new situation. It can finally symbolize finding one's place within a family, a community, a group, an organisation or a network.

The dark side of the rune: It is represented by issues related to the past, by a complicated inheritance, by problem-causing past lives or ancestral memories, by confusion and madness, by disturbing ghosts, by a genetic code issue, by a lack of help from one's family, social group, health care organisation or society, by a family conflict or a conflict with a government or private organisation, by a splitting apart of structures that are not rebuilt correctly, by a difficulty in having a house and a home, by delays and things not coming out as expected, by a difficulty in correctly managing a legacy or in settling down somewhere and by a difficult crossing or journey.

Its sound: This rune is related to an « o » sound as in the word top.

Key words: Spiritual, psychological, family and material legacy, a data structure enabling to go from one state of being to another, preparing a journey leading to a new life cycle, a place where growth and transformation takes place, a place where one experiences wellness and where one can recharge one's batteries (a home, a wellness centre), genealogical or past life imprints, ancestral lands, land and property, collective memories, making the best of one's legacy, managing smartly a heritage (lands, property, companies, skills, knowledge and knowhows), a rental fee or pension, help from family, from the community or from society, transmitting one's heritage, expressing one's legacy in a manner adapted to present times. This rune is strongly related to the Hindu concept of Karma, to liberation from Karma and to adapting to Necessity.

People and jobs related to this rune: Someone greatly influenced by his or her past, someone known in some distant past, someone managing a legacy or a data structure, someone master in his or her art and an ancestor. Jobs related to handling data, change, genealogy, projects, land and property.

Gods related to this rune: This rune is related to the god Loki who could pervert, spit apart and destructure any situation and who could also create illusion replacing the truth. It is also related to Odin as the true magician master who could protect life and evolution. It is finally related to the god Vidhar/Vidarr or Vitharr who put an end to the forces of chaos and destruction represented by Loki and the wolf Fenrir and who brought about the arrival of a new day, of a new cycle.

Places and objects related to this rune: Lands, property, testaments, financial documents, insurance policies and contracts.

Colors connected to this rune: Iridescent colors.

Animals connected to this rune: Human beings and viruses.

English, Norwegian and Icelandic poems:

The English poem:
An ancestral home is very dear to every man
If he can enjoy prosperity there in his house
That which is right and filling

This poem is about wellness, joy and prosperity at all levels, within a protected space, thanks to doing what is right and to managing one's global life and evolution well.

This rune does not exist within the Viking Futhark so the Norwegian and Icelandic poems don't mention it.

Using this rune to do magic: Rune Othala can be used as a box to place and protect different objects, to experience in daily life the connection with "The Source of all life", to become aware of one's roots, to find one's legacy and make the best of it, to store energy that will be used at latter times, to creates bonds and alliances within a group or family, to find a house and settle in it comfortably, to make a structure or a situation break apart so as to later rebuild it differently, to create events and to gain access to a superior state of awareness, knowledge, richness, prosperity, wellness and happiness.

Links with other information systems:

I Ching: This rune can be related to Hexagram 23, "Splitting apart", to Hexagram 59, "Dissolution" and to Hexagram 63, "After completion".
Mayan Astrology: Rune Othala can be related to the "Night" and "Storm" glyphs.

Tarot: The group who created Tarot cards wisely decided that in 1426, the time was not ripe to create a 24 card system and so they stopped at 22. The time will come when two new cards, representing numbers 23 and 24, can be created. Rune Othala, which is a very special rune, can be related to card 4 "The Emperor" who represents structures and managing the lands and the "empire", to card 12, "The Hanged Man" (genealogical memories one is hanging on to and switching to spiritual faith and evolution), to card 12, "Death" (splitting apart, a crossing to a new world and the end of something), to card 16, "The House of God" (change of structure and connection with "The Source"), to card 18, "The Moon" (Home, a living cell, cleaning up one's memories), to card 20, "Judgment" (becoming free from one's past and evolving towards a higher vision and towards a new world) and to card 22"The Fool" (mastering one's inner genius and magic).

Astrology: This rune is a mix of Sun, Moon, Venus, Uranus, Neptune and Pluto.

Rune 24 : DAEG

Various names given to this rune:

Old Norse: Dagr. Daylight, the coming back of daylight, daytime.
Name and meaning in Old German: Dagaz. Day.
Name and meaning in Old English: Daeg. Day.

Its graphic design and form: This rune's icon can be either seen as made up from two Isa runes ❘ framing a Gefu rune ✕ or as four Ken runes ‹ with three of them rotated at angles of 90, 180 et 270 degrees. It is made up of two closed triangles and two opened triangles. These triangles describe the various light cycles repeating over and over again for eternity but also the particular moment when they meet and when the two forces are balanced. The two main cycles are the day-night light cycle where day and night meet at dawn and dusk and the yearly Earth-Sun cycle where the two projected equators meet at the spring and autumn equinox. The icon does look a bit like a compressed infinity icon. It also looks like a Mann rune ᛗ without its legs, which are no longer needed. Rune Daeg is no longer dependent on matter. It exists everywhere, at all levels, in every dimension. It is always in motion and always changing.

Comments about the name: For German people of ancient times, the day began at dusk and lasted till sunset of the next day. They believed that daytime was born out of night, that spring was born out of winter and that the sun was pulled by a horse called Skinfaxi.

Its number: Daeg is rune number 24 and the last rune of the original German Futhark. Number 24 doesn't have any specific meaning by itself but there are 24 bones or vertebrae in the human vertebral column so it reveals a structural unit. It can be obtained by putting side by side 2 and 4 (day and night getting organized), from 20+4 (consciousness and a higher vision organizing life), from 2 by 12 (cycles of daytime and night time) or from 3 by 8 which can mean infinite motion of joy and sharing.

Comments about placing rune Daeg in potition 24: Some people have placed this rune is position number 23 and not 24. What I see and feel is that when runes were created, there were strong bonds between German Shamans/healers/priests and their colleagues much further east, in Asia.

These people met in the invisible worlds in specific places or temples, during out of body experiences. There was and still is in Asia a numerological system, the I Ching, used for divination. The first 22 symbols of the I Ching, called Hexagrams, very strangely match the meanings of the first 22 runes. Number 24 within the I Ching is about the returning or coming back of daylight and of a situation and about the returning of Eternal Day, which is when an evolved human being has permanently reconnected through God with "The Source of all light". So placing rune Daeg in position 24 seems right and obvious. I have not checked and calculated, within all archaeological discoveries with complete Futharks, the percentage of cases where Daeg is in position 23 and 24.

Summary and essence of this rune: I reveal your landmarks, what is important for you and where you place your consciousness, your light or your attention. I symbolize abandoning the old and the creation of a new world with new rules, new points of view and new landmarks. I make things clear and bring about a new vision where "what is" and "what is required" are obvious. I enable complete awareness, expressing one's inner light and being the best version of one's self. I bring about a new day after night time, a new vision, the ability to overcome any duality, the returning of light after dark times, a new start after an old situation ends, a new way of life or the discovery, after a long journey or an important transformation or after experiencing illumination, of a new self, a new land and a new world.
A new balance and a new life are been implemented. All potentials come to be. Light always ends up being triumphant.

The dark side of the rune: It may represent an issue concerning self-image, deep identity, being aware, expression of one's light, radiance, an imbalance between opposite forces, a duality or excessive self-importance.

Its sound: This rune is related to the "d" sound as in the word day.

Key words: The shining daylight, awakening of consciousness, putting things of one's life and identity back in order or back on track, a new balance, taking care of one's image, experiencing positive thoughts, behaviour and vibrations, becoming visible, returning on the right path, a new step, a new birth, a new start, the coming back of better times, working with light, balance between two opposite forces, getting over opposition, making an alliance, using creative power, success, self-realisation, abundance, prosperity and intensive and long lasting joy and bliss.

People and jobs related to this rune: A radiant, brilliant, very successful and very happy person, someone arriving in a new situation or a new world, jobs related to bringing light and awareness.

Gods related to this rune: This rune is related to the German day god Daeg, to the light god Baldr who is worshiped during the summer solstice, to the god Heimdall son of the night who reveals the great fight taking place when the end of the worlds comes and to the new couple who survive over Ragnarok and repopulate Earth, to the Goddess of life called Lif and to the Goddess symbolizing continuity of life Lifthrasis.

Places and objects related to this rune: Bright, glittering, radiant, beautiful and precious places and objects.

Colours connected to this rune: White.

Animals related to this rune: Animals seen at dawn.

English, Norwegian and Icelandic poems:

The English poem:
Day is the creator's (The Source) glorious light sent through by the lord
It is loved by men and is a source of joy and happiness for rich and poor
It serves the world and everyone

The poem shows how light comes from the Source and is channeled through the lord or within the spiritual body. It shows that light is love, joy, creative power and happiness, that it generously gives to all and that it serves humanity above any specific considerations.

Rune 24 does not exist within the Viking Futhark so the Norwegian and Icelandic poems don't mention it.

Using this rune to do magic: Rune Daeg can be used to overcome duality, to experience light, to make someone or an object come back, to keep dark forces out, to become the best version of oneself, to make a new dawn happen and to create a new and positive situation.

Links with other information systems:

I Ching: This rune can be related to Hexagram 24.
Mayan Astrology: Rune Daeg can be related to the "Sun" glyph.
Tarot: Rune 24 can be related to card 19, « The Sun » and eventually to car 8, "Justice" which rules over balance between different forces.
Astrology: This rune can be related to the Sun with a bit of Venus.

Chapter 4: Runic spreads

Questioning the runes consists either in throwing them on a white sheet, either in picking them intuitively out of a leather bag or in spreading them face down on a table and in choosing a few runes that are displayed in a certain manner, in specific predefined positions. Each rune is then interpreted according to its nature but also according to its position and to nearby runes. When you undertake a runic spread, you implement a flow of data between your subconscious and your consciousness, in the present moment, in order to answer a question. There are many runic spreads, especially since tarot spreads have proliferated. This chapter offers a selection of them.

Getting prepared to question the runes: Before questioning the runes, it is advisable to be clearly aware of your intention. Why are you really questioning the runes? What is your question precisely? What do you want deep down? What do you really want to know? What will you do when you get your answer? When your question has been clearly put into words, you can then choose the most appropriate spread. It is then auspicious to set yourself in the appropriate psychological mindset and to organise your environment so as to obtain the answer that is right for you.

Being in the right mindset: Questioning the runes implies being connected to your deep intuition, to your spiritual self and to your inner guide. This requires humility, respect, seriousness and a state of calm free of any desires, expectations or fears. The right mindset is being brave enough to just accept what comes, feeling inner clarity, a peaceful joy, serenity and a relaxed alertness. It is not advisable to undertake a runic spread in a non harmonious atmosphere or with people addicted to drugs or alcohol.

The best time to question the runes: You can either question the runes when you feel it is time to do so or take into account the day of the week, the day number of the month or the hour of the day. Each day of the week is related to a god. Sunday is related to Baldr and to the sun, Monday to Frigg and to the Moon, Tuesday to Tiw/Tyr, Wednessday to Odin, Thursday to Thor, Friday to Freya, Njord and Aegir and finally Saturday is related to Vidhar and Loki. Every hour is also related to one of the 24 runes. The first hour after sunset can be related to the first rune and so on.

Every day of the month has a number and this number can be related to a rune through what is called "the significant symbol" or just "the significant" which is the symbol for something specific. You can identify the significant related to your question and then choose the best time of the day, week or month in connection with it. If for example you want to publish a book, the significant of books would be Odin and so the best time to question would be Wednessday, the third day of the month of the third hour after sunrise. According to the roman historian Tacitus, Germans believed that the best time to question about something new or to start a new business was just after the new moon while the best time to question about ending something or to finish something was between full moon and the next new moon.

Choosing the right place and creating the right atmosphere: It is advisable to find a place where you are not disturbed by the surroundings. It you feel that it is right to do so, you can then organize a ritual with music, incense and candles or do a meditation session before questioning the runes. The important thing is that you feel well, calm and connected with your inner life.

The significants: Choosing a symbol to represent your question: You don't have to do this but it greatly helps in getting a more clear answer. In astrology and tarot, a significant is a symbol that represents your question. Using significants implies that you have previously decided and thus encoded that each rune means for you at all levels and to have classified everything in life into 24 categories (colours, days, people, emotions, skills, strengths and weaknesses, objects, time and events). This is why there is such classification of what the 24 runes can mean in the previous chapter. Significants are also classified further down in this chapter.

Writing down your question in a notebook: You don't have to do this but writing and putting the date often helps you find the right words and feel what you really want deep down. It also helps having a more realistic vision. Looking at your notes some days, weeks or months later can help you see how the situation evolves and where you want to go.

Before questioning the runes, you can speak or chant a gratitude prayer where you thank Freya, Odin and all the runic masters: By doing so, you connect with the gods and with the sacred parts of your soul which are symbolized by Freya and Odin.

What is important here is your intention, being in a sincere state of gratitude and being alert, aware, awake, here and now and yet calm, as if something very special was going to happen and you do consider that getting the right answer is something very special don't you?

Here is an example of chanted or spoken poem or prayer: You can of coarse create your own, ones that make you vibrate and feel great.

I salute, greet and honour you precious Freya, Goddess of love and beauty.
Guardian of joy, trance and inspiration
Thank you for opening my soul and my heart to the secrets of the present moment
Thank you for blessing this runic spread
I salute, greet and honour you dear Odin, God of mysteries, knowledge and magic
Guardian of profound visions, of right words and of efficient actions
Thank you for opening my mind to the present moment's Necessity
Thank you for blessing this runic spread
May my heart be joyful, may my vision de clear and may my words de relevant. So be it.

1-The one rune spread:

If you are a beginner, this spread can help you become familiar with runes and their messages. If you are an experienced rune practitioner, this spread can give you a simple and efficient message that will be grasped intuitively. You can either pick a rune in your bag while intensively thinking about your question or spread the 24 runes down on a table, face down, pass your hands over the runes and choose one that makes your hand or fingers feel cool, hot or that gives you a tickling sensation or a subtle feeling saying this is the rune i want just now. That will then be the right rune, the one that vibrates with you in the present moment.

Exemples of questions you can ask: How is this day/relationship or situation turning out? In what atmosphere will this day/situation/relationship take place? What is the deep meaning of this situation or relationship? What is the most advisable way to be or thing to do concerning this situation/relationship? What will today be like? Where do i have to focus my attention today?

What do you recommend me doing today? What do i have to take into account just now? Here are some examples of possible answers through keywords that are all "significants". However, what is important is to use your intuition, to listen to what it whispers to you and to feel what the rune means for you.

Rune 1: FEHU: Very busy day where your creative power and masculine qualities (as for example defining a goal and undertaking smartly so as to achieve it) can be expressed. It is a great day to clarify your intention, to set a new goal, to start off something new, to do what must be done, to be assertive with spontaneity and enthusiasm, to use your will power efficiently, to use your skills in daily matters or to use at best available tools, to grasp an opportunity, to get results and to create wealth. There may be someone young involved in the situation.

Rune 2: UR: This is potentially a very fertile day where feminine qualities (imagining and fulfilling your dreams, taking care of life) can be expressed. It is a great day to have faith, to observe, see what you feel, think things over, study and learn, to prepare and nourish a project or to nourish yourself correctly at all levels, to question what is in your memory, to dive into your subconscious to pull out secrets or souvenirs, to listen to your intuition and to be inspired, to process data or to manage data media, to take care of someone and to increase your wellness, wisdom and serenity. You may have to use a lot of energy preparing something.

Rune 3: THORN: This is a day where you have to express your personal power, your life instincts, your intelligence and your ability to communicate and to adapt and so as to organize chaos, overcome obstacles and create new forms or a new situation. It is a great day to implement a new project, to organize a lot of data, to go somewhere, to send and receive messages and to manage a situation in a smart, elegant and balanced manner with whatever authority required. This may be a lively and vibrant day with lots of communication, movement and sharing or trading with people. You may have to do a lot of thinking and organising. There may also be a strong connection with Mother Nature or with your mother.

Rune 4: ASS: This is a very busy day with lots of work to do, where you have to use your authority, your will power and your confidence, where you have to make sure that things go your way thanks to appropriate communication, organisation and discipline. It is a great day to work in a determined and passionate manner, to do business, to be firm, strict and accurate, to build and structure, to manage a team, to deal with important business issues, to make sure rules are applied, to act as a responsible person, to control your territory and to make sure that the world around you works as it should. There may also be a strong connection with leaders, with important people or with your father.

Rune 5: RAIDH: This is a rather a lucky day where mastering knowledge, teachings, travelling or moving around and awareness can play an important role. It is a great day to support and foster or to get support, to communicate, to travel or to prepare a trip, to go on an adventurous journey, to negotiate, to become more aware, to be meaningful, to gain knowledge, to deal with a data systems, tech or to find required information, to prepare and give teachings or to make sure teachings bring about results. It is also a great day to find the right direction thanks to a clear vision, to trust and be trusted, to take religious factors like gratitude into account, to act as an expert with a keen and sound judgment, to find a solution, to sign a contract, to gather and unite people, objects or situations, to make something official, to bless and be blessed, to protect and be protected and to experience an inner shamanic-like journey so as to gather the different parts of one's soul. There may also be a strong connection with a wise person or with your grandfather.

Rune 6: KEN: This is a bright, joyful, happy and sensual day with lots of possibilities and where there may be a lot of relationships or artistic activities to handle. It is a great day to express your inner fire, your inner artist, your feelings of love and your desires, to see and listen to your true desires, to see beauty where it is, to create bonds with people, to do what brings you joy and pleasure, to make balanced and relevant decisions, to be committed to someone, to have a good time with your partner and take good care of her or him, to decorate and adorn, to create objects and to be a master of your art. There may also be a strong connection with very nice, pleasant or young people. If you don't listen to your true desires or take other people's happiness into account, there may then be an unpleasant situation.

Rune 7: GYFU: This is a great day to be focused, to see every part of a situation, to express your talents with both your feminine (preparing efficiently, listening to your intuition, taking care of the situation) and masculine skills (clarity, goals and action), to show generosity and to give the best of who you are, to clarify your goals, to take relevant decisions, to get organized efficiently so as to achieve your goals, to balance what needs to be balanced, to structure or create a new structure, to go out on a mission, to help someone or to accept someone's help and to share with body, heart and mind.

Rune 8: WYNN: This is a great day to be aware of the underlying order existing behind life, to see that every cause leads to a consequence, that what is happening today is the consequence of the past and that you create your own future, to organize and structure in the right manner, to form alliances, to be committed within a group and within society which implies setting aside part of your personal will, to undertake with great awareness, with your heart and with the will to bring about joy and to share with others in a joyful atmosphere. It can also be a very good day to deal with bureaucracy, paperwork, administrative formalities, legal papers and tax issues. There may be a wide range of social, cultural, club or even artistic activities to be dealt with. It can be a very balanced, pleasant, graceful day where things go right. You reap what you have sawed or what you saw.

Rune 9: HAGL: This is a great day to plant seeds, to handle a building site, to undertake important achievements, to work on structures or long term goals, to make plans and prepare, to ask the right questions and do research, to take some distance or see things from a certain distance, to abandon what must be left behind, to end something, to deal with quality or safety issues, to go deep within and practice meditation, to see things from a deeper perspective, to show wisdom and to experiment inner peace so as to move forward on the path that leads to your deep inner truth. It can be a quiet, calm and peaceful day. Something new can symbolically come from the sky. It may also be a difficult day and building-site like day with obstacles to overcome, with delays and setbacks, with people finding excuses to resist or with a lot of work to do.

Rune 10: NYD: This is a great day to use your technical intelligence so as to serve and adapt, to deal smartly with constraints or technical challenges, to fix what needs fixing, to see both your own needs and necessity and take them into account, to take care of your health and hygiene, to use numbers and to take cycles into account, to trade, to work, to copy, improve or innovate, to experiment the laws of destiny and to accept that there are things you cannot control. Destiny may knock on your door today or things may get along like clockwork. There may be ups and down or things may go one way and then take a totally different turn. It can also be a very good day to try your luck, to change repetitive schemes, to free yourself from any slave-like situation and to start a new cycle.

Rune 11: EIS: This may be a powerful, harsh and significant day where you have to bravely fight your way though like a Jedi, organize things efficiently, handle your anger and center yourself back in your heart, give the best of who you are, practice self-control and confidently master a situation with whatever authority required. It is a very good day to clarify your vision, to set clear goals, to gather various elements around a central one, to assert your essence and your priorities, to listen to your heart and to express your strength, your determination, your will power, your creative abilities, your inner light and the power of love. It is a day to be well centered, to be on the front stage, to highlight what is important, to be both autonomous and connected with others and to do what is required to succeed with greatness and nobleness.

Rune 12: YER: This is a day where you need to be in harmony with your feminine self, with your faith, your divine nature, your unconditional love or your ancestors, where you have to be devoted towards your community, where you must end a cycle and prepare for a new one and where you have to take into account either what has been sawed or handle what is been harvested. You may have to deal with a memory (ancestral memories, past life memories) or with a repetitive scheme that may show up. It could be a strange and deceitful day with appointments canceled or postponed and with a situation that seems to be blocked or tied up with knots or that ends abruptly. It can also be a delightful, enchanted, incredible day where things flow like magic and where miracles can occur. It is a very good day to see things differently, to relieve the misery and sufferings of body and soul, to show compassion, to sacrifice something, to let go, to let yourself be carried along by the flow of life, to dream and fulfill your dreams, to meditate, to experiment inner joy and bliss without there being any specific reason for it and to experiment unity with life and with divine presence.

Rune 13: EIH: It could be a stressful, complicated, extreme and unpleasant day with an issue or a drama to deal with. You may have a tendency to burry yourself somewhere, to be playing dead, to sustain an imbalance, to focus on the dark side of things and to be grumpy. This can also be an intense and vibrant day and a very good day to put an end to what no longer needs to be, to eliminate what is toxic, to heal wounds and regenerate, to transform something or someone, to implement a change and a new beginning, to see behind the scenes or work with subtle forces, to make discoveries, to gain access to revelations, to experience eternity, your deep spiritual truth or the world hereafter, though shamanic travel or an out of body experience so as to implement a new and liberating state of being.

Rune 14: PERTH: This is a great day to be aware, of coincidences, synchronicities and of connections between causes and effects, to balance what needs to be balanced at all levels by reducing extremes or whatever is in excess, to question chance, to connect with people or with intergalactic space, to expand your network or to do teamwork, to have some good time with friends, to share ideas and concepts, to work on your need for freedom, to relax and rest, to use your psychological or technological intelligence so as to find solutions and answers or create a better world or bring about progress, to work with hi-tech objects that require electricity or the use of waves, to find efficient help or to help someone, to go from one state of being to another, to fly off to other destinations of levels of awareness and to move forward on the tracks of your destiny. It can be a very harmonious, pleasant, serene and appeasing day where things flow smoothly and where there is hope, relief, liberation and healing. It may also be a multidimensional and paradoxical day with lots of connections between objects, situations of people.

Rune 15: EOLH: This is a great day to be clear-eyes and alert, to distinguish things, to listen to your survival instincts, to show a strategic intelligence, to fight fearlessly so as to achieve your goals, to transform what needs to be transformed, to break any enslaving chains or bonds, to work in the shadows, to enjoy sexuality, to earn money, to express your personal power so as to serve life, to work with metal or fire and to do what you are passionate about. It may however be an intense, passionate, tense, frightening and conflict-ridden day where you have to face and deal with your shadows and old demons, the dark aspects of people, ignorance, imbalance, excesses, flaws, wounds, unwellness, and jealousy. You may have to handle and channel a manipulative, perverted, vicious, unbalanced, fraudulent, illegal or spellbinding person. You may be tempted to bypass or defy the law or to disrupt a balanced situation by excessive behavior.

Rune 16: SIGL: This is a great day to go deep within, to develop more awareness, to make astounding discoveries, to say what needs to be said, to free yourself from any blocks or past emotional shocks, to deconstruct and rebuild differently, to handle vast and complex data structures, networks, projects or building sites, to play your role within a team or a network, to efficiently use your psychological or technological intelligence, to work with very tense forces, with fireworks or with dynamite, to express your need for freedom, liberation and independence and to adapt to modern life. It can be either a calm, quiet, solitary, inner orientated, and meditative-like day where you lock yourself up in your castle or tower to do a check up of your vision of yourself and to go in on a quest of your inner living god or it can be an electric, tense, explosive, shaky, enthusiastic, unexpected, shocking, overwhelming and liberating day that is full of surprises.

Rune 17: TIW/TYR: Today is a great day to channel your energy and resources so as to fight your way through and achieve a goal that you feel is absolutely right so as to restore harmony, beauty, rightness and the laws of the sky or the laws of life. It can be a great day to listen to your body and to your true desires, to take care of your inner garden or your inner sky (astral chart and Birth Diamond), to gat closer to the shining light in the center of your heart, to take care of your joy and pleasure, of your wealth and your relationship to abundance, of your body and life force, of your skills or weapons and of your life or of other people's lives. It can also be a great day to spend some time doing leisure or artistic activities, to foster harmonious relationships, to do what makes you feel thrilled, to express the "star" within you, to recharge your batteries in a beautiful place where nature thrives, to enhance your faith in life and to feel alive, to use your creative abilities to decorate, adorn and beautify, to be devoted to someone, to show compassion and forgive and to live happily at every level within the world of matter. Things may work out smoothly, nicely and happily. It can be a fertile, inspired and lucky day that is full of hope. There may also be an important "Thing-like" meeting, an intense debate, a very strong commitment and a great success for someone.

Rune 18: BERKANO: This can be a great day to stay at home, to take care of your home and your household or of your subconscious and your memories, to be with your family or experience fulfilling emotional relationships, to cook, nourish and feel nourished at all levels, to earn some money, to deal with your past and your souvenirs, to listen to your intuition, to express your imagination and your creative abilities, to fulfil your dreams, to be motherly-like and take care of yourself or of people and to express feminine values. If you cling onto to fears, disturbing memories, illusions or ghosts, you may then feel emotional stress. If you focus on life, on faith in life and if you use your imagination to make things flow and nourish positive images then things can flow smoothly, poetically and it can be a fertile, recharging, intimate and lovely day where you feel well and peaceful. You may experience a strong connection with a child, with a mother or with a woman.

Rune 19: EH: This can be a great day to get moving with great self-control, to work with horses, to listen to your heart and do what you love doing, to become more aware of who you really are, to go on the front stage and show the best of yourself, to focus on an ideal, on your values and on clear goals that drive you onto steady direction in life, to love yourself and others, to build an alliance or a partnership, to work with a partner and to express your will power, your creative abilities, your inner light, your generosity and a fatherly-like power of love so as to shine like the sun. It is also a great day to experience very nice relationships, to get organised very efficiently, to educate and teach, to enhance a feeling of gratitude and to enjoy sunshine. You may experience a strong connection with children, with a father or with a man. It can be a beautiful, joyful, sunny, lucky and successful day.

Rune 20: MANN: This can be a great day to dive deep within yourself, to clearly see what's there, to increase your awareness and to clean up old memories, to listen to your inner voice and to your intuition, to vibrate with music, to send or receive news and messages, to listen to a lecture, a speech or to teachings or to be the one on stage, to give or get very good advice or spiritual teachings, to experience a higher vision, to become more aware of what is sacred in your daily life and to hear a call for change or to implement significant change. It can be a great day to have a second chance, to regenerate and rise from your ashes, to liberate yourself from the past, to help someone have a baby or experience rebirth, to heal body and soul though speech and vibration, to share to people, to handle complex projects, to master very advanced technologies, to adapt to modern life or to unexpected events or to create a new life in a new world. You should avoid locking yourself up in guilt or judgments or painful past memories. It could be a very special and vibrant day, where you can fully express your potential and the real you, heal your soul and accomplish your destiny.

Rune 21: LAGU: This can be a great day to realize that you are like a little drip in the vast ocean, to understand your economic and legal environment and to play your role within it, to broaden your vision and to get connected with foreign lands and with the world. It can be a great day to dance, improve your organisation or processes, to master teachings, to achieve important goals or projects, to beautifully finish something, to give the best of yourself, to create more wealth or works of art, to reap what you have sawed and to awaken spiritually by experiencing the state of being called "God" and by being connected with "The Source of all life". It could be a very busy day where being in the world or dealing with legal matters takes a lot of time and energy. It can also be an optimistic, lucky, multidimensional, powerful, successful and happy day. Water may be important.

Rune 22: ING: This is a great day to express your curiosity and to feel wonder, to keep an eye out for coincidences, to see your most secret wishes, to go into the unknown, to express your uniqueness and the genius within you, to have great ideas, to try looking at things from many different angles, to do things differently and to go along new unexplored paths, to be guided by faith, intuition and by the currents of love flowing all over the universe, to take a leap of faith, to dissolve any blocks, to experience inner freedom and to live freely and happily in this world. It could be a very unusual and surprising day. There may be no limits and everything can be possible. If you are not focused then it may be a meaningless day where deep "past life or ancestral memories" pop up and make you careless, negligent, confused and even lost. If you are not well centered, if you think too much or if don't act with a smart judgment, you may seem to turn around in circles like a foolish person without doing the right things for the situation to evolve on the right track. Otherwise it could be a fantastic day filled with grace, where you feel free and where you experience the beginning of a new cycle.

Rune 23: OTHALA: This can be a great day to analyse in detail the structures and causes of your present day life or of a situation and to see the connections with your ancestors, to learn from your past, to express the best of your legacy, to go from one place or state of being to another, to let the truth come out, to end a situation, to drive your illusions or ghosts towards the light, to joyfully recharge your batteries, to take care of your home, your inner life or of people, to implement changes and to play a role within a group, a community, an organisation or a network.

Rune 24: DAEG: This can be a great day to clarify your life or a situation by seeing all its components and the connections between them, to be more aware of what's really important, to put things back on track and in order by going beyond opposition, to balance what needs to be balanced, to become visible or to work on your self-image, to express your light , your creative power, your joy and the best of yourself so as to bring about prosperity and abundance, to prepare your arrival in a new situation or in a new world, to start off a new cycle, to realise important achievements and to build your success story.

2- The Norn's spread.

This very old spread was and is used by German/Scandinavian people to answer a specific question. You question here with great respect and faith the three goddesses or Norns called Urd, Verdandi and Skuld. Before questioning, a small prayer or poem where you officially ask for their insight can be spoken silently or verbally. You place your runes in an opaque bag and when you are ready, you can then pick out a first rune that represents your question and its issues or what is at stake. You don't have to represent your question with such a rune but it can be very helpful to do so. You then pick out three runes and place them in a row face down as in the diagram below. It is also possible to place the 24 runes face down and to choose a first rune that represents your question and then three more.

Rune 1 or position 1: It represents the past in relation with your question.
Rune 2 or position 2: It describes what is occurring in the present moment
Rune 3 or position 3: It shows short and long term evolution.
You can if necessary choose a fifth rune to clarify the future.

The three runes can also be interpreted in the following manner:

Rune 1: How the situation begins
Rune 2: How the situation evolves
Rune 3: How the situation ends

or:

Rune 1: What are the roots of the current issue?
Rune 2: What must i do to overcome this issue?
Rune 3: What will the consequences be if i do what is required?

3- The German spread.

This is the spread described by roman historian Tacitus in the year 98 AD. It was used to have a global intuitive vision of a situation and of what must be done. It requires a perfectly clear knowledge of what each rune means and to be well connected to your intuition so that answers and visions just flow. To do this spread, you first place a square-shaped white sheet on the ground with the four sides facing the four directions. You then draw a large circle with a burned piece of wood or a pen and pinpoint the centre of the circle. You then stand with your back to the south and look northwards. You take the 24 runes in your two hands and recite a poem or prayer to thank Freya and Odin for giving you a clear answer. You then throw up the 24 runes so that they fall at the centre of the circle.

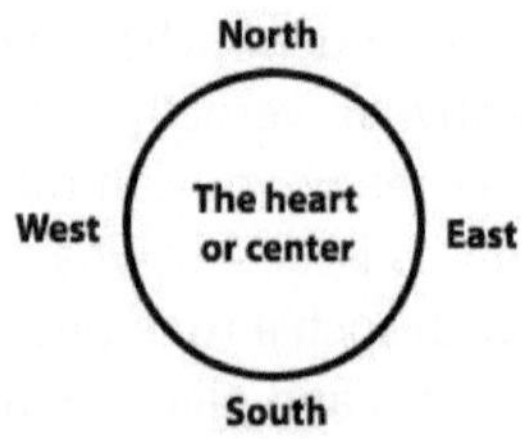

- runes with their face down are taken away and put back in their bag.
- The nearer a rune is to the center and the more important it is.
- The runes are read clockwise starting from the highest rune in the north-east quarter, at 12 PM.
- When you interpret a rune, you take into account the ones closest to it.
- East represents action, creation, beginnings, newness, enthusiasm and spring. It is related to wind and motion.
- South represents authority, control, organisation, building, awareness, stability, prosperity and summer. It is related to fire.

- West symbolises change, putting what has been done into its best form, working together, sharing, harvesting, ending something, managing data, decline and autumn. It is related to water.
- North symbolises retreat, going home, scarcity, working on structure, inner spiritual life and advancing towards your deep inner truth. It is related to earth.

To get the best out of this spread, regular practice is required. Another way to do it is to sit south and face north, to close your eyes, to silently speak your request and express your gratitude and to pick 5 runes from the bag and place them east, south, west, north and in the center.

4- The dagger spread.

This spread gives a very relevant answer that enables you to decide efficiently. Six runes are chosen and placed face down as below and then interpreted one by one from rune one to rune six.

Rune 1 or position 1: It shows how the consultant feels and sees the present situation in relation to the question but also what must be done to be successful i.e. the positive forces that can be expressed.
Rune 2 or position 2: It shows difficulties, issues, forces going against the consultant, what is not harmonious and what must be avoided.
Rune 3 or position 3: It shows the forces of destiny that impact the current situation and thus what must be accepted as it cannot be changed. It describes what comes from the sky and often an event impacting the situation. It also reveals the right path to be taken to adapt and evolve.
Rune 4 or position 4: It reveals the answer to the question and effective short term consequences.
Rune 5 or position 5: This position shows the heart of the question, the meaning of the situation and the teachings or lessons one can learn from it.
Rune 6 or position 6: It describes long term evolution.

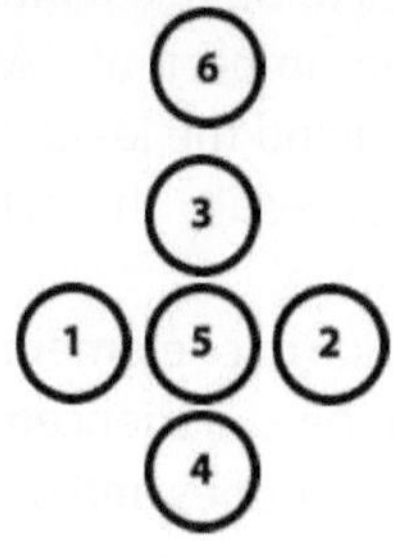

5- The high priestess spread

I created this spread from the Celtic Cross Spread. It gives a clear global and precise vision of a situation, of a person or of a period of time (a month, 3 months, six months or even a year). You pick 13 runes, one by one and spread then face down as below starting with rune one and ending with rune zero.

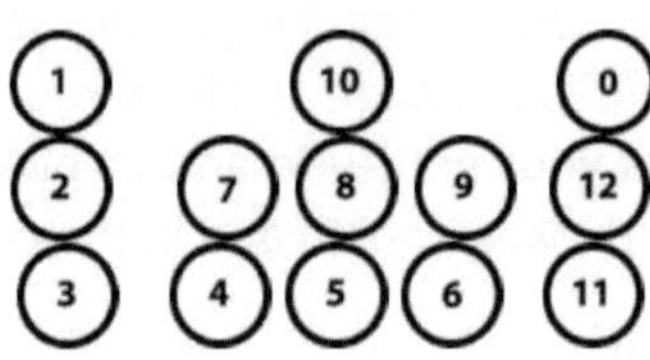

Rune 1: What impacts the present moment, the heart of the situation and in what state of being the consultant is.

Rune 2: Obstacles, issues, conflicts, fears, resistances and the main challenge with regards to the situation.

Rune 3: Deep beliefs, vision, conscious ideal, intentions and goals

Rune 4: Roots, causes and the origin of the present situation, unconscious schemes and unsaid hidden goals, souvenirs impacting the situation and hidden resources.

Rune 5: Means, actions, tools, solutions that can and should be used to achieve one's goal and succeed. What must be dealt with, finished and solved. Advice.

Rune 6: The consultant's self-image and the image showed to others. A choice that has been made. The right choice.

Rune 7: Available and visible help, resources in the outside world that should be used.

Rune 8: Risks and what should be avoided.

Rune 9: The environment, what it expects from the consultant, how the consultant is seen and the rules to be taken into account so as to adapt.

Rune 10: What is becoming important, what is coming, short-term evolution, the path of evolution and the ideal future.

Rune 11: The answer, the final result, the achievement, how healing can take place and long term evolution.

Rune 12: Genealogical and karmic elements that impact the current situation, the karmic healing to be experienced, the end of the cycle.

Rune 0: Chance, the unexpected, hopes and messages from the cosmos.

6- The nine world runic spread.

This typical runic spread is very interesting to look deeply into the structure of a situation and to have a deep global vision. It enables connectiong your inner world with what you create in the outside world. The nine world are those of Nordic mythology as shown in chapter two. Nine runes are chosen and displayed as below

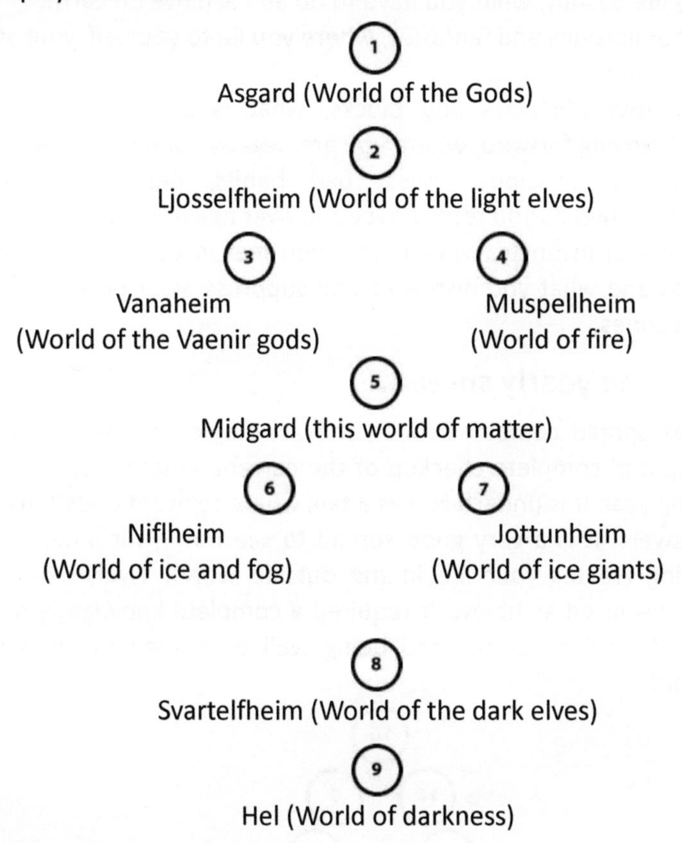

Meaning of the nine worlds:

Asgard: Necessity, your ideal, the right goal, what must lead your intention and your life, your spiritual self, expressing your creative power.
Ljosselfheim : The intelligence that guides you, efficient solutions and the help you can get.

Vanaheim: Your life force, your joy, your ability to create relationships, your feelings and emotions, your fertility and your ability to make a situation or a relationship blossom.

Muspellheim: Inner fire, your motivation, your fuel, your strength and your passion.

Midgard: You as a human being in the world of humans, your humanity, your earthly life destiny, what you have to do and achieve on Earth.

Niflheim: Your illusions and fantasies, where you lie to yourself, your stories and excuses, what is not clear.

Jottunheim: Your obstacles and blocks, what is preventing you from evolving and moving forward, where you are negative and pessimistic.

Svartelfheim: Subconscious drives, bad habits, personal or family memories, the schemes you repeat over and over again, sexual desires.

Hel: Your survival instincts, what makes you feel insecure, your shadow, your traumas and what you disregard and suppress, your personal hell or your darkest zones.

7- The 12 rune yearly spread.

This complex spread combines runes and astrological houses. It enables doing a deep and complete checkup of the current situation or describing the upcoming year. It is undertaken as a talk where relevant questions bring relevant answers. It is a very good spread to see how your inner life and state of being creates your life in the outside world. Twelve runes are chosen and displayed as below. It required a complete knowledge of both runes and astrological houses and being well connected to one's body, heart and soul.

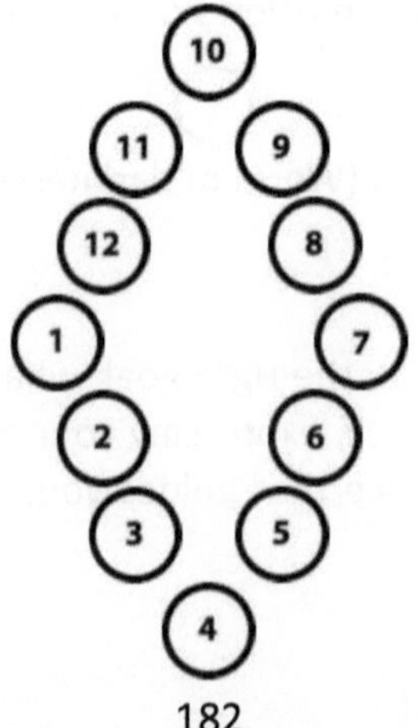

Defining the twelve houses or positions:

House 1: Your state of being in the present situation, your life force, your body and health, your point of departure, how you start things off, your vision of yourself and of life, your intentions and your goals, your motivation, what you show to others, your image, your personality and how you undertake or express your inner fire.

House 2: Your relationship to your body, to pleasure, to money and belongings, your wealth, personal resources, how you can earn money and the money you earn, your financial situation, your habits as a consumer, your budget, your acquisitions, your possessions, your sensuality, your joys and pleasures, your experience of matter and your happiness.

House 3: How you think, learn, analyse things, communicate and adapt to your surroundings, how you set yourself in motions and put things into form, your sales and trading intelligence, your surroundings, your brothers and sisters, the messages you send or receive, what you write, your short travels and your experience of selling.

House 4: Your home, your family legacy, your roots, how you seek wellness and emotional safety, your life at home, family atmosphere, your hidden treasures, your soul, your assets, your mother and how she educated you, your way of expressing motherly love and of taking care of life, your subconscious, your past, your personal history, how you nourish yourself at all levels, the very beginning and the very end of your life.

House 5: Your landmarks, your awareness of who you are, expressing your creative power and the love in your heart, the love you give, your generosity, your father and how he educated you, your way of expressing fatherly love and of showing the way, how you express yourself as a central element and how you put yourself in the highlights, your love life and love relationships, your creations, your first child, your leisure activities, your holydays and how you succeed.

House 6: Your technical intelligence, your health and how you take care of it, how you adapt to the world of matter, how you serve and do your daily work, your work environment, small daily issues, your obligations and constraints, what you repeat over and over again, your limits, your life hygiene, how you organize data and tidy things up, your relationship to numbers, your accountancy, your exams and your relationship to plants and animals.

House 7: How you relate to others, create harmony and participate in society, your behavior towards others, your partnerships, your opposites, what attracts you in others and so what you seek to find in others, your associates and partners, your contracts, your legal affairs, your social life, your faithfulness or unfaithfulness, your major challenge, your experience of marriage.

House 8: Your quest of truth, your initiatory journey, what is hidden or disregarded, and must be revealed, what needs to be destroyed, changed or expelled within you, your fears and dark zones, what spellbinds you, your access to eternity and to awareness of life in the hereafter, hidden treasures within you, legacies and money received from others, crises and major changes, sexual desires and sexual life, enjoying money and the world of matter, your relationship to death and afterlife.

House 9: You quest of expansion and fulfillment, how you explore the world and go out on adventure, how you broaden your vision and find your place in the world, social adaptation, your way of doing business and handling your affairs, the job you have come to do, your relationship to space, to society and to education, how you adapt in space, journeys of body and mind, graduate studies, how you organize your life, your philosophy of life and your relationship to religion, your ideal life, your relationship to foreign lands and to foreigners.

House 10: How you organize your life, your self-realisation path, your ambition, your social status, your career and how it evolves, your long term projects, your achievements and what you build, your relationship to government agencies and to organisations, your inner evolution, your major life lesson, your evolution towards serenity on the path to your deep inner truth., your mother and grandmother.

House 11: Expressing your technological and psychological intelligence, expressing your uniqueness, the help you give and receive, your network, your friends, your customers, how you deal with groups, group activities, teamwork, your projects, what you hope, your second child, your access to inner freedom and the solutions to be implemented so as to become autonomous and free.

House 12: Going from suffering to bliss, your deep inner life, how past life memories and ancestral memories impact you, what nourishes your faith, what makes you dream and feel delighted, what makes you suffer, important health issues, your griefs and sorrows, your experience of betrayal, your major tests and trials, major constraints, what is hidden and secret in your life, your experience of hospitals and clinics, how you flow in life, your psychic health and abilities, your spiritual evolution, your supreme long term goal, your experience of God and mystical experiences, your cosmic awareness, your way of ending things and what you leave behind.

How to deal with this spread:

- You can start with analysing runes placed in the most important houses which are backbone houses 1, 10, 7 and 4. These houses will reveal your state of being, your destiny/career, your home and your partner. Looking at the runes in these houses will enable you to see how vibrant, punchy and lively the spread is.

- You can then add these 4 runes and if the total is above 24, you can then add the two numbers. (e.g. 25 would become 2+5= 7). This rune will describe the global atmosphere and give you both a global vision and a summary of the situation. If the rune found here is also found in one of the 12 houses, then that house will be very important.

- You identify positive, neutral and difficult runes.

- You then interpret each rune in each house taking into account that either the rune will have a great impact of the affairs of the house or the house will help express what the rune symbolizes or on the contrary only allow a limited expression of the rune. To do this rightly, it is advisable to compare the rune and the house and see how they fit or don't fit together. Do the house and the rune want the same thing or are things tense in the sector represented by the house because the two are inconsistent and incompatible. If the rune and the house go well together, this creates luck and helps master what the house represents. Rune one fits well in house 1, rune 2 in house 2 and so on.

- Before doing the spread, you can mentally choose a rune that represents the consultant. This can for example be rune 2 or 3 if the consultant is a woman and rune 4 or 5 is the consultant is a man. You then observe if the chosen rune is in one of the houses and if so, what the house represents will be very important. If the rune representing the consultant isn't in any of the houses, you can then say that the consultant will deal with his or her life unknowingly, without much awareness.

- You can then analyse the six axes, i.e. a house and its opposite house or mirror house. (House 1 and House 7, House 7 and House 1, House 2 and House 8 and House 8 and House 2 and so on). The influence of a rune in a house tends to gradually flow in the opposite house. If you focus on a rune in a house, the rune in the opposite house can give you information about the future of the house you are focusing on. A house can be strengthened or weakened depending on the rune in the opposite house.

- You can then make a synthetic interpretation of the six axes by observing if the two runes in each house pair are similar or totally opposite. You can also add the two runes which will reveal a secret rune that summarizes the axis.

- You can then analyse each rune by comparing it to its two neighbouring runes. It's a bit as if the neighbouring rune popped in to say hello and gave its point of view in whatever is going on in the house concerned. Rune 1 can thus be analysed by taking runes 2 and 12 into account. Rune 2 can thus be analysed by taking runes 1 and 3 into account and so on. Combining runes implies that you are completely familiar with the keywords related to each rune. You then create sentences which combine the key words of the runes you are dealing with, in relation to the houses concerned.

- You can also analyse groups of houses with similar meanings like houses 4, 5 and 7 for life with a partner and love affairs, houses 6, 9 and 10 for work, houses 6, 8 and 12 for health matters and houses 8, 9, 10 and 12 for spiritual life. Houses are related to elements fire (energy and action, houses 1, 5 and 9), earth (organisation, achievements and evolution, houses 2,6 and 10), air (communication, relationships and adapting, houses 3, 7 and 11) and water (emotional and spiritual life, houses 4,8 and 12). You can thus also add the three runes in each fire/earth/air/water house and see for example how the consultant's energy and creative (fire) is getting along during the time span concerned by the spread.

- Finally, it is possible to add a secondary rune into one or more of the houses to give more precise information.

8 – Partnership spread for a specific life sector

This very powerful spread can be done for a specific life sector, for more than one life sector and for specific points. The left side rune represents the wife/woman, her state of being and her real life situation while the right side rune represents the husband/man with his state of being and real life situation related to the previously defined life sector. The middle rune show how the two interact and the result of this interaction. This spread is ideally done together by first choosing together which life sectors are to be dealt with and by writing this down. Then each person places runes in his/her side. The middle runes can be chosen by one of the partners and then by the other. The runes can be displayed as below. Doing this spread requires using your creative power and sincere communication between the two people involved.

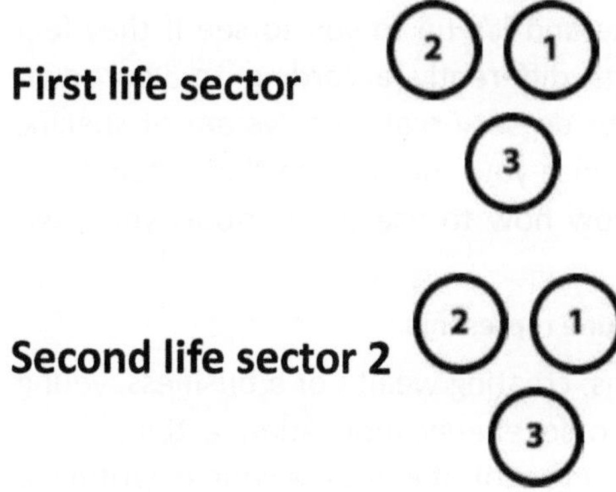

Life sectors or specific points can be:

- Why each partner decided to get together and create a partnership?
- Why is each partner staying and why he/she continues to be involved in the relationship?
- The positive elements brought about by each partner
- What is given or what is received
- What may be an issue, what needs to be improved
- Hopes, fears
- How the environment impacts each partner and the relationship
- How the relationship can be improved
- The body
- The financial situation

- The way of thinking and adapting
- Family environment and its impact
- How the heart feels and the way of expressing one's love
- Health or practical issues
- Relationships, sex life
- Work, spiritual life
- Projects, leisure activities
- How the relationship evolves in the short term
- How the relationship evolves in the long term

Working with « significants » or symbols:

Many people have created tables to establish relationships between different data systems. There aren't right or wrong relationships or matches but just those that work out for you. What follows are therefore suggestions based on my experience and it's up to you to see if they feel right for you and to match things differently according to your own experience if it feels right for you to do so. Creating a system of specific symbols (significants) helps you organize your intuition so that when it has something to say to you, it will know how to use the symbols you have encoded or predefined.

Key words that summarise what each rune represents.

Rune 1 – Newness, something begins, creating wealth or a business, young people, children, craftsmen, sales people, energy, motivation, action.

Rune 2 – Preparing something, spending a lot of energy, a course, writing, a book, seeking for something hidden, a family secret, mother (if old), grandmother, finding the key or information to open a door.

Rune 3 – Evolution in the coming months, formatting, a meeting, an encounter, communication, a message, the surroundings, using intelligence to overcome an issue, adapting, undertaking in nature, thriving life force.

Rune 4 – Work life, responsibilities, a man with authority or the father, territory, important business, managing an empire, building.

Rune 5 – Journeys of body and mind, teachings, studies, counselling, guidance, training, classes, lectures, specialised matters, contracts related to work, relationships or money, philosophical or spiritual issues.

Rune 6 – The torch of desires, commitment within a relationship, choices, love relationships, clothing affairs, youths, colleagues, producing objects, adorning, expressing art, making one's life a work of art.

Rune 7 – Expressing one's gifts and talents, giving and receiving, goals, commitment, enterprise, organizational and strategic intelligence, trips, work missions, results and victories.

Rune 8 – Expressing truth and one's will to create joy, creating harmony and happiness, art and civilization, sharing with others, justice, legal matters, contracts, government and private agencies, putting things back into order.

Rune 9 – Planting seeds, building-site management, dealing with the unexpected, abandoning, the past, ending a work situation, retreating, retiring, doing research, working on structure, meditation, deeply observing, deep beliefs, wisdom, advancing on one's path towards serenity.

Rune 10 – Needs and constraints, hazards of life, opportunities, technical or financial matters, serving life and others, ups and downs, evolution, destiny, cycles, becoming free from enslavement or repetitive schemes, starting off a new cycle.

Rune 11 – Struggle, being centered, loving oneself, deciding, motivation, autonomy, being a master of an art, self control, sports, creations, psychological matters, strengths and weaknesses, resolving a conflict, overcoming blocks, immobility, coldness or the power of love.

Rune 12 – Reaping what one has sowed, managing cycles, health and spiritual matters, genealogical blocks, feeling delight and communion with life, going from suffering to delight and bliss, good harvests.

Rune 13 – Lucidity, insight, significant changes, leaving, departures, breakups, unemployment, undertaking surgery, pains and traumas, eliminating toxins, regeneration, connecting with afterlife.

Rune 14 – Awareness of connections between causes and effects, relationships with friends, games of chance, questioning chance, helping or being helped, solutions and progress, leisure and holidays, high-tech communication devices, working with costumers or within a club, travelling by plane, using free energy, seeking freedom.

Rune 15 – Survival instincts, struggling, protection, safety, earning money, doing business, handling power or expressing one's personal power, being passionate or doing what you feels passion for, sexual intercourse, dealing with your dark zones and your inner saboteur, excess.

Rune 16 – Changes in structures, new products, upheavals, disasters, confinement, sudden changes, moving from one living or working place to another, sudden awareness, enlightenment, risk-taking, demolition and scrapping, reconstructing, building sites, data systems, hi-tech, technological evolution, liberation, modern life, working within a group, unexpected events, surprises, success.

Rune 17 – Fighting to implement justice and order locally, working on one's inner sky or astral chart or Birth Diamond, affairs related to the body, to the soul and to nature, love life, joy, happiness, pleasure, artistic activities, forgiveness, bliss, commitment and victory.

Rune 18 – Emotions, fears, home, family, public places, taking care of people, family legacy, food, nourishment, feeling depressed, ghosts, memory, wellness of body and soul, going from stress to wellness.

Rune 19 – Being consciously in motion, alliances, partnerships, what is in one's heart, expressing love, the couple, support, children, summer, summer holidays, horses, feeling gratitude and experiencing light.

Rune 20 – Healing your subconscious, experiencing a sacred or higher vision, receiving news, messages and legal results that change you, activities related to sound, vibrations and music, multimedia, extremely advanced technology, complex projects, drastic changes in lifestyle, resurrection, newness, expressing one's skills, accomplishing one's destiny, changing the world.

Rune 21 – Matters related to water, work, working with costumers, training, dancing, teaching, obtaining a diploma, important international legal matters, economy, organising life, travelling, going to live elsewhere, foreigners, luck and to harmoniously finishing something.

Rune 22 – Expressing curiosity, uniqueness and inner genius, very far away journeys, what is outstanding, going beyond limits and what seems possible, living freely and happily, a new cycle, exiles, excessive mental energy, genealogical memories pouring into consciousness, confinement in unharmonious mental schemes, confusion, chaos, stupidity.

Rune 23 – Issues related to deep and old causes and changes, to one's very deep truth, to the house of gods or to one's spiritual body where one's living inner god lives, to one's legacy or property, to data structures, to something breaking apart and being gathered again differently, to a departure from an old world or life and to reorganizing.

Rune 24 – Experiencing a comeback, a new start, a new life in a new world, bringing clarity, becoming totally aware, working with light, visibility, a new day, a new cycle, expressing one's creative power, achievements, great success, unity with light.

Matching runes and tarot cards

Rune 1 – Card 1: The Magician
Rune 2 – Card 2: The high Priestess and card 18, The Moon
Rune 3 – Card 3: The Empress
Rune 4 – Card 4: The Emperor
Rune 5 – Card 5: The High Priest or Hierophant
Rune 6 – Card 6: The Lover or Lovers
Rune 7 – Card 7: The Chariot
Rune 8 – Card 8: Justice
Rune 9 – Card 9: The Hermit
Rune 10 – Card 10: The Wheel of Fortune
Rune 11 – Card 11: Strength and card 8, Justice.
Rune 12 - Card 12: The Hanged Man and card 10, The Wheel of Fortune
Rune 13 – Card 13: Death
Rune 14 – Card 14: Temperance
Rune 15 – Card 15: The Devil
Rune 16 - Card 16: The Tower of House of God and card 19, The Sun
Rune 17 – Card 17: The Star and card 8, Justice
Rune 18 - Card 18: The Moon
Rune 19 - Card 19: The Sun and card 6, The Lovers
Rune 20 – Card 20: Judgment, the Archangel or Sacred Vision
Rune 21 - Card 21: The World and card 12, The Hanged Man
Rune 22 – Card 22: The Fool, the Joker or "The Source"

Choosing a significant or symbol that defines who you are: This can be done as follows and what is important is that the symbol you choose to define yourself feels right for you. If you are a woman, you can choose a rune that expresses a state of being, a knowhow or a skill that you possess. The feminine and female aspect of a woman can be represented by runes Thorn, Ken, Wynn and Tiw, in relation with planet Venus or Freya while the more motherly and nourishing aspect of a woman can be related to Runes Ur and Berkano in relation to the Moon and to goddess Frigg. The wise and deep aspects of female energy can be represented by runes Hagl and Eis in relation with planet Saturn. The fairy-like aspect of a woman can be represented by runes Yer, Tiw and Lagu in relation with planet Neptune. The shamanic and spellbinding aspect of a woman can be represented by runes Eih, Eolh, Mann and Othala in relation with planet Pluto.

If you are a man, you can choose one of the runes that can be matched with one of the numerous male characters in Nordic mythology or you can choose a rune that expresses a state of being, a knowhow or a skill that you possess. The masculine and male aspect of a man can be represented by runes Fehu and Gyfu in relation with planet Mars. The more fatherly aspect of man can be represented by runes Ass, Raidh, Eh and Daeg in relation with the Sun and with Jupiter. The angel or technological aspect of man in relation with planet Uranus can be represented by runes Peordh, Sigl and Mann. The shamanistic aspect of man related to planet Pluto can be represented by rune Mann.

Significants of the various age groups:
Children from 0 to 8 years old: Rune 18: Berkano
Youths from 12 to 20 years old: Rune 1: Fehu
Men from 20 to 35 years old: Rune 7: Gyfu
Wemen from 20 to 35 years old: Rune 3: Thorn.
Men from 35 to 60 years old: Rune 4: Ass
Wemen from 35 to 60 years old: Rune 8: Wynn
Men older than 60 years old: Rune 9: Hagl
Wemen older than 60 years old: Rune 2: Ur

Significants related to work and work life:
Major significant for work: Ass
Secondary significant for work: Gyfu and Hagl
A letter related to work: Thorn and Ass
A contract related to work: Wynn and Ass
A choice or love relationship related to work: Ken and Ass
A block related to work: Eis and Ass or Yer and Ass
A professional exam: Wynn and Mann
A new and stable job: Fehu and Ass A well-payed job: Eolh and Ass
A part time job: Ass and Ken
Important work achievements: Daeg and Ass
A brilliant victory: Gefu and Eh or Tiw and Daeg
Great success in one's job: Daeg and Eh. Fame: Eh and Mann
Celebrity: Eh and Lagu

Significants related to various specific jobs:

An expert: Ass and Raidh
A teacher or adviser: Raidh

Someone working in the building industry: Hagl, Sigl and Ass.
Techmen or technicians: Nyd
A notary: Wynn and Eis
A head secretary: Thorn and Isa (communication and mastering)
An administration supervisor: Ass and Wynn
A farmer: Hagl and Eih
A computer supervisor: Ass and Peordh
A TV/radio presenter: Peordh and Mann
A doctor: Raidh and Yer
A wall builder, construction worker or mason: Fehu and Hagl
A building supervisor: Isa and Hagl or Isa and Sigl or Ass and Sigl
A lawyer: Ur and Wynn
A smith or someone working with metal: Eolh

Significants related to money and finance:
The significant that represents the creation of wealth: Fehu
The main significant that represents money: Eolh
The secondary significants that represent money/wealth: Nyd, Tiw and Ass

Significants of studies, training and books:
The major significants: Ur and Raidh
The minor significants: Thorn and Hagl
Success with exams and obtention of a degree/diploma: Lagu and Mann

Significants of trade and communication:
The major significant: Nyd
The minor significants: Fehu and Mann
A letter: Thorn. A phone call: Peordh.
A text message or sms: Thorn and Peordh. A mail: Mann
From abroad: Lagu

Significants of Home and family:
The major significant: Berkano
The minor significant: Othala
Moving to a new home: Berkano and Sigl or Raidh and Sigl
The house: Berkano. An old house: Berkano and Hagl

Significants of various emotions:
Rune 6: Feelings and desires
Runes 3 and 15: Passion, violent drives, impulses

Rune 10, 13 and 15: Stress, anguish, fear
Rune 8, 17 and 19: Joy, pleasure, happiness
Rune 18: Anxiety, feeling frightened but also wellness
Rune 19 and 8: Sharing with love and happiness
Rune 21 and 24: Thriving, blossoming, completeness, complete happiness

Significants of creations, achievements or works of art:
The major significant: Isa
Minor significants: Eh and Fehu

Significants of sports:
The major significant: Gyfu
Minor significants: Fehu and Eh

Significants of health:
The major significant: Yer
Minor significants: Nyd can symbolize global health, Eih can represent an investigation requiring X-rays or surgery, Ur and Tyr can represent the body and Sigl can represent an emergency.

Significants of love life and partnerships:
The major significant: Ken
The minor significant: Eh
A new encounter: Fehu and Ken
A child soon to be born: Berkano and Fehu
Breakdown of a relationship: Eih and Ken
Adultery or treason: Eolh and Ken
Love at first sight: Sigl and Ken
Passionate relationship: Thorn and Ken or Ken and Eolh
An encounter while on a trip: Ken and Raidh
Marriage: Ken and Wynn

Significants of art:
The major significant: Ken. Minor significants: Wynn

Significants of sexuality:
The major significant: Thorn
Minor significants: Eolh

Significants of change and transformations:
The major significant: Eih
Minor significants: Nyd, Sigl, Mann and Othala

Significants of traveling:
The major significant: Raidh
Minor significants: Gyfu, Eh, Lagu and Ing
Means of transport: Gyfu if it's manmade, Eh for raveling on horseback
Traveling far away: Lagu and Ing

Significants of various transport means or solutions:
Traveling by foot: Hagl or Eih
Traveling on a bicycle: Nyd and on a motorcycle/motorbike: Mann
Traveling by car: Gyfu
Traveling by truck: Raidh
Traveling by high-speed train: Hagl and Nyd
Traveling by airplane: Peordh and Ing
Traveling by spaceship: Mann and Ing
Traveling by boat: Lagu

Significants of various public buildings:
The major significants: Hagl, Sigl and Wynn
Rune representing the public: Berkano
A company: Hagl and Fehu
A bank: Hagl and Eolh
A shop Hagl and Thorn
A nursery or a swimming pool: Hagl and Berkano
A saloon: Hagl and Ken
A palace: Hagl and Daeg
A garage: Hagl and Gyfu
A pharmacy: Hagl and Nyd
A leisure place, nature: Hagl and Tiw
A laboratory or a morgue: Hagl and Eih
A police station: Hagl and Eis
A shopping mall: Hagl and Mann
A training center: Hagl and Raidh
An administrative building: Hagl and Wynn
A court or jail: Hagl and Eolh
A sea port: Hagl and Lagu
An air port: Hagl and Peordh. A spaceport: Hagl with Peordh or Mann
A logistics center: Hagl and Sigl
A cinema or TV room: Hagl and Mann
A hospital: Hagl and Yer

Significants of time:
The beginning of time: Runes 1, 10 and 24.
The end of time: Runes 9, 13, 22 and 23.

The various concepts of time: Linear time where one moment follow another, related to Chronos in Greek Mythology, can be represented by Hagl. The time concept called Kairos which is instant time synchronized with Necessity, the right action at the right moment and the time where past, present and future meet can be represented by runes Peordh, Sigl and Mann.

The past: Runes 2 and 18.
The far away past: Runes 9 and 13.
The present moment: Runes 1 and 7.
The near future: Rune 20.
The future: Runes 14 and 16.
The far away future: Rune 17.

Significants of different times of the day:
Dawn = Fehu and Daeg. Dusk = Wynn and Othala
Daytime = Sigl and Daeg. Nighttime = Berkano and Othala

Seasons:
Spring runes: Fehu, Ur, Thorn, Ken, Gyfu and Daeg.
Summer runes: Ass, Raidh, Gyfu, Yer, Berkano and Eih.
Autumn runes: Wynn, Nyd, Eih, Eolh, Ing and Othala.
Winter runes: Hagl, Eis, Peordh, Sigl, Tiw and Lagu.
Feoh, Ken and Eih, combined with the rune representing a season, can represent the beginning of a season, midseason and the end of a season.
Next winter = Hagl and Peordh. Next summer = Eh and Peordh.

Hours of the day: The 24 runes can be related to the 24 hours of the day. You can either start by matching rune 1 with sunrise hour or do as the Germans did, by matching the beginning of the day at sunset and match rune one with the hour of sunset.

Seven days of the week: Each day of the week has a specific vibration and can be related to the moon, planet or star after which it is named. Specific runes can be related to each day of the week. When it is possible to do so, it is auspicious to do something on the day of the week that symbolizes that something. Lets have a look at this in more detail.

Monday: This day is related to Nordic goddesses Frigg, Mani, Hler, Vé and Erda, to the Moon, to water and to runes 2, Ur and 18, Berkano. It is a good day to make things flow, to feel inspired and to focus on family affairs, wellness, emotional bonds and magic.

Tuesday: This day is related to Nordic gods Tiw/Tyr and to Hel, to Mars and Pluto, to fire and to runes 1, 7, 11, 13, 15, 17 and 23. It is a good day to use one's strength and to spend energy, to feel motivated and to focus on action, combat, efficiency and victory.

Wednessday: This day is related to Nordic gods Odin, Kari, Loki and Wald, to Mercury and Uranus, to air and earth and to runes 1, 3, 4, 10, 14 and 16. It is a good day to speak and write, to do paperwork, to learn, to trade, to adapt, to find solutions, to focus on health and to do magic.

Thursday: This day is related to Nordic God Thor, to Jupiter, to fire, air and water and to runes 4, 5, 7, 19, 20 and 21. It is a good day to do business, to do a lot of work, to travel, to teach and to focus on wealth and prosperity.

Friday: This day is related to Nordic gods and goddesses Freya and Freyr, Hlin and Hnossi, to Venus and Neptune, to earth, air and water and to runes 6, 8, 12 and 17. It is a good day to focus on relationships, art, beauty, pleasure, joy, love and social activities.

Saturday: This day is related to Nordic gods Heimdall, Rig, Ull and to the three Norns, to Saturn, to earth and to runes 9, 11 and 13. It is a good day to do hard work, to handle a building site, to kook inwards, to meditate and to focus on one's destiny and inner peace.

Sunday: This day is related to Nordic gods Baldr, Sol, Idun, Iduna and Villi, to the Sun, to fire and to runes 11, 19 and 24. It is a good day express love and creative power, to define and focus on what is really important, on one's goals, on one's vision and on one's spiritual life. It is a good day to experience inner light and one's inner living god.

The 24 half runic months: A year can be divided into 24 fortnights. Each rune can be related to a fortnight in various manners. The correct solution is the one you feel is right for you. One possibility is to start at spring equinox (usually march 21rst) and to connect the first rune with the first fifteen degrees of the astrological sign of Aries and to move forward in time from there. A clever way to do so is to connect the first 12 runes with the first fifteen degrees of each astrological signs and then the second 12 runes with the last fifteen degrees of each astrological sign. Rune 13 would then be related to the last fifteen degree of Aries and so on.

The 12 months of the year with their matching planets, gemstones, animals and runes.

Month of Aries, planet mars, red jasper and hematite, the ram: Rune Fehu.

Month of Taurus, planets Venus and moon, amber, sapphire, carnelian, the cow: Rune Ur.

Month of Gemini, planet Mercury, blue calcite, chalcedony, crows and dogs: Rune Thorn.

Month of Crab or Cancer, the Moon, moon stone and pink quartz, turtles, owls and cats: Rune Ass.

Month of Leo, the Sun, sun stone, agate, opals and diamonds, lions and swans: Runes Raidh, Eh, and Daeg.

Month of Virgo, planet Mercury, sardonyx gems, monkeys, insects and rodents: Rune Nyd.

Month of Libra, planets Venus and Saturn, kunzite, rhodonite, turquoise, does and deers, lovely birds: Runes Wynn and Tiw/Tyr.

Month of Scorpio, planets Pluto and Mars, flint and obsidian, snakes, scorpions, crocodiles and eagles, scavengers: Runes Eih and Eolh.

Month of Sagittarius, planet Jupiter, jade, imperial topaz and goldstone aventurine, horses and elks: Runes Raidh and Lagu.

Month of Capricorn, planets Saturn and Mars, shungite, onyx and black tourmaline, goats, bears and buffaloes: Rune Hagl.

Month of Aquarius, planets Uranus and Saturn, lapis lazuli and labradorite, seagulls: Runes Peordh and Sigl.

Month of Aquarius, planets Uranus and Saturn, lapis lazuli and labradorite, seagulls: Runes Peordh and Sigl.

Month of Pisces, planets Neptune and Venus, sugelite and amethyst, fish, dolphins and whales: Runes Yer, Mann et Lagu.

You can also match the first 12 runes with the first 12 months of the year.

Other times:
The beginning of a new time: Runes Fehu and Daeg
The end of time: Eih
Time in motion: Raidh
Time standing still: Eis
Logical cycles of time: Nyd, Yer
The evolution of time: Nyd and Hagl.
Going from one time or place to another: Peordh

Synchronized time: Peordh and Sigl
Questioning time: Hagl and Sigl
Eternity: Eis and Eih
Holidays/week-end: Tiw and Eh
Summer holidays: Tiw and Eh
Winter holidays: Tiw and Peordh.
Meteorology: Peordh.

Significants of new technologies:
The major significant: Mann
Minor significants: Peordh and Sigl.

Significants of projects:
The major significant: Gyfu and Peordh
Complex projects: Sigl and Mann

Significants of spiritual development:
The major significants: Hagl, Yer and Sigl
Minor significants: Eih, Peordh, Sigl, Eh and Mann. Lagu and Daeg represent at their deepest level unity with God.

Slow and static runes verses fast and mobile runes: If you imagine that the 24 runes were about to race with each other and that the signal was given to start running, you would then have a list showing the fastest and slowest runes. Ur, Hagl, Isa, Yer, Tiw and Berkano are slow and they slow time down. Mann, Sigl, Peordh, Gyfu, Fehu, Nyd, Ing, Eh and Eih move forward, bring motion to a spread and speed things up.

Difficult and complicated runes: Thorn, Hagl, Nyd, Eis, Yer, Eih, Eolh, Sigl, Ing and Othala.

Positive and pleasant runes: Fehu, Raidh, Ken, Gyfu, Wynn, Yer, Peordh, Tiw, Berkano, Eh, Mann, Lagu, Ing and Daeg.

How do you use significants? You can either choose the significant of your question (which is a rune) from a second set of runes and place that rune in front of you or just define it mentally and see if it comes up in the spread. That special rune represents your question and the matters you are concerned about. Its position if it appears in the spread, and it should, will enable to make a specific interpretation.

Chapter 5: Learning to use runes as magical symbols.

Introduction: This chapter introduces runic magic as it was practiced by Germans. There are specialized books on this subject so you can refer to them if you want to go further. Magic was part of daily life for both German and Viking men and wemen. It was part of a global system of religious beliefs and practices. It was deeply linked to knowledge of the laws that rule nature and human destiny. Magic was part of a way of life. For men the art of fighting was at the centre of their lives. For wemen, who were highly considered and respected, the art of health, wellness, connecting with one's inner joy and creating happiness was crucial. Until guns were invested, magic and fighting went together. One of the key elements in magic was the ability to use extra sensorial perceptions so as to perceive subtle invisible forces such as those that surround people and telluric forces that flow on the earth. Nowadays, telluric forces are handled through subjects such as geobiology and Fend Shui. Magic was also closely related to dreams and to what is nowadays called "out of body" experiences or astral travel. Finally, magic implied a very strong relationship with the Nordic gods and goddesses who were questioned and whose help was asked for so as to find and implement solutions. In a hostile environment, magic brought both comfort for the soul and practical solutions to adapt.

What is magic: The first foundation of true magic firstly implies being aware of "Necessity" or of what is required at each moment so that life can flow the right way. It also requires seeing what is possible and the potential existing within a person or situation. Then, thanks to a special state of being where you are totally connected with your heart, with the earth and with the sky, in a state of harmony, joy, calmness and alertness, you make what is possible and what is right come true, you allow Necessity to manifest. The second foundation of magic is being aware that every action (thought, belief, behaviour and action) has a consequence. The third foundation of magic is humbleness and a sense of service towards life as you are using power lent to you by your inner God. Magic derives from using creative power by combining the power of intention, that is will and concentration, with focus and visualisation. It is accomplished though the power of love with faith combined with action in the form of rituals.

In ancient times, magic consisted in creating a strong and clear intention, in gathering sufficient energy and then in using the magical power of visualization with faith, poetry and runic symbols to make this intention manifest in a certain manner. Runes where then symbols filled through faith with magical energy so as to produce an effect in the visible world. True magic enabled people to create intentionally, to change something, to make an event happen or to avoid it happening. Nordic sagas include many stories showing the use of magic and we will see some examples later on. Magic was officially used until Christianity arrived. It was then gradually forbidden and banned by the Christian church and it almost completely disappeared. It started emerging again only a few decades ago, with a new understanding backed by quantic physics and without any religious fanatism. Runes are forms, shapes and patterns. Modern quantic physics explains that every form emits wave forms and that each wave produces a specific energy, a specific motion and thus produces a certain effect on its environment. This effect is then amplified by a ritual that sets in motion the power of intention, faith and visualization.

The importance of intention: At the very beginning of any magical action and of any desire to create something, there is an intention. It is crucial to be clearly aware of what you want to do and why you want to do it and thus to clearly define your goal but also to feel that you, your goal and what you are about to do are in harmony with life and with you evolution.

The required structure of any magical action:
1- Connexion with your heart and synchronisation with the life's will.
2- Awareness of signs and coincidences
3- Strengthening your will power and setting it in motion
4- Strengthening and using your ability to focus and concentrate
5- Strengthening and using your ability to imagine and visualize
6- Strengthening and using the power of faith
7- Strengthening and using your knowledge of each rune by feeling it, by feeling its effects with your body, mind and soul, by mastering the use of keywords and by being able to connect with a rune so that it vibrates within you.
8- Strengthening and using your ability to create poetry and put words together so as to create a strong impact.
9- Daily practice

Plants are sometimes used by drinking them mixed with blessed water or by burning them.

Structure of a rune or talisman making ritual:
1- Choosing the right moment to undertake the ritual.
2- Putting on special magician clothes and jewellery.
3- Defining and preparing the sacred space (Ve) where the ritual will take place.
4- Connecting with your heart and synchronizing with cosmic will.
5- Implementing slow and deep breathing.
6- Undertaking a ritual to protect and isolate the sacred space from any disturbing forces. This can be done by visualizing yourself in a sphere of white or blue light.
7- **Opening the cycle ritual:** Prayer to the god related to what you want to create. Defining and speaking out intention and goal with the request that it manifests in life at the best possible moment.
8- Connexion with the four elements, with your life force and with the energy of life.
9- Clear visualization of the rune or runes used in connection with the set goal, within the third eye, preferably in red.
10- Chanting out the name and identity of the rune or runes using phrases that make up a poem.
11- Engraving the chosen rune or runes on a specific object
12- Eventually adding color and waiting for it to dry up
13- Placing the rune or rune in their pre-prepared bag or box.
14- Sometime later, a birth ritual in undertaken using a ritualistic sentence where the rune is reminded of its name and given its mission.
15- Protection ritual and placing the engraved object in its pre-defined place.
16- **Closing the cycle ritual:** Expressing thanks and gratitude and closing sentence.
17- Undertaking specific actions in your life in connection with your initial intention and goal so as to achieve it and expressing gratitude when it is achieved.

The ritual should be done from beginning to end without any break as otherwise, it may not work. Kormak's saga shows an example about this. Germans believed that speaking out loud the name of a rune and engraving it a certain number of times increased its magical effects in a specific way. Doing it twice overcomes obstacles or binds two things. Doing it three times creates change through connection of body, heart (soul) and spiritual body. Doing it five times has a healing effect.

Doing it seven times helps achieve a specific goal and sets sexual energy in motion. Doing it eight times helps master an event in the world or experience astral travel. Nine times is for spiritual vision of truth and to amplify the power of faith while 12 times is to manifest good harvests.

How to dress when undertaking a ritual or creating a talisman: It may be auspicious, from a psychological point of view, to dress in a specific manner when performing a ritual, with clothes dedicated to rituals. What is important is to feel well, focused and happy with the clothes you wear. German magicians or Viktar wore leather shoes, Nordic style pants or dresses that were often red, a leather belt, a white or dark blue top and a dark blue coat with a hood. They also wore a wooden or metal bracteate or necklet engraved with runes and sometimes a ring also engraved with runes. Some rituals were done barefoot and some naked. They used a rune engraved and blessed wooden stick, a knife, a punch, a horn, a wooden mug and powders to colour the runes or talismans. Each object was blessed by a magical sentence and by sacred signs or forms drawn in the air like Thor's hammer or the Cross of Life.

Magic with daily life objects: Runes were sometimes just used to identify the owner of an object. But most times, they were used for magic. Magic was used in daily life in a very practical manner by engraving runes and by charging the engraved objects with a specific intention and energy so as to turn them into sacred and magic objects. Safety and protection were one of the major concerns. The magician or Vikti programmed the object with a specific vibration and then activated it when required. Objects could either be chosen amongst daily life objects or they could me made especially for magical purposes. Such objects are then called amulets or talismans. Germans changed their war shields into magic objects so as to be protected against enemy strikes. In Iceland, talismans even were created to win at games. Rings and wrist rings of different sizes were also engraved with runes and changed into magical objects through specific rituals. They were either worn or cast into swords or spears.

The anchor technique: Doing magic this way is a form of self-hypnosis. It calls upon a technique called the anchor technique which is often used in modern times by Eriksonian hypnotherapy and NLP. An amulet anchors an intention, an energetic process and thought forms in the world of matter. It then becomes a sort of living program and should be considered as any life form.

Before creating an amulet for someone else, it is auspicious to master the creation process and its magic used for yourself. With the help of your creative abilities, you can create all sorts of talismans.

A famous runic talisman: A combined rune created by rotating rune 15 in the four directions, has often been used as a talisman to be protected, to implement significant changes, to become invisible, to have a happy sex life, to live an exciting life and for financial abundance. The same 4 directional pictogram can be created using runes 8, 11, 17 or 21.

Magic in buildings: Houses and buildings were made using natural resources such as earth, wood and stone. Germans were very skilled at woodwork and carpentry. House walls were often structured and consolidated with wooden beams. Roofs were built using complex woodwork techniques. Runes were incorporated into wall and roof structures. This had several purposes. The first one was to easily recognize the house. The second was to protect it. The third was to attract harmony, abundance and wellness. Runes were sometimes combined to strengthen the power of runic symbols, to produce a nice visual aspect or a logo but also to hide them from Christian eyes. After the fifteenth century however, using magic to protect houses gradually ceased to be done. Until recently, engraving runes in houses became purely adornment or was used to write the name or initials of the original owner. As global awareness increases on the planet and as Feng-shui, the Chinese art of creating harmony in a home is spreading all over the world, the use of runes as wave forms in house structures is becoming more and more widespread.

Here is an example of a house in the French town called Strasbourg where you can see on the facade runes Ken ᚲ, Gyfu ᚷ, Isa ᛁ, Eolh ᛉ, Ing ◇ and three Thor's hammers (T).

Runes and cathedrals: Runes have surprisingly been used for centuries by master carpenters and their apprentices when they built cathedrals. Building a cathedral requires complex framework and the builders used a special marking system probably inherited from German builders, who were experts in woodwork. Marks were engraved on each piece of framework to help assembly it.

Some examples of these marks are the franc |, the countermark ᚱ, the goose claw ᛉ or ᛀ, the snake tongue ↑, the hook ᚱ, the double hook ᚠ and the rise ↑. There were also marks called in France "la plumée de dévers" ᛗ which was a Daeg rune, the cutting mark ᚷ which combines runes Eis and Gyfu, the Raide mark ᚷ and the Othala rune ᛟ. These marks showed both the final location, the order in which each beam was put into place and special technical tasks like for example trimming that were done on a specific beam. They enabled assembling the framework correctly on the building site. Did the master carpenters know they were using runes? At a certain level they certainly did.

If you go to the French city of Orleans and stop at number 36 rue de la Charpenterie or Carpentry Street, you will see a stone engraving on a wall pillar. If you look more closely, you will see the marking system (called the rainette alphabet) used by master carpenters. A rainette was the tool used to engrave the marks which is why it's called the rainette alphabet.

Tuning into a certain state of being and learning to know each rune using runes chants and runic postures: Chants called "Gald" or "Galdr" played an important role in runic magic. Many can be found in Nordic sagas. In the 1930s, German rune masters created new Galdrs for most runes. They also imagined body postures called stadhas. Then German rune masters Marby, Krummer and Karl Spiesberger created a specific runic yoga to connect with earth and sky and to learn how to channel energy within the body. As a person chanted the rune song and placed himself or herself in the defined posture, he could feel, experience and memorize the energy of each rune and observe the flow of energy both in the body and coming in and out of the body. Doing this also strengthened the efficiency of a person's intention before engraving a rune. You can find more information about this on internet for example here http://www.sunnyway.com/runes/stadha.html

Some historical examples of runic magic: Testimonies relating the use of Nordic magic can be found for example in the Ynglingasaga saga or in Hordr's saga. One of the most famous and well known stories where magic plays a very important role is found in the saga of Norwegian farmer, poet and rune master Egil Skallagrimsson, who immigrated to Iceland and who died in the year 990 AD. One day, when he was at a banquet or party, someone gave him a mug filled with a poisonous drink.

Being always alert, he engraved a runic formula, possibly ALU on the mug and cut his hand to pour a few droplets of his blood to activate the runes. The mug immediately split itself in half! Further on in the saga, he was invited by a man whose daughter was ill. He discovered a piece of whale bone engraved with runes under her bed, placed there by the lady's lover. But either the runes were not engraved correctly or the wrong runes were used. Egil scrapped off the rune carvings, engraved and tainted health runes and the young lady quickly recovered her health.

Earlier in this book, I mentioned that runes were more than likely created during the first century AD but that the first writings enabling to know their names, their properties and their use were written 800 years later. The most important of these writings is the Nordic poem called Havamal written between the year 900 and the year 1300. In a specific part of this poem called Runatal, there are 18 verses describing 18 possibilities to use runes in a magical way by engraving them and by chanting them to activate them. Runatal is the most explicit testimony we have about runic magic. It is said that Odin himself inspired its creation and spoke though the poet. It is tempting to relate each of the 18 verses to either the first 18 runes of the original Futhark or to the 16 Viking runes of the Viking Futhark. If you read the comments placed below each verse, you will see that the relationship between these 18 verses and the first 18 Tarot cards are quite surprising. These 18 verses reveal what the men and wemen of past times were concerned about and where they focused their attention. They describe human nature and are not at all outdated. I don't know why there aren't 24 verses…**Here are the 18 Runatal verses in three languages.**

	Scandinavian	English	French
1	Ljóð ek þau kann er kannat þjóðans kona ok mannskis mögr hjálp heitir eitt en þat þér hjálpa mun við sökum ok sorgum ok sútum görvöllum	I know the songs that no ruler's wife knows, nor anyone's son the first is called "Help" and it will help you with disputes and griefs and absolutely all sorrows.	Je connais les chansons Qu'aucune femme de dirigeant ne connait Ni aucun fils de qui que ce soit La première est nommée « aide » Et elle vous aidera avec les disputes et les chagrins et avec absolument tout ce qui vous rend triste
	Comment: Helps recover enthusiasm, joy of living and finding smart solutions to help things work out		
2	Þat kann ek annat er þurfu ýta synir þeir er vilja læknar lifa	I know a second which the sons of men need, those who want to live as physicians	J'en connais une deuxième Tous les fils des hommes en ont besoin Surtout ceux qui veulent savoir comment soigner et guérir
	Comment: Helps being a therapist, healing with plants and with runic magic.		

3	Þat kann ek it þriðja ef mér verðr þörf mikil hapts við mína heiptmögu eggjar ek deyfi minna andskota bítat þeim vápn né velir	I know the third if great need befalls me for a fetter for my enemy, I can blunt the edges of my enemies, so that their weapons and wiles do not wound	J'en connais une troisième Qui entrave tout ennemi Elle émousse les lames des épées ennemies Leurs armes et leurs ruses ne provoquent plus de blessures
	Comment: Helps neutralize weapons, evade guiles and adapt.		
4	Þat kann ek it fjórða ef mér fyrðar bera bönd at bóglimum svá ek gel at ek ganga má sprettr mér af fótum fjöturr en af höndum hapt	I know the fourth if men put fetters on my limbs, I sing so that I can go, break bonds from my feet and bond from my hands.	J'en connais une quatrième Si des hommes entravent mes membres Je chante afin de pouvoir m'en aller En brisant toute entrave De mes pieds ou de mes mains
	Comment: Helps suppress any impediment to motion, organization and action		
5	Þat kann ek it fimmta ef ek sé af fári skotinn flein í fólki vaða flýgra hann svá stinnt at ek stöðvigak ef ek hann sjónum of sék	I know the fifth if I see a spear, shot in malice to fly into a host, it does not fly so strongly that I cannot stop it, if I catch sight of it.	J'en connais une cinquième Si je vois une lance mal intentionnée envers un invité Elle ne va jamais assez vite Et je peux l'arrêter Si je la vois voler
	Comment: Helps stop or deviate a moving object (projectile) or a negative thought form.		
6	Þat kann ek it sétta ef mik særir þegn á rótum rams viðar ok þann hal er mik heipta kveðr þann eta mein heldr en mik	I know the sixth if a warrior wounds me with the root of a strong tree and calls forth hatreds from me, then the harms eat the man and not me.	J'en connais une sixième Si un guerrier cherche à me blesser ou me maudire Avec des runes gravées sur les racines d'un arbre La personne qui souhaitait me nuire C'est elle qui aura des problèmes et pas moi
	Comment: Helps mirror what is sent so that it returns to the sender. In occult sciences this is called the returning show wave.		
7	Þat kann ek it sjaunda ef ek sé hávan loga sal um sessmögum brennrat svá breitt at ek honum bjargigak þann kann ek galdr at gala	I know the seventh if I see a high hall to burn around my table-companions, it does not burn so bright that I cannot save it, when I can sing the spell.	J'en connais une septième Si dans le hall de hautes flammes Menacent de bruler mes compagnons Aussi chaud et étendu soit le feu Ma chanson saura l'éteindre
	Comment: Helps master fire and to extinguish it.		
8	Þat kann ek it átta er öllum er nytsamligt at <u>nema</u> hvars hatr vex með hildings sonum þat má ek bœta brátt	I know the eighth which is useful for all to take wherever hatred grows among the sons of the prince, I can quickly cure it.	J'en connais une huitième Très bénéfique pour tout le monde Si un guerrier éprouve de la haine dans son cœur Ce sortilège le soulagera et le guérira
	Comment: Helps restoring calm, harmony, love, joy and order within. Relief if brought by looking at the truth face to face, by accepting and forgiving and by being in harmony with the order of life.		

9	Þat kann ek it níunda ef mik nauðr um stendr at bjarga fari mínu á floti vind ek kyrri vági á ok svæfik allan sæ	I know the ninth if I need to save my ship afloat I can calm the wind on the wave and lull the whole sea to sleep.	J'en connais une neuvième Si j'ai besoin de protéger mon navire lors d'une tempête Je peux calmer le vent et adoucir les vagues Et amener la mer vers le sommeil
	Comment: Helps bring water to a state of calmness and appease storms		
10	Þat kann ek it tíunda ef ek sé túnriðir leika lopti á ek svá vinnk at þeir villir fara sinna heimhama sinna heimhuga	I know the tenth if I see witches playing in the air I can so arrange it that they go astray from their proper shapes and proper thoughts.	J'en connais une dixième Si des fantômes, sorcières ou entités chevauchent à travers le ciel Le sortilège que je chante les égare Leur forme et leurs pensées se perdent et se dispersent
	Comment: Helps push aside any harmful visible or invisible life forms or thought forms		
11	Þat kann ek it ellipta ef ek skal til orrostu leiða langvini undir randir ek gel en þeir með ríki fara heilir hildar til heilir hildi frá koma þeir heilir hvaðan	I know the eleventh if I must lead old friends to battle. I sing under the shields, and they go victoriously: safe to the battle, safe from the battle, they come safe from everywhere.	J'en connais une onzième Si j'emmène de bons camarades au combat Et que je chante ce sortilège derrière mon bouclier Ils se battent victorieusement Et reviennent sain et sauf
	Comment: Helps fighting efficiently without being wounded		
12	Þat kann ek it tólpta ef ek sé á tré uppi váfa virgilná svá ek ríst ok í rúnum fák at sá gengr gumi ok mælir við mik	I know the twelfth if I see up in a tree a hanged corpse swinging, I carve and color the runes that the man moves and speaks with me.	J'en connais une douzième Si je vois un pendu se balançant dans un arbre Quand je grave et colore ces runes Il descend de l'arbre et parle avec moi
	Comment: Helps revive a hanged man and communicate with genealogical memories		
13	Þat kann ek it þrettánda ef ek skal þegn ungan verpa vatni á munat hann falla þótt hann í fólk komi hnígra sá halr fyr hjörum	I know the thirteenth if I will throw water on a young warrior, he cannot fall, though he may come to battle, the man does not fall before swords.	J'en connais une treizième Si je verse de l'eau sur le fils d'un guerrier Il ne tombera pas même dans les pires batailles Et sera protégé des épées et projectiles
	Comment: Helps protect warriors and successfully defend a person or a place		
14	Þat kann ek it fjórtánda ef ek skal fyrða liði telja tíva fyrir ása ok álfa ek kann allra skil fár kann <u>ósnotr</u> svá	I know the fourteenth if I must reckon up a troop before gods and men, I know the details of all the Æsir and the Elves the unwise man knows that not at all.	J'en connais une quatorzième Si je dois prendre en compte un groupe, un réseau une armée Sous le regard des dieux et des hommes Je connais les détails de chacun La différence entre les ases et les elfes. L'homme ignorant ne sait rien de tout ça
	Comment: Helps see the psychological structure and uniqueness of a person and to manage a group or network		

15	Þat kann ek it fimmtánda er gól Þjóðreyrir dvergr fyr Dellings durum afl gól hann ásum en álfum frama hyggju Hroptatý	I know the fifteenth, which Thjothreyrir sang, the dwarf, before the doors of Dellingr: He sang the might of the gods, the courage of the elves, the understanding of Hroptaty.	J'en connais une quinzième Le nain Thjodraerir la chanta devant la porte de Delling (l'aube) Il chanta la puissance des dieux Le courage des elfes L'intelligence de Hroptaty (Odin)
	Comment: Helps express courage, strategic intelligence and personnal power		
16	Þat kann ek it sextánda ef ek vil ins svinna mans hafa geð alt ok gaman hugi ek hverfi hvítarmri konu ok sný ek hennar öllum sefa	I know the sixteenth if I wish to have all the heart and pleasure of a cunning girl, I turn the feelings of the white-armed woman, and I change the whole of her mind.	J'en connais une seizième Si je veux obtenir le cœur et le plaisir d'une fille rusée J'oriente les sentiments De la jeune fille aux bras blancs Et je modifie sa disposition d'esprit
	Comment: Helps seduce by putting a spark in someone's heart		
17	Þat kann ek it sjautjánda at mik mun seint firrask it manunga man ljóða þessa mun þú Loddfáfnir lengi vanr vera þó sé þér góð ef þú getr nýt ef þú nemr þörf ef þú þiggr	I know the seventeenth, that the youthful maid will never avoid me Loddfafnir, you will be lacking these charms for a long time, though it be good for you if you get them, useful if you take them, needful if you receive them.	J'en connais une dix-septième Pour que la jeune femme reste aimante et ne cherche jamais à m'éviter Loddfafnir, ces sortilèges te manqueront longtemps Ils te seraient pourtant très utiles et bénéfiques
	Comment: Helps make a partner stay et create a happy life		
18	Þat kann ek it átjánda er ek æva kennik mey né manns konu alt er betra er einn um kann þat fylgir ljóða lokum <u>nema</u> þeiri einni er mik armi verr eða mín systir sé	I know the eighteenth which I never teach to maid or man's wife, everything is better when one person understands it, it belongs at the ending of spells to none but she alone who is wrapped in my arm or is my sister.	J'en connais une dix-huitième Que je n'enseigne jamais aux jeunes filles ou aux épouses Sa place est à la fin du sortilège Je la réserve à l'amour que je serre dans mes bras Ou pour la chanter à ma sœur
	Comment: Only used with very close relationships to nourish, maintain and strengthen emotional bonds.		

White magic or black magic: A person doing white magic serves others, life, the Source of all Life and the Universe. Attention is focused on what is positive and on what creates happiness and inner peace. Such a person is aware of eternal life, of life in the world hereafter and of the returning path to light. Being connected to the Source of all life and thus receiving abundant energy from there though the heart, he or she has no need or desire to go and take energy from other people.

Such a person puts aside personal desires and will and acts with humbleness to do what must be done. Other people's freedom is always fully respected. Such a person acts to discover and master who he or she is in order to progress on the path that leads to his or her deep inner truth and then gives her life to life so as to create a better world.

*

A person who does black magic does not deeply understand how life works, where he or she comes from and where she needs to go to be a happy and joyful person. Such a person feels separated from the Source of all life and focuses his or her attention on negative things and on satisfying personal desires, where each unsatisfied desire brings frustration and where each satisfied desire just leads to another new desire. Such a person nourishes his or her wounds, his or her ignorance, a desire to get revenge, fear, anger and hatred and tries to control and manipulate others to rob energy and to satisfy personal needs. There is neither awareness nor care of consequences on present and future life. As Nordic literature shows, such magic existed in past times. Getting revenge, destruction and wishing for others disharmony, misery, poverty, lack of fertility and misfortune are related in Nordic sagas. Different stories mention a procedure where a misfortune stick called Nidhstong was used. This piece of wood influenced the spirits in a place so that they disorganized the life of people living nearby. Other people's freedom is not respected by people doing black magic and when such people die, what happens to them is very sad. At best, such a person spends a very long time in an astral jail where he or she sees the causes and consequences of what has been done and feels the suffering he or she has caused until she or he can find forgiveness, start a new life et get back on track on the path that leads to light and to unity with the Source of all life. At worst, such a person becomes totally disintegrated into cosmic dust.

*

Organizing runes according to their effects and finding the appropriate runic symbol for what you wish to create:

Your knowledge of each rune and your feelings are your best guides. In chapter 3 where each rune is described, there is a section showing how the rune can be used to do magic. Germans were very fond of grouping runes together according to their effects and of classifying runes into this or that category.

211

In Nordic literature and for example in a text called Sigrdrifumal, there are numerous mentions of runes of this or that, like for example runes of victory, runes of joy, runes of health and so on. The texts unfortunately don't specify which runes are of what type. Only deep intuitive knowledge and common sense can enable you to correctly match a rune and a state of being or a specific effect. Below are some suggestions.

Rune families: (structured here in the order of astrological signs)

Newness Runes: Fehu, Nyd, Sigl and Daeg.
Victory Runes: Thorn, Gyfu, Sigl, Tiw and Eh
Self-confidence Runes: Féhu, Raidh, Gefu, Isa, Eh and Lagu

Joy Runes: Ken, Wynn, Gefu, Yer, Tiw and Eh
Fertility Runes: Féhu, Ur, Thorn, Eolh, Mann, Ing and Lagu
Rainfall runes: Ur, Hagl, Yer, Sigl and Berkano
Runes to attract money: Féhu, Gyfu, Eolh, Tiw Berkano and Lagu

Runes to attract costumers: Sigl, Peordh, Tiw and Berkano.
Speech Runes (Malrunar): Thorn, Ass, Raidh, Sigl and Mann
Growth generating Runes: Thorn, Nyd and Lagu

Runes for magic: Fehu, Ur, Thorn, Nyd, Berkano, Eh, Mann and Othala
Binding Runes: Gefu, Nyd, Eis, Eh and Mann.
Intuition runes: Ur, Yer, Eih, Peordh, Eolh, Sigl, Berkano, Mann and Ing

Awareness Runes: Raidh, Gyfu, Eis, Sigl, Eh and Daeg
Love Runes: Ken, Raidh, Gyfu, Wynn, Eis, Yer, Tiw, Berkano, eh and Daeg
Runes to attract a partner: Ken, Raidh, Gyfu, Tiw and Eh
Runes to strengthen love between partners: Ken, Wynn, Ass, Eh and Daeg.
Success Runes: Féhu, Gyfu, Wynn, Isa, Sigl, Eh and Lagu.

Health Runes: Féhu, Ur, Ken, Nyd, Tiw, Eh and Lagu

Runes to create strong bonds and relationships: Thorn, Eh and Othala
Runes to create harmony: Ken, Wynn, Tiw and Eh

Power Runes: Thorn, Ass, Raidh Gyfu, Eis, Eih, Eolh, Sigl and Lagu
Initiation Runes: Féhu, Eih, Eolh and Mann.
Runes to cut bonds: Ass, Ken, Isa, Eih, Eolh, Ing and Othala

Runes to find the right job: Fehu, Ass, Raidh, Gyfu, Hagl, Eh and Lagu
Safe and happy travelling Runes: Raidh, Gyfu, Peordh, Eh, Lagu et Ing
Luck Runes: Fehu, Raidh, Gefu, Nyd, Tiw, Eh et Lagu

Runes for success in legal matters: Ass, Raidh, Wynn and Tiw

Protection Runes: Ur, Thorn, Ass, Raidh, Hagl, Eis, Eolh, Tiw, Eh, Berkano and Lagu
Defense Runes: Thorn, Eih, Eolh, Tiw, Eh and Othala

Meditation Runes: Hagl, Isa, Ing, Othala and Daeg
Deliverance (Biargrunar): Peordh, Sigl, Berkano, Eh, Ing, Mann and Othala
Healing Runes (Limrunar): Ur, Raidh, Peordh, Sigl and Mann
Ending Rune: Hagl, Eih, Yer and Othala

Choosing the best time to do magic:

Being aware of the structural energy related to the present time is crucial when doing magic. Identifying the best time, that is the time where the greatest amount of life energy, in relation with what needs to be done is thus very important. Certain specific results can be obtained much more easily at certain specific moments. Each time has structural energetic vibrations and properties. Certain rituals are only carried out during the old German-Nordic feast calendar. As mentioned before in the chapter dedicated to runic spreads, you can either undertake a ritual when you feel it is the right time to do so or either take into account the hour of the day (first, second, third hour after sunset or sunrise for example), the numerical hour of the day, the part of the day (dawn, morning, noon, evening, dusk, night), the day of the week, the moon phase, the numerical day of the month, the month of the year, the eight ancestral feast days and the season. Runic practitioners often work with graphics called time circles which divide time and relate it to different runes and gods. A typical time circle is divided in 4 (the four seasons and the 4 Moon phases), in 7 (the seven days of the week), in 8 (the 8 ancestral feast days and the eight direction is space), in 12 (the 12 astrological signs and in 24 (the 24 runes and the 24 hours of the day).

If a day of the week has to be chosen for example, each day is related to a planet and to a god. Sunday is related to Baldr and to the Sun. Monday is related to Frigg and to the Moon. Tuesday is related to Tiw/Tyr and to Mars. Wednessday is related to Odin and to Mercury. Thursday is related to Thor and to Jupiter. Friday is related to Freya, to Aegir and to Venus. Saturday is related to Vitharr and to Loki and to Saturn.

Each of the 24 hours of the day is then related to a rune. The first hour after sunrise can be related to the first rune and so on. Working in base 24, each day of the month can be related to its corresponding rune. Day 25 gives 2+5=7 and is related to rune 7 Gefu. You can also identify the key symbol or significant of what you want to achieve. Before doing any magic, it is auspicious to be aware of "the energy of time". It is well known that times change and that past times aren't the same as now. What is important is your personal relationship with time and your way of perceiving time cycles. This specific form of awareness grows with practice. What is below can help.

Awareness of time: Complementary information.

1: Division by two:

The moon and invisible light are strong during nighttime while visible light and the Sun are strong during daytime. Daytime emerges or is born from nighttime.

2: Division by four:

This number is related to the four seasons that structure a year, to the four phases of the Moon that structure a month and with the four phases of the day. It can also be related to the four main directions and to the four elements and main psychological profiles.

Phase 1: Spring. East. Intuition. Air.
Phase 2: Summer. South. Energy. Fire.
Phase 3: Autumn. West. Analytical and emotional power. Water.
Phase 4: Winter. North. Matter and structure. Earth.

3: Division by seven: This division is based on the number of times the earth spins around itself in a quarter of the lunar 28 day month.

4: Division by eight: This division is based on 8 central moments in the year where feasts have been celebrated since thousands of years by the people from the East, i.e. by our ancestors who came from the East, the Celts and then the Germans. These feasts are related to the two equinoxes (when the Sun's equator and the Earth's equator are on a same line), to the two solstices (day with greatest light or least light) and to the 4 central times between equinoxes and solstices. Number eight can also be related to the eight directions in space.

Spring equinox feast: Around March the 21rst. In the northern hemisphere, it occurs when, from the Earths' point of view, the sun crosses the projection of the Earth's equator and is about to rise above it. This specific moment can be related to rune 1, Fehu, creation of new wealth but also to rune 7, Gyfu, giving one's life to life. It can be related to the astrological sign of Aries.

Celebration of nature, fertility, Eternal feminity, Mother-Earth and life: Around May the first. This is a time where life and nature thrive, when the earth is prepared so it can nourish and where raids where planned on Earth and at sea. This specific moment can be related to runes Ur, Tiw and Lagu. It can be related to the astrological sign of Taurus.

Summer solstice feast: Around June the 21rst. In the northern hemisphere, it occurs when the Sun is at its highest yearly position up in the sky. The longest day, when daytime lasts longest, is celebrated. This specific moment can be related to rune Daeg, daylight and to rune Berkano, Life at its fullest. It can be related to the astrological signs of Gemini and of the Crab (Cancer)

Celebration of outer light: Around August the first. This is the time when the Sun is most powerful. It is related to master runes Thorn and Ass and to solar runes Eis, ice and Eh, the horse. The power of love, of light and of "The Source" are then celebrated. It can be related to the astrological sign of Leo.

Autumn equinox feast: Around September the 22nd. In the northern hemisphere, it occurs when, from the Earths' point of view, the sun crosses the projection of the Earth's equator and is about to drop down below it. There is the same amount of daytime and nigh time. The two are balanced, in harmony but night time is about to take over. This specific moment can be related to runes Ken and Wynn. It can be related to the astrological sign of Libra.

Celebration of inner light and of the world of life beyond: Around November the first. This is a time when the power of invisible forces and of darkness reaches a peak. This specific moment can be related to runes Eih and Eohl, to rune Hagl which symbolizes inner life and the path to initiation but also to rune Othala which symbolizes the world of ancestors. The awakening of one's inner fire, magic, relationship to life beyond, death and renewal are celebrated. This day was the beginning of the solar year for both the Celts and the Germans. It can be related to the astrological sign of Scorpio.

Winter solstice feast: Around December the 21rst. In the northern hemisphere, it occurs when the Sun is at its lowest yearly position up in the sky. The shortest day, when daytime lasts shortest, is celebrated as it announces the coming back of an increase in light time. This specific moment can be related to rune Hagl, hail falling from the sky and the long returning path towards light and towards the Source of all life and also to rune Ing, the Source itself. It can be related to the astrological sign of Capricorn.

Heart of winter celebration: Around February the first. In the northern hemisphere, this is the coldest time of the year where in the last the land was under deep snow, reducing available resources to a minimum. This specific moment can be related to runes Eis, Ice, Peordh, the dice cup and to rune Sigl, sun lightning or sun flash. It can be related to the astrological sign of Aquarius.

Below is an example of a yearly wheel. It takes into account past times, modern times and the eight German ancestral celebrations. I seems quite adapted to present times.

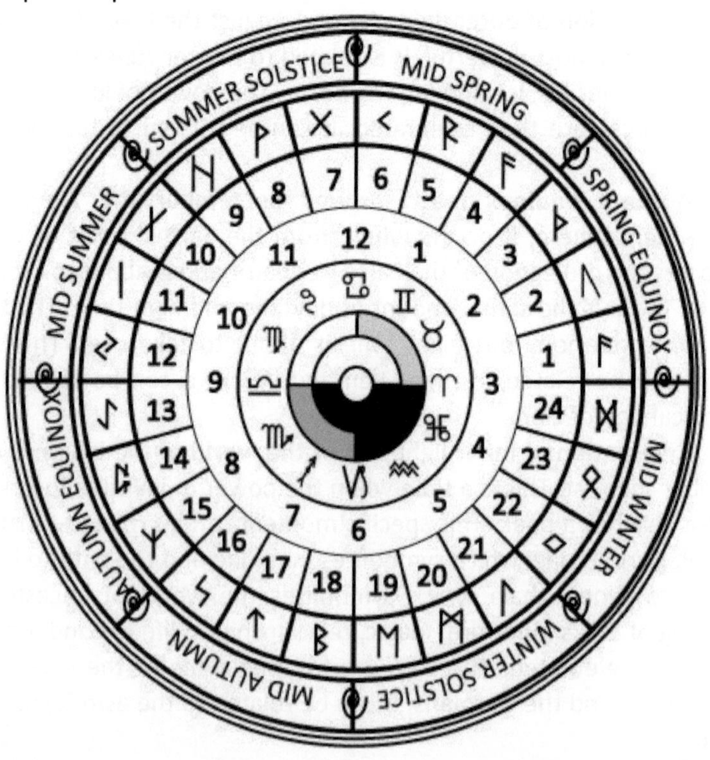

5-Division by twelve: This division is based on the yearly rotation of the Earth around the Sun and on the number of full Moons occurring in one year.

6-Division by sixteen: This division is based on two cycles of eight, on the structure of how energy sets in motion and on the Viking Futhark.

7-Division by twenty four: This division is based on two cycles of twelve, on the 24 runes and on the structure of a human being whose physical body has 24 vertebrae and whose soul has 24 major parts (see the self-knowledge tool called the Birth Diamond).

Magic formulas, incantations, chants, prayers: They are spoken silently or loudly in a certain state of being during a ritual and when so, runes are also visualized. This state of being is a state of calmness full of life and of peaceful joy, a state of relaxed alertness and of being 100% here and now. There are two types of magic formulas. The first type gathers all the traditional formulas found in poems and sagas or passed on by rune masters. They are used to activate a rune during a ritual so that its energy is released and so that its form waves create something in the real world. The second type of formula is created for very specific purposes and depends on what is required and on the intention. These formulas are created by the Vikti or Magician. The most efficient formulas are simple, in the present tense, clear and rhythmic. What is required here is to be connected with the magic of life, to become the poet or poetess that lies within you and to express what is there. The right formula usually puts a discreet smile on your face, triggers a state of unexplainable joy and makes you vibrate.

Example: If you are a lady and if you want to encounter a gentleman to create a long-lasting and beautiful relationship then your magic formula could be: "I, (your full name and date of birth), meet in this physical world the man that suits me perfectly, as our souls have already met." Visualising rune Fehu and Ken together strengthens this formula.

Poetry exercise: Below are a list of major reasons why people created talismans. A talisman and the poem in the form of a prayer that goes with it can be created for each reason or for the one you are concerned about. You can also create a poem for each rune to help it manifest itself in your life.

Postures and incantations: As we have seen before, each rune can be related to a body posture (stadha) and to a specific incantation (galdr). Different postures have been suggested for each rune and it is best to test and find for yourself the postures that are right for you. Combining a posture and an incantation can help you vibrate each rune with your whole body.

More hints for practicing magic: When you have felt what you want to create, you can then choose one, three or five runes that you feel are relevant. You can then clearly define and write down your goal in the form of a magic formula or poem on a piece of paper. Your wish should be written in the present tense and include your name and date of birth. It should be achievable or at least realistic. It should also be beautiful and make you feel joy and enthusiasm. A wish well expressed makes you feel and say "Yes, this is what I really want".

While intensively visualizing your wish happening in your life, you can then engrave your runes on wood, on metal or on stone or write them down on the piece of paper where you have written your wish. You could also paint them or draw them, either in white on a red background or in red on a white background. You can also write them down on a piece of cloth and tie it around your wrist or upper feet with the runes face down so that they touch your skin.

You then link and bind the runes to the object or paper on which your goal is written by a special incantation. You can then light a red, green or white candle during your ritual and place your wish paper and your talisman at the foot of the candle and firmly speak out three, seven or nine times what you want to create in your life.

To activate your runes, you can pour a few drops of your blood or your saliva on them while speaking your wish out loud or silently, as you wish. You can then take some time to visualize what you wish again and this time see your chosen runes in the picture and bind them to your wish. You can end your ritual by thanking the runes and the gods for their help.

Runes related to an event can be secretly engraved in the place where the event will occur or on an object closely related to the event. This is called a symbolic magic action.

Chapter 6: Making your own runes and amulets or talismans.

The Nordic poem called Havamal and the section of that poem called Runatal verse 144 reveals the building blocks to make, activate and use runes. This is what is says.

Verset 144

Veiztu hvé rísta skal?	Do you know how you must cut and carve them?
Veiztu hvé ráða skal?	Do you know how you must read and interpret them?
Veiztu hvé fá skal?	Do you know how you must paint or color them?
Veiztu hvé freista skal?	Do you know how you must try them?
Veiztu hvé biðja skal?	Do you know how you must ask and invoke them?
Veiztu hvé blóta skal?	Do you know how you must sacrifice them?
Veiztu hvé senda skal?	Do you know how you must send them?
Veiztu hvé sóa skal?	Do you know how you must kill or erase them?

Runatal shows that a series of tasks must be accomplished and that a certain order must be taken into account when making runes. It suggests that it better not to ask than to sacrifice, or in other words it is sometimes better to do nothing than do wrongly or to act in an excessive manner. It also suggests that it is right to let what is coming come and to let what is leaving leave. It also says that what is given will come back and therefore shows that it is important to be aware of the cause-effect laws and to respect the runes as if they were life forms. It finally says that fire, thunder and lightning engraved runes long before Men did.

Many sets of runes can be found in shops or on websites. If you use the keywords "rune sets", "pebble rune sets", "stone rune sets" or "wooden rune sets" you will find them. Purchasing a rune set can be a transitory first step because normally, a rune set is not bought nor sold nor lent but is made by the person who uses it or given by a true rune master. Stone is usually for the dead and for burial sites while wood is used for the living but again, it is right to do what you feel. Gemstone sets are used for special sacred ceremonies. Creating and using your own rune set does give more relevant results. There are various ways of creating a rune set as we will see. The 24 runes should fit in the palms of your hands.

Pebble runes: If you love stones and water, you can go to the river or to the sea side, sit down for a while, thank Mother Earth and tell her you want to borrow 24 stones to make a rune set. You can choose a specific moment to find your pebbles (day of the week, day number, Moon phase...). You can then find 24 or more stones that have the same shape and size that seem beautiful. They should be round or oval in shape. Once home, you can clean them and let them dry in the sun. In ancient times, Germans painted runes with their own blood or with a mixture of red-purple berry juice, saliva and blood. The idea in doing this is to place part of your life force on each rune so that they become part of you and you a part of them. If you feel that doing so seems somewhat too extreme, you can use organic paint made from plants and pigments. You can directly paint your runes in brown or black on each pebble, having previously felt which rune goes on each pebble or paint your pebbles in white, allow required time for drying and then paint the runes in red having added some saliva in the paint. The right color is the one that makes you vibrate and feel joy. You can eventually varnish your runes but that does tend to isolate the natural energy or life force of the stone. Again, you should do what you feel is right for you.

Site : etsy.com   Site : eydisdewdrop.wordpress.com

Baked earth or ceramic runes: If you can find a person or a ceramics club where there is a pottery kiln, you can make runes with baked earth. They can be circular or elliptical in shape. You create the required shape, engrave the runes, color them and put them in the oven. It is also quite possible that one day, runes will be made with a tree dimensional printer. Runes made out of resin, baked earth and ceramic are available on internet as can be seen on the next page.

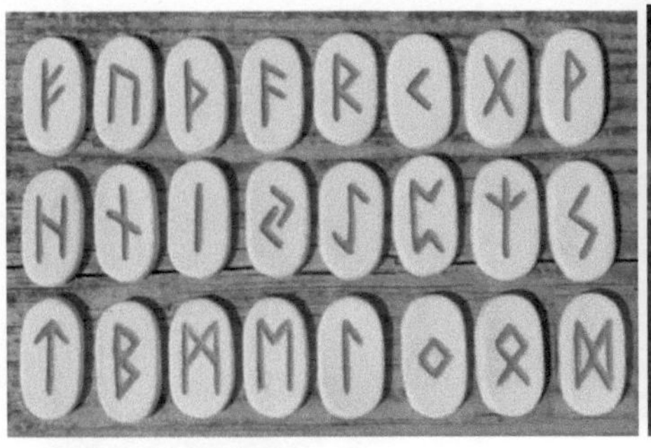 

Site : deviantart.com   Site : maginrose.com

Wooden runes: Germans, as the Celts before them, love trees. To make a set of runes, they sometimes took a peace of bark from the tree, after having asked the tree and thanked it. They often picked up a branch on the ground or used branches of trees cut down to make houses, tools or weapons. They sometimes picked up already cut branches along the riverside or in the forest again thanking the tree to which the branch belonged and Mother-earth for its gift. Seeking rune branches was often done at dawn, at noon, at dusk or during full Moon. Nowadays, it is possible to buy beech branches in specialized shops or supermarkets. Once the raw material was found, runes where then engraved at a chosen time within a ritual, in a state of meditation and clear alertness of one intention, often just after new Moon time. Breaking or sawing a living branch from a living tree is not done, except on very special occasions, when making a special amulet, with the permission of the tree. The tree is then thanked and a gift, like water or urine, is offered to it in exchange for its sacrifice.

Sawing: When the branch is clean, you wedge it tightly on a vice as on the picture below and saw 24 runes of same thickness, ideally about 1 cm, making sure you do this safely. You can use an electrical saw or a hand saw as below. It is often auspicious to saw more that 24 washers or discs in case you are not satisfied with what you have. Gardening claws can be used to cut a branch into smaller sizes but they are not suitable to cut rune discs as they chip the wood. Once cut, you can then use sandpaper to smoothen the surface. It is possible to find already cut and smoothened wooden discs on internet but it is better to create your own.

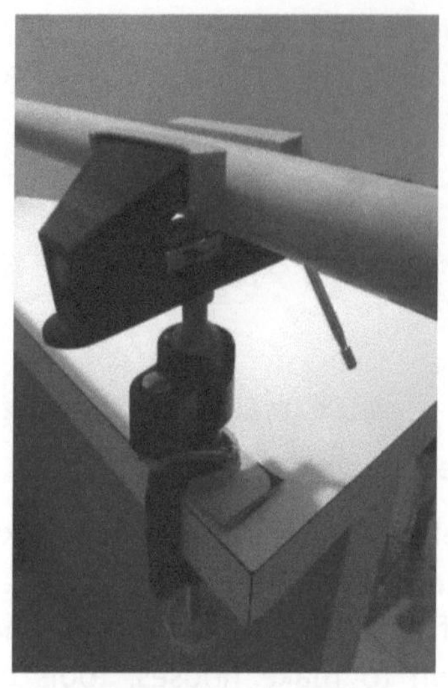 

Engraving and painting: There are various options. You can directly paint the runic symbols on the previously chosen discs. You can draw them with a pencil and paint them. You can use a tool, such as a cutter or a knife, to engrave them and then paint them. You can also burn them with a previously heated tool, using a wood burning tool like a pokerwork machine or a pyrography station. Safety and alertness are very important here. I draw the runes with a pencil, make a carving with an American X-ACTO knife as seen below and then engrave them with an electrical pyrography tool.

If you feel that it is right for you to do so, you can finally taint or varnish your runes. Varnishing does help conserve the wood but it also isolates its life force. Runes are engraved starting with rune number one, Fehu and finishing with rune number 24, Daeg. Rune masters' favorite trees to make runes are apple trees, ash trees, birch trees, beech trees and yew trees but yew trees are nowadays very rare and therefore need to be left at peace. We will see more about engraving later on.

Site : pinterest.com   Site : mysterylodge.co.uk

Here are the small, midsized and large rune sets I made

Making, consecrating or blessing and activating runes or any other talisman: This is done when deeply connected with your heart, thanks to organization, concentration and visualization. The best days of the week to do this is Wednessday (Day of Odin), Friday (Day of Freya) and Sunday (Day of the Sun). A talisman made to create is made during rising Moon days while a talisman made to put an end to something is made during falling Moon days.

It is very important to be in a quiet place and to be in a sacred space that you previously define and protect with a ritual. It is crucial to be in a relaxed, peaceful, joyful, lively and alert state of mind. The process structure has been described in the previous chapter.

The opening ritual: First there is an opening ritual which begins with a formal statement. You then declare to the Gods, to the Universe and to "The Source of all life" that you (name and date and place of birth and son or daughter of) that you are going either to make or to bless (sacralize) a set of runes and that your intention is…When creating or blessing, it is crucial to visualize what you want the rune or the talisman to do, undo, maintain or change and how your life will be when that happens, when the magic of the runes woks out and when your goal is achieved.

Preparing the ritual space: You place:

- A white square shaped table cloth
- A small recipe with large salt crystals
- A bowl filled with water
- A candle, matches or a lighter and some incense
- A wooden plate where you put the runes
- Your engraving tool (knife, cutter, punch or pyrographic blade)
- A recipe with pigment mixed with water if you taint your runes
- A small needle sterilized with alcohol or boiling water
- A branch made out of a tree whose vibration matches your goal (see further down the texts about the various trees)

You can then light you incense and thank it for protecting your sacred space. You then light the candle, take it and walk clockwise around your sacred space declaring that this space is now dedicated to your ritual, that it is closed to any outside forces and that it is protected by light, by life and by the Source of all life. You then sit down comfortably.

You then invoke Freya, Odin and Mother-Earth though a special speech or formula. This invocation firstly consists in revealing your identity (first and family name, date and place of birth, identity of mother and father). You then warmly thank Freya, Odin and Mother Earth Erda for having created the runes and for helping you to create or bless a set of runes that brings truth, freedom and what is best for life and evolution. You can then feel the feminine power and the beauty of Freya, the masculine power of Odin and his sparkling intelligence and the love of Mother-Earth, Erda or Gaia.

Your speech ends with a "thank you very much" and with a "and so be it". Runes are engraved and loaded with life force one by one, separately and in order, starting with Fehu, the creation of wealth and ending with Daeg, the light of the eternal day.

Creating a runic life form, engraving and tainting: Once in the appropriate state of being, calm, alert and joyful, you firstly pick up the first wooden disc that will bear rune Fehu and stamp it down gently in the salt, on one side and then on the other.

You then raise your disc in front of you, chant the name of the tree it is made, thank it, chant the name of the rune and then you make the disc touch the center of your forehead (third eye). At the same time, you visualize the runic symbol and energy coming out of your heart and pouring into the disc.

You then bring the disc down to your throat, name the rune and you tell her who she is, what potential qualities and skills she has and how she can help you (if the rune set is for you, you name yourself), a specific person (that you name) or other people. You can bless the rune with the four elements by pronouncing a phrase connected with each element.

You then bring it down to your heart and express your gratefulness, your kindness, your joy to work with it and your love for this life form that is willing to help you. You then bring it down to your belly button, which you touch for a few seconds or as long as you feel necessary and focus on the life energy that is there. You then bring it down to your sexual organs so as to anchor it in life and so as to create a connection with Mother-Earth, whom you can thank.

If you feel that it is right for you to do so, you can then take your pencil and draw the rune. You then take your carving tool and carve the symbol of the rune and visualize it at the same time. **Picture 1.** I then use a pyrographic tool to engrave each rune.

If you are making very large runes, you will then have to carve differently. Having made a first carving as just explained, you then carve small lines about 2 mm large on the extremities of each line so that you define the limits of the runic symbol as in **picture 2.** You then gently carve two lines or series of dots on each side of the first line so as to define the width of the runic symbol. These are only visual marks and are only about a half a millimeter deep. **Picture 3**.

You then pick up your cutting tool and holding it at an angle of 45 degrees, you place it on the marks on each side of the main line and take away the wood between the outer marking line and the central line as in **pictures 4, 5 and 6.** Your rune is now engraved in the wooden disc.

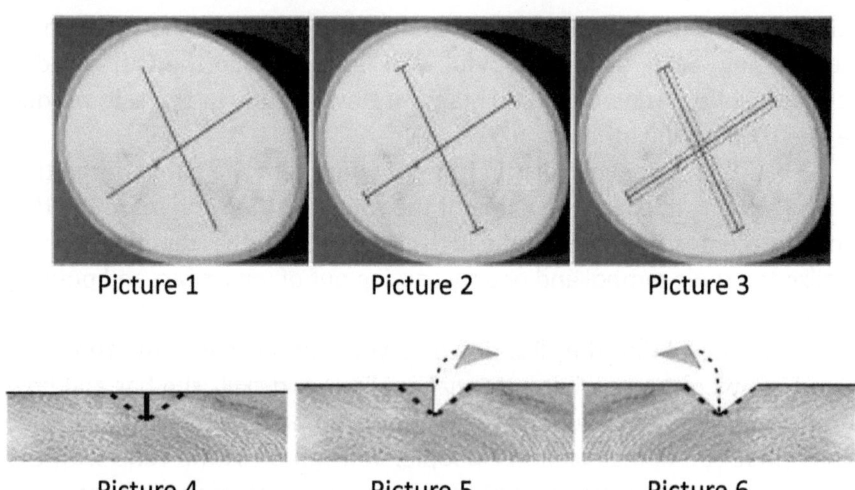

| Picture 1 | Picture 2 | Picture 3 |

| Picture 4 | Picture 5 | Picture 6 |

You then declare that the rune, which you name, is presently engraved. If you have decided to taint your runes, you then take the engraved rune and dip in into the recipe containing the pigment solution. You then blow on the rune, so as to either dry it up or just to give it your breath of life. You can now varnish it if you have decided to do so. It is auspicious to visualize and feel life force pouring into the rune or talisman all along the production process. Doing this right comes with practice.

If you are creating a talisman, you then wrap your talisman in a cloth three, five or nine times and place it in darkness, in a box where it will rest or a pre defined period of time that can be 7, 9, 12, 24 or 108 minutes, hours or days. You also place a piece of paper or a card where you write your intention. This will charge and prepare the talisman for the activation ritual that will follow. Then, when the time has come, you place yourself in a very alert and yet relaxed state of mind and you take the talisman out of the box just as if it was a baby being born from its mother. You then raise it above your in the light and present it to life. You then connect it with the 4 elements while saying what you are doing, by passing it over the candle, by making it touch the earth, by blowing on it and by dipping it in water. Your talisman is now ready for consecration. It is ready to be blessed.

If you are making a talisman for someone else, it is auspicious to advise that person as to when you will be doing the rituals so that he or she can participate or focus but from his or her home only. It is then important, when doing the ritual, to visualize the new life that the person wishes to experience and to include the person in the visualized scenery. You can then firstly engrave the name of the person in runic alphabet on the talisman, then the rune and then bind the two with a formal declaration.

Consecrating and blessing engraved runes:

In order to activate, consecrate and bless wooden runes, Germans performed a ritual called "blodvekya" meaning activation by blood. What is this? To undertake this ceremony, you pick up for first rune and make it touch the salt on one side and then on the other. You then raise the rune in front of you, chant its name and then you touch the center of your forehead (third eye) with it while visualizing its runic symbol. You then bring it down to your throat, chant its name again and tell her who she is, why she was created, what she can do and most important what her mission is. You can also chant one of the 18 verses of the Havamal poem shown in the chapter dedicated to introducing runic magic or a poem that you have created for the rune. This binds the rune or talisman with its mission and you sort of sign a contact with it. You then bring the rune down to your heart and gratefully thank it, either silently or out loud. You then bring it down to your belly button and feel its energy while visualizing it. You then rub it along your sex so as to anchor it to life.

You then put the rune on the salt, take your needle and gently sting a part of your body that will give you a few drops of blood. You then place the rune in your left hand, place your hand along your heart and with your right hand you put some of your blood on the rune and you tell her that you are giving her some of your own blood, that is of yourself so that she can create, manifest and speak truth, results and what is best for your evolution. If cutting yourself to consecrate each rune does not suit you, you can also prepare a small recipe, fill it with water and add a few drops of your blood or eventually some of your saliva. You then dip each rune in the recipe. When tainting, you first taint the blank side or if it's a talisman the side when the name is engraved and then the side where the runes are engraved. You then clearly declare who you are what your intention is. You declare that you are now activating the rune (which you name) as a tool to manifest in the world of matter so as to serve life.

You blow on the rune three times and you thank it for manifesting what she represents. You undertake this process for each of the 24 runes.

When you have finished the ritual, you then place the 24 runes in a recipe, box or bag that you have previously chosen for them. You then close the rune making and consecrating process by a closing ritual where you declare what you have done and that the rune ceremony is now finished. You can recite a poem, thank Freya, Odin and Erda and then pick up your candle and walk around your sacred space to give it back its freedom. You then tidy everything up. You can also go for a walk or do some meditation to create a transition between what you have done and the next part of the day. The best ritual is the one you have designed for yourself and the one that makes you feel joy, strength, gratitude and serenity.

Creating an amulet or a talisman: Amulets and talismans have been created for thousands of years. Germans quite often made some. Metal talismans were worn as necklaces. These were called Bracteates and they were often very beautiful, which made their magic even stronger. Gemstones were sometimes engraved in talismans. Most talismans however were made with wood or baked earth. Before creating an amulet, it is crucial to perfectly master both your knowledge of runic symbols and the process of creating and consecrating an object. It is also very important to have faith, joy in your heart and enough energy.

The first step is to define your intention and to check that it is in harmony with your evolution, with cosmic order or Necessity and with what is possible in present times. You then choose the rune or the combined runes that will be engraved. Runes can be engraved in a straight line, in a circle or as bindrunes. The amount of runes you chose can match the symbolism of your intention.

Three runes can be chosen if your intention concerns adapting, evolving or communication, five if what you want to create is related to traveling with body and consciousness or to protection, teachings and meaningful social integration, seven for love and efficiency and nine to influence destiny. The first rune in the sequence will show how you want the process to start, the middle one how you want things to take shape and the last rune how you want things to end. Runes engraved in a circular pattern are sometimes called power emblems and they are usually made up of 4, 6, 8 or 12 runes.

The best way to proceed is to have your intention clear in you mind, body and heart and then to choose runes that give you a vibrating, flashing or tickling sensation because they match your intention, your goals and your needs. A runic sequence may be highly efficient for one person and not work at all for another person. Once you have chosen the runes, you then choose where or on what you will engrave them, the type of three for wooden runes and the shape of your talisman. Talismans can be square shaped, rectangle shaped, oval shaped, pentagram shaped or even diamond shaped. What is important is that you see it as beautiful and vibrating. Choosing a tree depends on the personality of the tree, on your intention and also on what is available in your surroundings. Here is some data about this.

Describing the symbolism, personality and energy of a tree: Trees are classified into two categories. Leafy trees are those who have leaves while coniferous trees are those with needles who produce resin. The best way to get to know a tree is to consider it as a person or a life form, to go towards it, to tell it who you are and that you would like to get to know it, to put your hand on it or hug it and to ask it to show you who it is.

When you tune in with your sensitivity and feelings and put your thinking mind at rest, you can experiment connecting with trees and see what wonderful life forms they are. You then need to match what you feel and perceive with key words.

Choosing a type of tree to create a talisman depends on you, on your experience, feelings and particular connection with such and such a tree. Here are some hints describing the energy and symbolism of key trees.

Symbolism of trees: A few examples:

Birch tree: Female energy, sparkling life force, joy, sense of humor, fertility, imagination, simplicity, things flowing smoothly, tranquility, purity of soul, wellness, motherly love.

Cherry tree: Female energy, joy of being alive, sensuality, charm, power of attraction, social intelligence, kindness, harmonious relationships, abundance, artistic abilities.

Hornbeam tree: Female energy, Being well anchored in life, long lasting beauty, manual artistic abilities, charisma, inner beauty and strength, kindness and sense of sharing but also firmness, common sense and determination.

Chestnut tree: Male energy, dignity, integrity, smartness, autonomy, efficiency, generosity, productivity, abundance, strength of character, straightforwardness.

Oak tree: Inner spiritual strength, love, benevolence, caring, goodness, power and wisdom, depth, solidity, bravery, majesty, robustness and harmony.

Ash tree: Structure, balance between male and female energy, liveliness, alertness, protection, seriousness, rightness, autonomy and reliability.

Beech tree: Smoothness, kindness, sensitivity, flexibility, health, smartness, precision, good advice.

Walnut tree: Organisation, determination, self-sufficient, autonomy, severity, inner beauty, solidity, ability to see the right path.

Hazelnut tree: Tolerance, fertility, nourishment, protection, healing power, restores harmony, finds water and springs, fairy-like, delight and bliss.

Olive tree: Life force, power to create harmony, deep awareness, lucidity, seeing memories of time, power to create change, flexibility and smoothness, resistance and endurance.

Pine tree: Smartness and strong ability to adapt, flexibility, joy of living, inner beauty, grace, smoothness, harmony, sociability.

Poplar tree: Communication, sense of humour, joy, wisdom, adaptability, flexibility, mobility, communication, memory, inner balance.

Apple tree: Love, benevolence, goodness, generosity, inner joy, wisdom, creative power, optimism, healing power.

Fir tree: Inner strength, spiritual growth, calmness, dignity, majesty, protection, ambition, work force, determination, heals inner wounds, adaptability and mobility.

Linden tree: Brings harmony, lightness, smoothness, strong sensitivity, vision of what is right and of human destiny and it relieves human sufferings and misery of both body and soul.

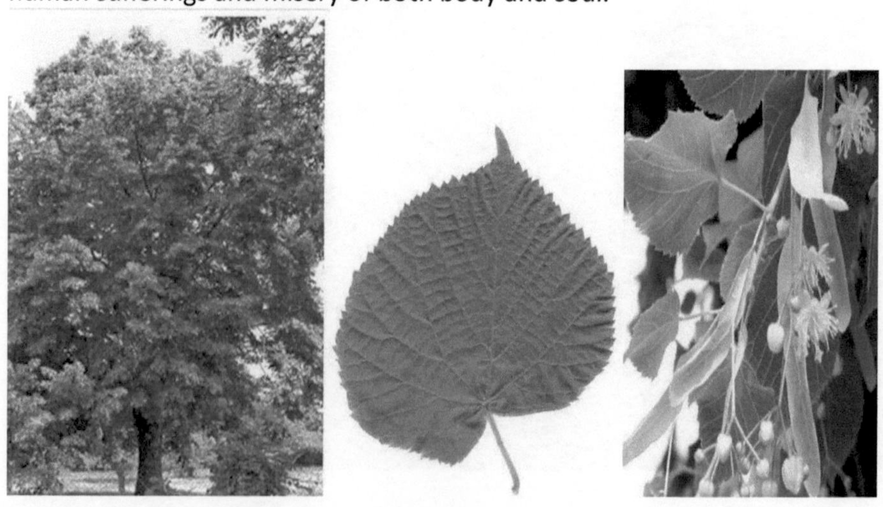

Some other interesting trees to work with: Nannyberry tree, alder tree, holly tree, plane tree, willow tree. All of these are leafy trees. Cedar tree, cypress tree, spruce tree and larch tree. These are coniferous trees.

Matching trees and astrological signs or periods of time: Between the first and ninth centuries AD, people living in Ireland and England created a 20 to 25 character alphabet, named the Ogham, based on the symbolism of trees. The name of each character was derived from the name of a tree.

In 1948, the poet Robert Graves wrote a book called "The White Goddess" in which he invented a fictional calendar with the new year starting on December the 23rd and where he matched trees and time periods. He was inspired by the work of the Irish historian Ruairí Ó Flaitheartaigh.

Some people took this calendar very seriously and since then, different authors have created various calendars with trees! The Celts and Germans loved trees. Their teachings were not written down however. They may have designed a calendar matching periods of time with trees but as far as I know there are zero archaeological proofs of this.

However, trees do have a personality and specific symbolic patterns so it is theorically possible to create a sensible data system and to match trees with astrological signs for example. Everyone could then choose a tree that matches his or her Solar, lunar, Venusian, Martian, Ascendant or Jupiterian astrological sign to make runes, amulets or jewellery.

Research is wide open here!

***

Here is a fictional tree calendar invented in the twentieth century.

• December 23rd to January 1st t - Apple tree	• June 25th to July 4th – Apple tree or Pine tree
• January 2nd to January 11th – Fir Tree	• July 5th to July 14th – Fir or Chestnut tree
• January 12th to 24th – Elm or Linden	• July 15th to July 25th – Elm or Beech tree
• January 25th to February 3rd – Cypress or Birch tree	• July 26 to 4th August - Cypress or Oak tree
• 4th February to 8th February - Poplar	• August 5th to August 13th - Poplar or Hazel nut tree.
• 9th February to 18th February – Cedar or Olive tree	• August 14th to August 23rd – Cedar or Maple tree
• 19th February to 28th February - Pine	• August 24th to September 2nd – Pine or Apple tree
• March 1st to March 10th – Willow or Chestnut tree	• September 3rd to September 12th – Willow or Fir tree
• March 11st to March 20th – Linden or Beech tree	• September 13th to September 22nd – Linden tree
• March 21st – Oak tree	• September 23rd – Olive tree
• March 22nd to March 31st – Hazel nut tree or Oak	• September 24th to October 3rd – Hazelnut or Birch tree
• April 1st to April 10th – Rowan or Hazelnut tree	• October 4th to October 13th – Rowan or Poplar tree
• April 11th to April 20th – Maple tree	• October 14th to October 23rd – Maple or Olive
• April 21st to April 31st – Walnut or Apple tree	• October 4 to November 11th – Walnut or Pine
• May 1st to May 14th – Poplar or Fir tree	• November 12th to November 21st - Chestnut
• May 15th to May 24th – Chestnut or Linden tree	• November 22nd to December 1st – Ash or Beech tree
• May 25th to June 3rd – Ash or Birch tree	• December 2nd to December 11th – Hornbeam or Oak tree
• June 4th to June 13th – Hornbeam or Poplar tree	• December 12th to December 21st – Fig or Hazel nut tree
• June 14th to June 23rd – Fig or Olive tree	• December 22nd – Beech tree
• June 24th – Birch tree	

Examples of circular runic talismans and emblems of power

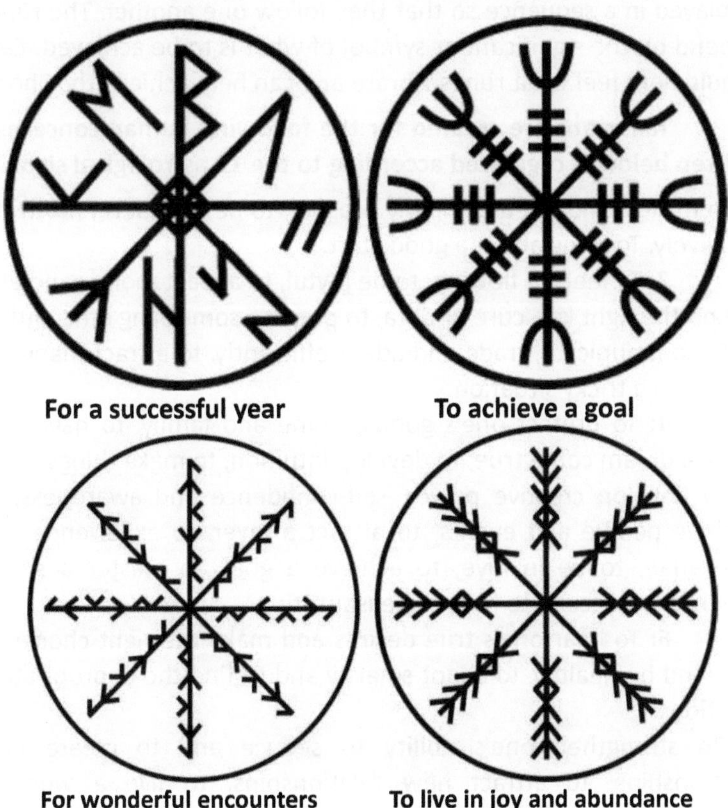

For a successful year

To achieve a goal

For wonderful encounters

To live in joy and abundance

Examples of talismans with combined runes

ALU divine joy

GA Luck and success

For a happy love relationship

Talismans with rune sequences: Three runes are chosen and displayed in a sequence so that they follow one another. The runes chosen depend on the significant or symbol of what is to be achieved. Each person should here feel what runes vibrate and can help achieve the chosen goal.

Talismans are created for the following human concerns: What is written below is organized according to the 12 astrological signs.

1: To make a shop or a company prosper, to be confident, motivated, brave and lively. To bring about a good start.

2: To feel life flowing, to be joyful, to attract money and abundance, to find the right key, cure or data, to prepare something efficiently.

3: To communicate, trade and adapt efficiently, to attract many customers, to handle a tricky situation.

4: To protect one's goods, home and family, to have children, to make a dream come true, to develop intuition, to make things flow.

5: To develop creative power, self-confidence and awareness, to attract positive people and events, to attract a lover, to experience a delightful love affair, to be in love, to achieve a goal, to master a situation and experience success, to have a pleasant trip.

6: To hear one's true desires and make the right choice, to relieve pain and be healthy, to adapt smartly and to find the appropriate technical solutions.

7: To strengthen one's ability to seduce and to create harmonious relationships, to attract new relationships, to live a wonderful love relationship, to efficiently express one's abilities, to implement the right strategy, to be efficient and successful.

8: To be protected against enemies, dark forces or jealous people, to cut bonds and to end a relationship harmoniously, to experience a delightful sexual relationship, to transform a difficult relationship, to overcome fear of death, to safely experience astral travel, to experience an intense and fulfilling social life.

9: To define and play one's role in life, to travel safely, to find a new job or a new home, to be protected and to be lucky.

10: To understand one's destiny and life mission, to make the wheel of destiny turn the right way, to pass an exam, to experience silence, inner peace, wisdom and one's deep inner truth.

11: To attract appropriate help and to find the right psychological or technological solution, to become free from addictions, to experience inner freedom, to be liberated from fear, choc or phobias, to make new friends.

12: To relieve suffering and heal, to experience communion with God, to become open minded concerning what is invisible, to develop psychic abilities, to be inspired and enlightened, to experience non conditional love, to forgive and to become free from Karma.

When you have found the right runes, the ones that vibrate in relation with your intention, you can then choose a name for your talisman. This name is often a key word in connection with the role it will play (for example prosperous shop, success in an exam, quick recovery, encountering a lover and so on) or with the desired result.

The right moment: You then choose the place and time (hour, day of the week, date) where and when you want to create your amulet. (see previous chapter). You then create and consecrate your amulet as previously explained. You can then wrap it up in a piece of cloth three times or nine times. While doing this, you can declare that it will soon be baptized with its name, name its power and abilities and the connection or relationship it has with you. It is a good time to feel its energy as if it was a person. You can then lovingly place it in its special box or bag so that it can have its home and rest there.

You can then leave your talisman in its home during a symbolically defined time. Then, at a chosen time, you can undertake the birth and baptism ritual. You use salt to purify it and you connect it to the four elements, by pouring spring water over it, by passing it over a candle or by raising it towards the sun, by putting it into earth a few seconds or minutes if possible in a forest or in the countryside and by blowing on it three times. For each action, you declare its name and you explain what you do.

You can take a special blessed branch engraved with runes and gently tap on it three, five or nine times. You can also gently strike a gong or a chime so as to awaken it and so as to turn it alive, declaring again who it is, why it was created, what it is capable of doing and for how long it will live. You can then express your gratitude, declare that the ritual has now come to an end, place it back in its box so as to use it during special occasions or you can wear it.

It is now your ally and it is very important to realize that you have created a new life form that has its own will and that is full of life and energy. The talisman is the physical support, house or frame for this life form. This life form has a mission to accomplish, the mission you programmed it to undertake and it is very important that you do everything you can to make sure that this mission is accomplished.

Storing and carrying runes and amulets: You can either build or create a special box or a bag made of cloth or choose one in a shop or on internet using the key word rune bag. Historians say that rune bags were stored along with a piece of one meter square shaped white cloth that defined the sacred space where runes where used. This piece of cloth was neatly folded and placed in the rune bag or box along with the runes.

Putting an end to a talisman's magic: Some talismans are designed to last forever or until the material they are made of is destroyed. Other talismans are made to achieve a specific goal and cease to operate once that goal is achieved. When the goal has been achieved, it is auspicious to give the life form or entity that was connected to the talisman its freedom. This is done with a short ritual. You can go to a place you like, in a forest or in the countryside or at the river side for example. You take the talisman out of its bag or box. You thank the talisman, the gods, Mother Earth and the Source of all life and you explain to the talisman that you are going to give it back its freedom and that you are giving it back to Mother Nature and Father Sky. Then, with love, gratitude and respect, you either scrape off the runes, burn it, burry it somewhere where no one will disturb it or throw it in a river or in the sea, while saying good bye.

Chapter 7: Knowing yourself using runes.

Getting to know a person:

If you want to obtain some land marks concerning a person you make a talisman for or with whom you have a relationship, then you can use the following three numerological self-knowledge methods.

First method: The numerical structure of a person's first name

Here, you can ask a person what his or her name is, write it down and note underneath each latter the number corresponding to each letter. The letters in the first name Sophie for example have the corresponding numbers 1, 6, 7, 9, 8 and 5. You then take the runes 1, 6, 7, 9, 8 and 5 and line then down one after the other. Sophie's personality is a mix of the forces symbolized by the runes that make up her first name. If you want to go further, you can match the meaning of the position of a letter with the meaning of the corresponding rune. Example: The first letter shows how a person expresses himself or herself and how he or she affirms his or her identity. The second letter and rune shows his or her feminine aspect and his or her richness and how he or she can experience and create pleasure and wealth. The third letter shows how that person communicates and adapts while the fourth how she structures and builds. The fifth shows how that person gives a meaning to things and how she becomes more aware and so on.

Second method: The numerical value of a person's birth date, first name and last name. This will give you more information than method 1.

This self-knowledge method is an extraction from the numerological tool called the Birth Diamond that I created in 2011. You can ask a person his or her name and date of birth, write them down and note the value of the letters and numbers concerned as below.

Rune 1: Day of birth. If that number is above 24 then you add the two numbers so 25 becomes 7. This rule applies to every rune. This describes how a person expresses his or her male forces (goals, action, assertion, motivation, use of one's abilities to get results). This is the first house or inner space of the Birth Diamond.

Rune 2: Addition of the rune in house 1 and the month of birth. This describes the richness and beauty of the female forces within a person and how that person can experience pleasure and wealth. This is the second house or inner space of the Birth Diamond.

Rune 3: Addition the month of birth and the year of birth reduced to 24. This shows how that person communicates, learns and adapts. This is the third house of the Birth Diamond.

Rune 4: Addition the year of birth and the year of birth reduced to 24. Example: 1995=1+9+9+6= 25=7. This describes how a person can be part of the world, play his or her economic role in the world and blossom. This is the ninth house of the Birth Diamond.

Rune 5: Addition of rune 1, of the month of birth and of the year of birth reduced to 24. This is the runic life path and it describes the path leading to inner peace, the major life teaching, the type of destiny and how a person evolves. This is the tenth house of the Birth Diamond.

Rune 6: Addition of rune 5 and the numerical value of both the first and last name. Each letter is converted into its number from 1 to 9. A is 1 and I is nine and so on. This gives the self-realization number of the Birth Diamond or how a person can experience fulfillment.

Rune 7: To know the temperament or the nature of a person (how a person is when he or she is natural), you can add rune 1+ month of birth+ rune4+ month of birth. This is the Temperament house of the Birth Diamond.

Rune 8: To see a person's life mission and how that person tends to express himself or herself, you can add the numerical value of first and last names. This is the expression house of the Birth Diamond.

The book called "The Birth Diamond "shows you how to undertake a complete structural analysis of a person's soul and how to see that person's soul architecture and evolutionary plan. A Birth Diamond done with runes which can be called a Runic Birth Diamond can be done in base 24 as just explained earlier and not in base 22 as with the classical Birth Diamond. You will find more about The Birth Diamond just now.

Method 3: The Runic Birth Diamond to see and use the keys of your destiny and your soul's evolution plan.

Introduction:

Why Birth Diamond? As a Human being created by "The Source of all life", you are a beautiful diamond that wants to shine through all its facets. When each facet or part of your soul is experienced in full awareness, expressed in its best possible manner and gathered within your higher Self, your Diamond or spiritual body, which has the shape of a diamond, comes to life and shines. You then give and radiate the best of who you are and succeed.

What is a Runic birth Diamond? It's a self knowledge tool that reveals the soul's architecture and evolution path. It's a map of your soul. The Runic Birth Diamond is a coaching tool, a self-knowledge tool and a self-realization tool. It reveals the 24 main parts of your soul. It shows your structure, your potential skills, your schemes, your resources, your difficulties, your solutions and your possible evolution. It helps you become aware of what parts of you create what in your life. It can help you see what you really want, how to make relevant choices and how to implement successful actions so as to achieve your goals. This brings about changes in your life.

How is it organized? The Runic Birth Diamond is firstly made up of 12 houses called astrological houses (these houses are the same than those found in an astrological chart) and then of 12 numerological houses. It actually is a synthesis of astrology, numerology and runes. It is built using your first and family names and your date of birth. Just like an astral chart, it shows how your soul was split apart into many different pieces during embodiment into a material mammal body, but in a more specific way than an astral chart. A Birth Diamond is like a village made up of 24 houses where each house represents a place within you. This place is occupied by a rune corresponding to the number living in that space. The Runic Birth Diamond is interpreted by observing what rune is in what house, by observing similar runes that may be living in different houses and by observing what is called complementary runes. This will be explained further on. Here is what a Runic Birth Diamond looks like.

Birth Diamond - Classical Presentation

Date of Birth :
First Name :
Family Name :

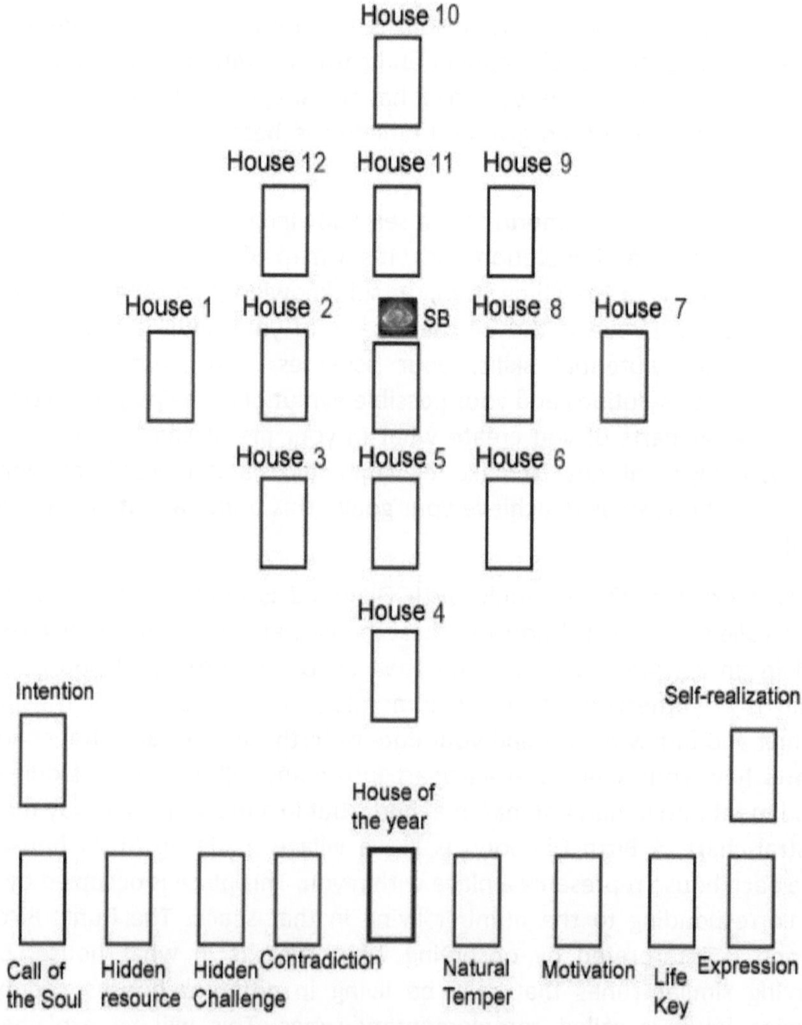

Creation : Eric Jackson PERRIN

What the 24 houses of the Birth Diamond reveal:

House 1 or Ascendant : The state of mind that you have come to experience, the way in which you affirm who you are, the way you start things out, your appearance, the image of yourself that you show to others, your weapons, your strength, the masks you put on to have "an ascendant" on the world.

House 2: Incarnation, your wealth, your main resources, the way you handle matter, how you experience pleasure, how you can earn money and how you relate to your physical body, your artistic abilities or the way you put things into shape.

House 3: Your way of thinking, of learning and of communicating, the way you adapt to your environment, the way you move and create movement in your life. How you express your commercial intelligence.

House 4 or « Bottom of sky »: Your origins, your roots, your family heritage, how you create wellness, your childhood and its conditionings, your subconscious mind, the dwelling place, your source of well-being and where you feel at home.

House 5: Your deep self (who are you really and what do you want), your personal marks, your awareness of yourself, your creative power and your creations, your ability to succeed, your will, the expression of your heart, your way of loving.

House 6: Your technical intelligence, your adaptation to the world of matter, your sense of service, your search for well being, good health and hygiene, recurring problems caused by a tendency to try and find solutions with your mind.

House 7 or Descendant: The way you engage into relationships with others, the couple, associations or rivalries, the opposite but complementary part of you, your antipode, how you go away from your center to meet others, the source of adversity that you must transform into an ally and the main challenge.

House 8: What is hidden inside you, seeking initiation and your deep truth, the dark side of you that needs to be brought to light, the hidden treasure you have inside you, crisis and transformations, sexuality, the unconscious feminine part, discoveries and revelations.

House 9: Finding your place in society, expanding your horizons, exploring space, travelling, studies, using authority and power to do your work, negotiation and business, your behavior at your workplace, your philosophy or life, your spiritual research and beliefs and how you can blossom.

House 10 or "Mid sky": Your ambitions, the way you organize your destiny, your relation to structures and organizations, career, important achievements, the major lesson of your life, the path to yourself, seeking your deep truth and the laws of life.

House 11: Expressing your specificity, experiencing group activities, adaptation to modern life and it's technologies, friends, psychological evolution, experiencing helping and being helped, compulsory solutions that you must experience to free yourself, experiencing inner freedom, psychological et technological intelligence.

House 12: What makes you suffer, how to go from suffering to delight and bliss, the tests that make you grow, how you can transcend, spiritual evolution, your source of faith, ancestral and soul memories, mystical experiences, experiencing unity with God, the end of the story and what you leave behind.

Source of Brilliance: The house is strongly connected to your self-realization house. How can I radiate the best of who I am? How will I be successful in life? How can I get access to my heart, to the very center of myself? How can I express all of my resources and overcome all of my challenges?

Soul intention house: Why have I come to live on planet Earth? What is my ideal life? What have I come to experiment and work on in this life? What is my soul's goal? Long before being born on earth, you had a specific need, an ideal, a clear intention and a goal concerning what life you wanted to live on Earth. The Soul Intention card answers the question "What do I want to achieve during my life on Earth and how can I do it?" it shows a deep and often unconscious need. Hearing the soul's intention enables you to connect with your deep self and to grow towards you self-realization.

Soul call house: Deep inside your soul, there is a call, a cry that echoes as a deep need. This house answers the question: What does your soul want? What is my soul crying about? What are the deep needs of my soul that make me growl if these needs are not answered?

Hidden resource house: This resource is like a seed you bring with you when you are born. It is a gift of life. Like any seed, it needs the right soil, water and sunshine to be able to grow. This card brings you certain abilities that lie deep within you. They need to be revealed and used. When so, growth occurs. What is one of my major resources that I can use with some effort so as to make progress on my evolution path? What seed inside me wishes to become a beautiful tree?

Hidden challenge house: What spine must I take out of my foot so as to move forward much more freely? What taboo must I accept and take into account? What is the hidden challenge that I must overcome?

Contradiction: Hidden deep inside you is a conflict-causing contradiction which is at the same time your strength and your weakness, your wealth and your challenge, something that attracts you like a magnet and yet deeply disturbs you.

The contradiction card show a state of being, which is at first a state of unwellness, that you personally create in your life. This state of mind and the skills that you can show, strange as it might seem, are a powerful force at the centre of your soul. Your contradiction initially manifests as an inner conflict which hinders your growth and which is one of the main causes of your difficulty to move on towards a better life. It forces you to challenge yourself, to change your vision of the card in this house and to do work on yourself so as to change the structure of what you are, in connection with the card. If the challenge is not overcome, if you continue to "feed" your contradiction, you make very little progress and you stay stuck in the problems connected with the card. This conflict is quite often projected on others and it manifests within relationships. In a second phase, your contradiction card describes the available solutions to overcome your inner conflict and it can give you the keys to open the closed door so that you can move on to a better life. When the background problem connected with the card is solved, your contradiction then becomes a great strength, a stepping stone, a catalyser to achieve self realization and transcendence. The card opens a door to a new life. What is my greatest strength than I strangely seldom express? What conflicting memory must I transform? What is the cause of my main problem deep down?

Annual card: What skill will I have to express this year? What opportunities and challenges does this year offer? What will I need this year? What will the atmosphere be like this year?

Temperament or natural temper house: What do I need to feel well? How do I behave when I'm natural? What are my unconscious needs? What type of person am I?

Deep motivation house: What drives you and motivates you? What helps you set in motion? What organizational strength helps you accomplish your destiny?

Key Resource house: What resources can I always use to find a job and be successful in doing it in the outside world? What is the magical key that I can always use? What is my Joker?

Expression number house: What is the numerical vibration of my first and last names? How do I express myself? What do I need to express myself and thrive? What are my conscious needs? What must I do in life?

Self realization card: How should I organize my life? What can I do with who I am? How can I achieve self-realization? How can I go to the very end of my path? How can I accomplish my life mission and accomplish my personal legend?

Here is how to calculate the runes that go into the 24 houses

TECHNICAL FILE – PUTTING TOGETHER THE BIRTH DIAMOND MANUALY

HOUSE 1: Day of birth.   HOUSE 8 : Month of birth

HOUSE 9: year of birth. (1968 = 1+9+6+8=24 and 2+4=6)

HOUSE 10: Day + Month + Year.

HOUSE 2: H 1 + H 8.   HOUSE 3: H 8 + H 9.

HOUSE 7: H 8 – H 9.   HOUSE 5 : H 2 + H 7

HOUSE 6: 22 – M 5.   HOUSE 4 : H 6 + H 7+ H 9

HOUSE 11: H 1 + H 8 + H 9 + H 10.

HOUSE 12 : H 2 + H 8 + H 10

CENTER OF THE DIAMOND: Source of brilliance: H 2 + H 10.

Hidden facets :

- Soul Intention : H8+H9+H10
- Deep hidden need or Call of the Soul: Sum of vowels of first name and family name.
- Hidden resource : sum of year of birth's last two numbers
- Hidden challenge : H 1- H 9 or H 9- H 1
- Contradiction : H6+H7

Annual card: H 1 + H 8 + numerological year (2011=2+0+1+1).

Visible core :

- Natural temper: H 1+ H 8 + H 8 + H 9.
- Motivation number: H 1 + H 5 + H8.
- Key Resource : H 2 + H 10 + H 11
- Expression number: Numerical value of first name and family name.
- Life Axis: Expression number + House10

1	2	3	4	5	6	7	8	9
A	B	C	D	E	F	G	H	I
J	K	L	M	N	O	P	Q	R
S	T	U	V	W	X	Y	Z	

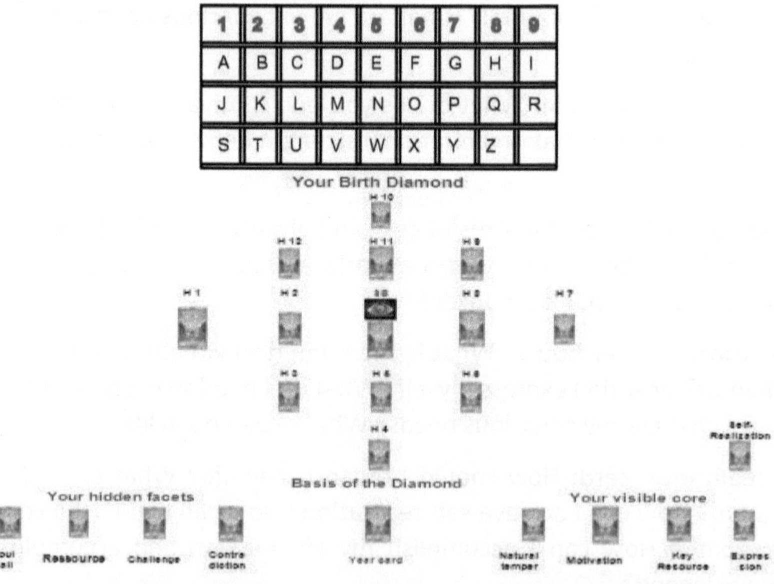

How to interpret the Runic Birth Diamond

Interpreting the Runic Birth Diamond consists in interpreting runes in houses, runes existing twice, tree times, four times or more and in comparing houses occupied by similar runes. In order to do that, it is crucial to be completely familiar with symbolic key words related to each rune, especially keywords that are psychologically orientated. That implies being aware of the essence and purpose of each rune and more specifically of its bright and dark aspects and then to be able to feel how a rune in a house expresses itself within a global psychological structure.

Here are some land marks to interpret the Runic Birth Diamond

1: The aim of the RBD is to gather the different parts of you within the centre of yourself and to become the best version of yourself so as to express the best of who you are. This is done by expressing each rune in your unique manner in a way that matches your evolutionary path.

2: The first level of interpretation consists in interpreting the runes in the 24 houses. A rune in a house is linked to that house and tends to express itself in the life sector represented by the house. It is very important to see how the rune is currently experienced by a person and what beliefs are related to it (example: the rune in house 2 shows what triggers pleasure and how a person can earn money by using a key resource)

4: There are no good or bad runes! Each one has a role to play within evolution. What is important is how you personally express a given rune and how you use it to move forward towards your deep inner truth. However, some runes can be more easily expressed than others, or expressed more harmoniously, in a given house. This can be analysed by comparing the purpose of a house and that of the rune occupying it.

5: At first, in a person's life, the runes that are usually well used, beneficial and helpful are those found in houses 1, 2, 3, 5, 9 and 11, in the Source of brilliance house, in the key resource house and in the self-realization house. Difficulties, issues, blocs and prohibitions are usually brought about by runes in houses 4, 6, 7, 8, 12 and by those in the hidden challenge house and in the contradiction house.

6: The second level of interpretation takes into account identical runes found twice, three times, four times, five times or six times. It then takes into account what is called complementary runes. These are runes that add up to a certain number and that can help express and achieve what is symbolized by that number. We usually consider number 24 which symbolizes daylight and total happiness but we can also consider number 22 (joy due to freedom) or 21 (success in the world, gathering oneself so as to feel complete and connecting to God) or 19 (love) but also 13 (relationship to the world hereafter and to death) or 12 (how to go from suffering to delight).

Coaching with the Runic Birth Diamond: Coaching enables you to define the right goal, to find the resources to achieve it and to implement a series of appropriate actions.

You can calculate and build your Runic Birth Diamond, choose a house you want to work on and either coach yourself or be coached by a trained expert. You can proceed in the following manner. Settle down and relax for a few minutes and then answer the following questions on a notebook. What are your goals in life? What goals have you achieved and what goals remain to be achieved? You can then choose one that you want to work on just now. You can then read the texts that describe the 24 houses and match your goal with one of the houses and see what number is in that house. You can then read the text describing the rune concerned.

You can look deeply and intensively at the rune for a few minutes while asking yourself: What does this rune say to me? Firstly observe your thoughts. What do you think? What ideas spring in your mind in relation with the question when looking at the rune? I could be an "I don't know" or a flow of ideas! Then observe your feelings. When you consider the house you have chosen and look at the rune in that house, what and how do you feel? What emotions pop up? What does it suggest? You can then observe your body sensations without doing anything. When you consider the house you have chosen and the rune in it, what body sensations can you feel? You can write this down.

How do you currently express the rune in the sector represented by the house it's in? Are you expressing the best of that rune? What could you do to improve the way you express that rune? What could you be like if you expressed that rune in its best possible form of expression?

You can now consider what you have written in your notebook. What awareness does your reading generate in relation with the goal you have chosen? What is your main awareness? In relation with your main awareness and with your goal, what actions can you do to make things progress? When precisely can you do what you have decided to do?

When would you like to do a check-up with yourself or with a coach, to acknowledge and validate the results obtained and to go on to the next step, or to deal with a problem or an obstacle encountered when putting your plan into action? You can also do this with each of the 24 houses and the runes in them. This process can help you move forward in life and gradually express the best of who you are.

There is more information about the Birth Diamond on my website **http://www.coaching-evolution.net** and if you want to experience the Birth Diamond you can purchase a special Birth Diamond phone session which lasts between 1 and 2 hours and which costs 80€.

Conclusion of this book: Runes can be used with love and respect as visual magic tools that can make your subconscious mind, your conscious mind and the forces of life, nature and of the cosmos work together. They can be used to answer questions and they can also be a very interesting self-knowledge tool. I hope you enjoyed this book! It is now up to you to create your own unique manner of using the runes and it is though practice that you can gain confidence and improve.

Thank you for your attention.

May you experience health, love, success, joy, happiness and prosperity!

Kind regards

Eric Jackson Perrin

Annex - Proposal for a system with 64 runes

The 24 runic system is complete as it is. A very long time ago however, there were other systems on this planet with much more numbers, from eastern Asia to Western Europe and elsewhere. Here is a proposal that goes up to number 64 with symbols and names. The essence of the numbers shown here have connections with Chinese Archangel "Lao Tse"'s numerology system.

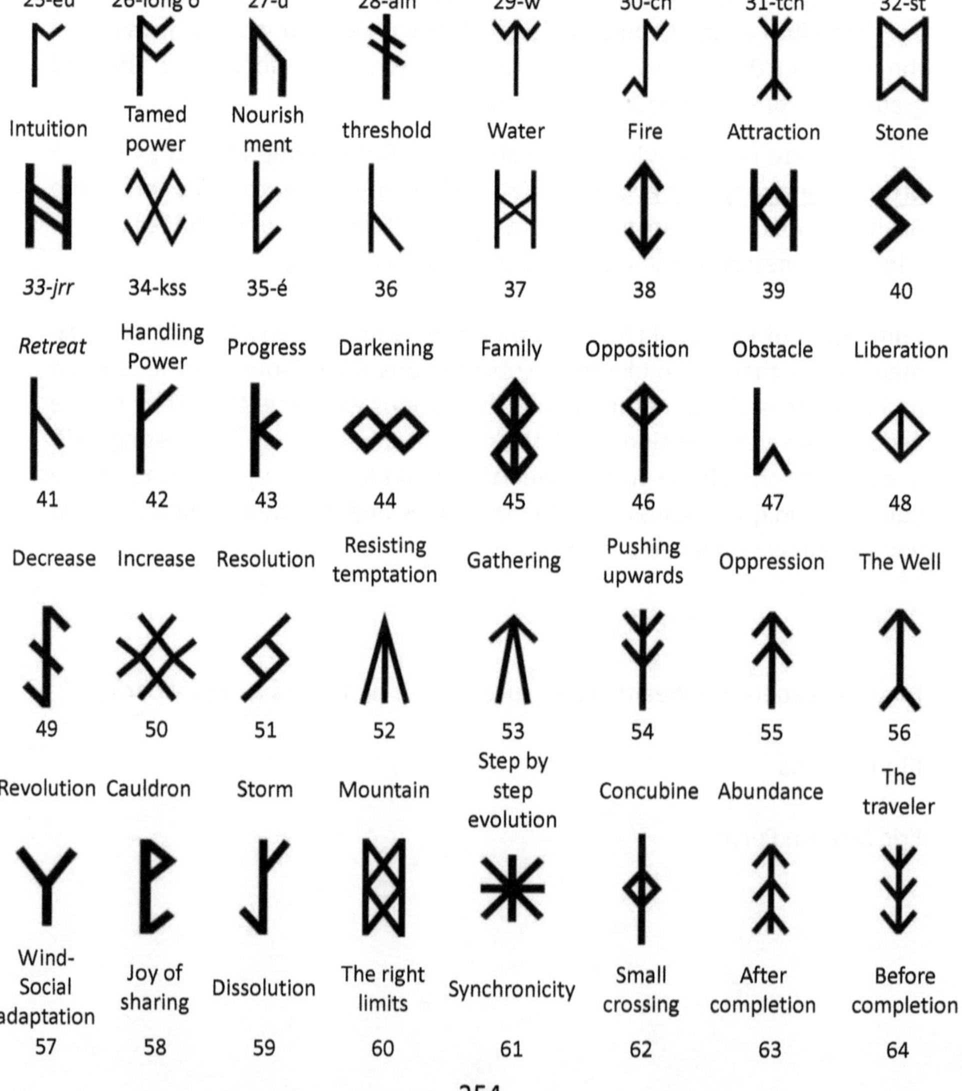

Bibliography

Runes and Magic by Nigel Pennick

An introduction to English runes by R.I. Page

Les runes by Dominique Agnus

Manuel de magie runique by Edred Thorsson

L'Edda poétique by Régis Boyer

Workshop making Celtic and Nordic jewelry

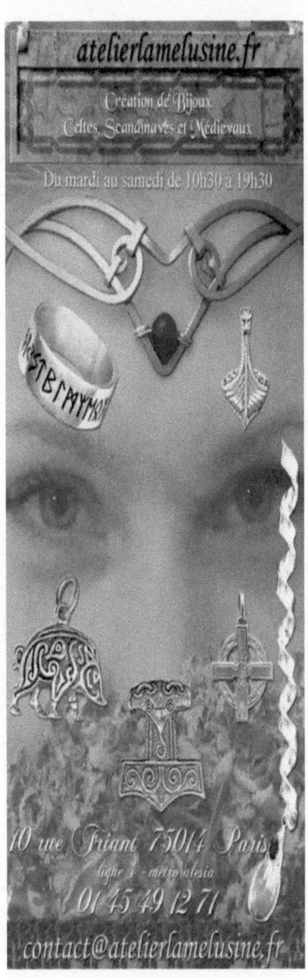